ON WINGS OF FIRE

# ON WINGS OF FIRE

A narrative of odd and unusual characters and queer, remote places along the flamingo coast from Swakopmund to the Cape

LAWRENCE G. GREEN

HOWARD TIMMINS PUBLISHERS

Southern & East Africa · United Kingdom
North America · Australia · New Zealand

Reprinted 1982

ISBN 0 86978 212 6

Published by Howard Timmins (Pty) Ltd.
P.O. Box 94, Cape Town 8000, S.A.
Printed by Citadel Press, Lansdowne, Cape

## *CONTENTS*

## *ILLUSTRATIONS*

*Chapter One*

# AT THE FLAMINGO CAFÉ

IF you knew Swakopmund soon after the Kaiser's war then you may remember the Flamingo Café with its tame seals and a brilliant flamingo painted on the wall in the beer-garden. A stuffed flamingo stood on the bar counter; and the café owner, known as "Hasenpfeffer" Schmidt, looked something like a flamingo himself; long-necked, gracious, and all curves as he weaved among the tables bowing to his patrons.

Paul Schmidt's nickname, however, arose because the long-legged hare of the surrounding desert appeared regularly on his menus and he always recommended it. I dislike rabbit and hare as a rule, but I must say that *hasenpfeffer*, saddle of hare simmered with gammon, onions and red wine, was a memorable dish. Schmidt had been a ship's steward. When his old Woermann steamer was wrecked he decided to remain in German South West Africa. Someone told me that he called himself Schmidt because he was trying to escape from his wife. She traced him, and that was the end of the Flamingo Café, for Schmidt moved on. But in its day, during its short period of glory, the Flamingo brightened the whole Swakopmund scene. It left a faint aroma of well-being which deserved the status of a legend.

Swakopmund is one of those places where it is better to gaze inwards than to look out and shudder. When I had a window table at the Flamingo the wide streets were almost as grim as the Namib desert. People walked in deep sand. Trolley tracks ran everywhere, the flat trolleys drawn in Russian style by three little horses side-by-side. Drivers jumped off hurriedly to turn the points at crossings. Parcels from the shops, firewood, passengers on chairs, all went by trolley. I saw a trolley funeral one day. It was a relief to stare at the sculptured cupids on a tall corner building not far away. In the German colonial days this mansion had been reserved for amorous officers. Later it became a respectable apartment house; but the legend never grew dim, like memories of the Flamingo Café; and never did old Swakopmunders need such dainty reminders as the stone cupids to bring visions of the madames and the girls.

Let me do justice at last to a man who gave more honest value than the people in the house across the way. Paul Schmidt was a master of atmosphere and the Flamingo Café was his own creation. It had been a store, looking into an enclosed yard where cargoes were brought up from the jetty and stacked. Schmidt turned the yard into a beer-garden. In the centre he built a fountain with a small ornamental pond where two baby seals played and snapped with marvellous accuracy at the rollmops and herrings flung to them by the drinkers. Hasenpfeffer Schmidt made the Flamingo more than a café. It was a *backerei* and *konditorei* offering such delicacies as hot cheese rolls, rye bread, strudels and a magnificent cake named Kaiser-creme. The restaurant served many fine platters apart from the famous *hasenpfeffer*: *suppe* with dumplings and force-meat balls, *fischgulasch* sprinkled with paprika, huge craw-fish served hot with grated cheese, the pickled beef called *sauerbraten*, venison steaks, grilled *bratwurst* and blood sausage. Fresh tomatoes and other vegetables came from Hrabovsky's farm in the bed of the Swakop river, and this weird oasis also supplied roses. I am glad that I kept one of the Flamingo Café menus, for it recalls the smoked ham Schmidt imported from the Black Forest, the *schokoladen-flammeri* and various rich pastries. But this cheerful *gast-haus* was also a *weinstube* and *bierkeller*. Most people drank the South West *helles* or *dunkles*, or wine from the Klein Windhoek mission, or *schnapps* with beer as a chaser. For the children there was *himbeersaft* or *trauben-saft*. On special occasions the Germans ordered sparkling *sekt*, Rhine or Moselle wines. Schmidt had fruit brandies, the cherry, plum and raspberry. After meals he served Mokka, and some of his patrons laced it with rum. No doubt there were millions in Germany during that hard post-war period who would have opened their eyes in wonder if they could have entered the Flamingo Café during a Sunday morning beer session.

Swakopmunders called Schmidt's place "the Schloss" because it had corner turrets like a castle. As I have indicated, there was no *schönblick* from the windows, no beautiful view; but there was soft comfort within and the promise of satisfaction. Schmidt had secured a cuckoo clock from a Black Forest *kukukenfabriek*, and not only the children watched for the regular appearances of the brightly-painted bird. Hand-carved lamps, dark panelling and a large open fireplace helped customers to forget the sand outside. On certain evenings there was a pianist rendering a Strauss waltz with restraint; or there might be an inconspicuous zither-player. Food and drink came first at the Flamingo, and the true music of the place was the clinking of glasses and bottles and the crackle made by carving knives as they broke into the roast pork. Every piece of equipment aided the atmosphere. For a Bavarian customer there would be an earthenware *bierstein*. Wine came in glasses with green stems. On the bar counter the drinkers found an array of herring salad with diced cucumber, pigs trotters with *sauerkraut* and the finest *kartoffelsalat* south of the line.

Naturally one heard strange talk in a place like the Flamingo. Some patrons travelled great distances to answer the call of Schmidt's *hasenpfeffer*. My journeys in South West Africa really started at the Flamingo. I listened to stories which aroused in me an uncontrollable desire, and I became firm in my resolve. I, too, must penetrate the dunes of the coast, the lands of the Ovambo, Herero and Hottentot; and beyond all, the far wildernesses in which the Bushmen survived. In the German time the Bushmen were classed officially as "vermin", like baboons or jackals, and they were shot at sight. Not only that, but the government paid a reward for each Bushman head brought to the nearest police post. After the surrender in 1915 the South African Mounted Rifles took over from the German police. A corporal in the fine old first regiment S.A.M.R.

Food and drink came first at the Flamingo, and the true music of the place was the clinking of glasses and bottles.

assured me that while he was stationed at Grootfontein a German farmer rode in with several Bushman heads tied to his saddle and demanded five marks apiece. The farmer was tried for murder but acquitted after the German ex-chief of police, one Ulrici, had given evidence for the defence. Ulrici, who was employed by the S.A.M.R. as interpreter, quoted the German proclamation of the Bushmen as vermin and pointed out that this had not yet been repealed. The farmer was most indignant over his treatment, even after he had been found not guilty; but no more Bushmen were shot as vermin. However, the corporal had no illusions about the Bushmen, especially the tall Heikum Bushmen of the Etosha Pan area. "They were cannibals," he told me. "They used to eat the Ovambos who came south to work on the copper mines. It took years to put a stop to that game."

My friend the corporal often tested the skill of the Bushmen with bows-and-arrows. He would throw up a matchbox at a distance of ten or fifteen yards and challenge a Bushman to hit it in mid-air. It could only be done on a still day, and never at the first shot; but some Bushmen could hit the box at the third attempt. The corporal was even more impressed by the staying power of the Bushmen in following and running down game. Not only the young men succeeded in the chase. He knew a Bushman who looked ninety; and he declared that this wrinkled old man could have beaten all the youngsters in the Marathon race at the Olympic Games. The course of twenty-six miles would have suited the old fellow admirably. The corporal became an officer between the wars, and when he was sent to England on duty he took with him a number of Bushman arrows, the poisoned ones. He handed them to the toxicologists at London University for analysis. "Poisonous, deadly poisonous," they told him. "Unfortunately the poison defies analysis. It is not snake venom but some vegetable poison unknown to science."

Another old policeman spoke of the days when they patrolled the Kaokoveld on horseback, lived on the country and followed the elephant trails because they always led to water. "We went in there for adventure and had a wonderful time," he declared. "I'd like to go back. We rode through the bush and if we picked up a strange spoor we followed it in the hope of finding a poacher or some other sort of criminal. When we came to a native village the chief supplied us with firewood, water and meat, usually a goat. Our native informers knew everything that was going on. One fugitive eluded us, a reckless fellow who threatened to shoot any policeman who followed him. He just vanished into that wilderness of fifty thousand square miles. I remember finding 'Snowy' Walker the prospector at the Hoarusib River mouth. He died of thirst, close to water, with a pocket full of diamonds." This constable spoke of another man who perished along that coast; Walter Matthews, the beachcomber who became wealthy as a result of his discovery of the Cape Cross guano. He could have lived well in civilisation but he preferred exploring the desert coast. Matthews left Swakopmund with four Hottentot servants and pack donkeys. He went down with malaria far from medical aid and died.

Some of the white people in South West Africa led strange lives. At the Flamingo I heard of a German farmer who built a house with an enormous circular thatched roof supported by poles but without any side walls. Curtains were drawn when it rained. Under the thatch stood a beautiful grand piano and a pile of music. The farmer played the violin, his wife was the pianist and a son played the cello. This was in the Otavi district, far up in the north where the narrow-gauge railway threw out its forks. A music-lover who stayed there informed me that he had seldom encountered such a marvellous library of music, and it was a gifted trio to find in the Bushman country.

Not far from Otavi is the Tsumeb copper mine. Before the Germans surrendered they hid thousands of cases of rum down the mine, army rations which they did not intend the enemy to enjoy. But the South African troops found this cache and brought the rum to the surface. "We were drunk for days," an ex-soldier told me. "Officers were drunk. The sentries were drunk. Everyone was drunk. The war in South West was over and we felt like a celebration. When a stranger arrived at the mine he was not offered a tot or a bottle of rum. We gave him a case."

At the Flamingo I heard one story that I kept to myself for fear of ridicule. An old German farmer, on holiday from the far interior, declared that the Hottentots of the territory had always used tame baboons to guard their sheep and goats. This caused so much laughter and disbelief in the Flamingo that I decided not to spread the legend. The farmer admitted that he had never seen a baboon shepherd, but one of his labourers had told him the story. Female baboons were employed as they were more conscientious. They led the herd to water and grazing, rounded up stray animals, and uttered warning cries at the approach of danger. In the evening the baboon would lead the flock back to the homestead and continue to guard it at night against such raiders as wild dogs, jackals and leopards. There was a schoolmaster present at this discussion, and he said that he knew the origin of the yarn. It came from Sir James Alexander's book on his expedition in the territory during the eighteen-thirties. I looked it up and found this statement: "The Namaquas said that a man had brought up a young baboon and had made it his shepherd. It remained by the flock all day in the field and at night drove it home to the kraal, riding on the backs of the goats which brought up the rear. The baboon had the milk of one goat allowed to it and it sucked that one only and guarded the milk of the others from the children. It also got a little meat from its master. It held the office of shepherd for twelve months and then was unfortunately killed in a tree by a leopard. Possibly the tale of the hairy shepherd may be quite true."

Probably it was true. My old friend the late Dr. Walter Hoesch, and Professor Raymond Dart, investigated a similar tale not long ago and confirmed the legend. They found that Mrs. Ashton, aged sixty, was running the farm Otjiruse near Okahandja with the aid of two native piccanins and a female baboon. This was the third baboon she had employed. The first was torn to pieces by strange dogs after six years' service and the second had been shot by someone who was unaware of its position of responsibility on the farm. The third baboon, captured as a baby, had served for seven years and was still on duty. All three baboons had been fed on goats' milk, and I think this diet must have had some bearing on their behaviour; it was a prized reward. The baboons looked after about one hundred goats and kids. They knew every one of them, and brought the kids to their mothers. Mrs. Ashton said the baboons were far superior to the natives she had employed previously. The third baboon had formed the bad habit of riding home on a goat (like the baboon of Alexander's story) but otherwise it was a perfect goatherd. It cleared the goats of ticks and dragged high branches down so that they could feed easily. When a leopard attacked the flock it gave the alarm by screeching wildly. So the baboon is more useful than a sheep-dog, and more efficient than a native. It has a highly developed social sense, not only in its own community but in the service of man. Those scientists who claim that the baboon is closer to man than any of the other primates will find support for their views in this old story which has proved to be true. I only wish that I had gone in search of baboon shepherds and goatherds forty years ago.

Yes, I sat on a high stool at the Flamingo bar counter listening, and the past of this desert coast seemed to rise before me. Castaways and runaway sailors were among the explorers last century; bold spirits from whalers and schooners; men who discovered rivers and mountains and died without leaving even a trace of their adventures for the historians. One expedition after another has searched the coastline to the north of Cape Cross in the hope of solving the mysteries of the lost ships, the fragments of old wooden ships (with their human skeletons) which lie scattered and half-buried in the sand. They have returned with old-fashioned wooden blocks and gratings, and one porcelain vase. That vase provided a clue. It was identified by experts in London as a type of Persian vase used in Dutch East India Company's ships three centuries ago, at a period when Chinese porcelain was unobtainable. Archives have been ransacked for details of that lost Dutch ship but the story remains untold. She lies there shattered with the skeletons of her crew. They were drowned or they died of thirst on that waterless coast. No one could have walked north or south to civilisation. It was too far. Those expeditions also found the skeletons of whales some way inland among the dunes. Were they thrown up by a tidal wave? No one knows the old secrets of that coast of wrecks. I have been there myself and come away with my curiosity unsatisfied.

I gathered strange tales of Swakopmund, too, at the Flamingo, tales of the old Swakopmund that grew up before the town lost its port and became a collection of seaside houses and hotels and camps for holiday visitors. Swakopmund's story opens with a mystery. When the Dutch East India Company sent the *Meermin* to the Rostro da Pedra (now Walvis Bay) at the end of the eighteenth century, a daring hunter named Pieter Pienaar marched up the coast to the Swakop river mouth. He came out of the sheer desert and the dunes and found himself among clumps of ana and *kameeldoring* trees, in a land where elephants roamed in herds of hundreds, a land of rhino and gemsbok. Near the river-bed Pienaar came upon a number of abandoned huts and relics which proved that white men had camped there. They may have been British or American whalermen, collecting water in casks from the river-bed for their ships; but their adventures have been lost completely in the dust of the years.

Apparently the first real settlers were two German seamen who deserted from a sailing ship at Walvis Bay in the middle of last century. These nameless pioneers lived in a mud hut, traded with the natives and supplied visiting ships with sheep and cattle. Their lonely enterprise might have gone unrecorded if the missionary Scheppman had not encountered them during an exploring journey.

Captain Curt von Francois, the first German army officer to be stationed in South West Africa, put up the first building in Swakopmund. It was a small fort designed to shelter troops, built in 1892; dwelling-houses and stores followed. Von Francois also surveyed the coast as far as Cape Cross. Only the Germans would have turned the open roadstead at Swakopmund into a busy port. They ran out a wooden jetty before the end of last century, and surf boats brought the cargoes from the ships lying offshore to the cranes. So much freight was lost, however, that a curved stone mole was built to give more shelter. I knew an early Walvis Bay magistrate who was invited by the Germans to attend the opening ceremony at the mole. At that time the only British resident in Swakopmund was the operator at the cable station. He met the magistrate on arrival from Walvis with a light cart drawn by four mules. The two British guests wore tophats and frock-coats; but the German governor and other officials were in evening-dress. "The formal procession to the mole, with a German band leading, was ludicrous," the magistrate told me. "Everyone enjoyed the champagne afterwards." I gathered from the magistrate that the Germans might have saved a great deal of money by using the safe harbour at Walvis Bay, but a dispute arose over the passage of German troops. Thus the port of Swakopmund arose, an act of folly, grandiose but contrary to all the principles of harbour construction. The port never paid its way. All the harbour works silted up, and after World War I the ships moved south thankfully to Walvis Bay. Swakopmund's great harbour dream had crashed for ever.

When you approach Swakopmund from the desert, the old, absolute Namib desert, it may seem that you are driving into an oriental town of palaces and towers. Minarets and cupolas rise from the yellow dunes. It is the mirage, of course, though bygone German craftsmen built well on this unpromising ground and most of the old, elegant architecture has survived. The desert is so overpowering that Swakopmund is inclined to forget the menace of floods. Down the tremendous gorge of the Swakop comes a muddy, raging torrent forty, fifty feet high. Decades may pass between floods. No one can work out the pattern, for the records go back no farther than a part of last century. But when the flood comes it is terrifying. Houses and a steel bridge at Swakopmund were swept away during the 1934 floods. Trees in the town, some of the few precious trees were cut down to form a barricade against the waters so that other threatened homes might be saved.

At the river mouth the flood was four hundred yards wide. The bewildered people of Swakopmund saw monkeys and snakes being carried out to sea on logs. One baboon was washed up on the beach alive, clinging to a tree-trunk. And when it was all over the great pier, the pride of the Germans, was found to be three-quarters of a mile from the sea. So much silt had come down the river that the ocean turned the colour of chocolate.

I am glad to have known Swakopmund in the days of the Flamingo Café. The old names are still there, Kaiser-Wilhelmstrasse and Von Moltke Strasse; but where are the old officers of the Kaiser with bristling moustaches and duelling scars? I remember the cinema, known locally as the *kino*, where a quick-witted interpreter sat at the back and boomed out a German translation of the English subtitles; for Swakopmund was German to the core in those days and many understood only German.

In every home there were portraits of the Kaiser and Bismarck, and pictures of the Franco-German War of 1870. I understand that old people still treasure pictures and relics of happier days, for the wars of the present century brought them no final victories. The handsome lighthouse goes back to the German colonial period, and the granite tower is still painted in the Kaiser's black, white and red. Do the thirsty prospectors and miners still come in from the desert and the Brandberg with their talk of metals and precious stones? I remember the Swakopmund of wooden duckboards when the wide streets lay deep in sand; when all the Ovambo houseboys and Herero maids swept the sand off the boards outside the homes of their employers. Swakopmund offered little shade, but there were avenues of *melkboom* at the bathing place, and the café at the mole had lanterns on the boughs.

In summer the Windhoek heat compels all who can afford it to make for the sea, and Swakopmund is still the choice of many families. Shrewd fathers have always discovered the date when the Administrator and high officials have decided to make the road journey of two hundred and thirty miles from Windhoek to the coast. They know the road of tar, gravel and finally salt will have been repaired and scraped for the elite of Leutwein Street. Careful inquiries are also made about the German cooks of Swakopmund, for a favourite boarding-house may have to be abandoned in favour of a rival establishment if the cook has been lured away. After all, one's favourite *rinderschmorbraten* or *zitronenflammeri* cannot be left to an inexperienced *haustochter*.

Swakopmunders have their favourite bars, open from eight in the morning until midnight. After midnight some bars become "night clubs" and the lights are dimmed. Skittles are played with all the old enthusiasm. "Skat" is the great card game. They still order a "Steinhager" with beer as a chaser. Visitors unaccustomed to the local water may have stomach-trouble, so a "kleine kleine" is safer. "When it rains in Swakopmund, you find everyone on the roof", they say. The corrugated iron becomes leaky in that peculiar climate, and it rains so seldom that many householders are taken by surprise. As there are no rainwater tanks the brackish local water has to be used for washing. It does not lather. Newcomers regard this water as a danger and a hardship and pay extra for Walvis water. Swakopmund was chosen as a port because of the subterranean water in the river-bed. The Hottentot name Swakop described the taste of this unpleasant water in a vulgar yet accurate way. However, I understand that some old Swakopmunders have become so fond of the nauseous liquid that when they travel they add salt to the sweet water, thus restoring some of the beloved flavour.

Although Swakopmund lives mainly on holiday-makers from the burning hinterland, it has a few odd sidelines. Salt comes from the lagoons along the coast, where Rudolf Klein piles the salt into dunes like icebergs. Swakopmunder beer (made from Walvis water) is famous far beyond the frontiers of the territory. Woollen garments have been made there in recent years. An older and more exotic industry is the curing of lion and leopard and antelope skins from the farms. You can order a rug or a pair of shoes made from soft kudu hide with soles of zebra skin; shoes that would survive a walk from the Kunene to the Orange and back. Elephant leather is also tanned at Swakop on the rare occasions when some old tusker is shot by special permit.

Suphur is the odour which brings unhappy memories to Swakopmund. Suphur eruptions occur in the bed of the ocean, millions of fish are killed and washed ashore, and then the holiday coast becomes a place for scientists, not swimmers. This strong aroma is not to be compared with the sweet perfume of the *kameeldoring* trees along the river when the yellow blossoms are upon them.

One fine spectacle at Swakopmund has remained unchanged through the centuries. Go down to the river mouth and you will see the flamingoes preening and stretching their powerful wings as they were doing long before Diego Cam discovered this desert shore. For this is the true flamingo coast. At favoured spots for nearly a thousand miles, from Cape Cross to the Cape Flats, you may see the flocks of flamingoes twisting their long necks, dipping their heads in vleis and rivers and lagoons, searching eternally for the insects and crustaceans and plant foods that give them such abundance of flaming life. When they are left undisturbed they strut like dancers, prancing ridiculously, giving out sounds like no other bird noises in the world; such a deep chatter, a gurgling and a gossiping that you would imagine they had great affairs to discuss. Advance on a flock and you hear a different sound, an urgent, rising note of alarm. Then they cease to be foolish and grotesque. Then the flamingoes become creatures of wonder, of grace and beauty, showing the most gorgeous wings in the world of birds. When you have heard those scarlet, black-edged wings beating in unison, long necks and legs streamlined as a vast flock of flamingoes takes to the air, then you have been present at a heavenly vision.

The fascination of the flamingo lies in those sunset colours; but for ornithologists the bird has another appeal. It's nesting habits formed one of Africa's great mysteries until recent years, and even now the flamingo must have secret breeding places along this lonely west coast. I think it was that brilliant flamingo on the wall of Hasenpfeffer Schmidt's place that aroused my interest in this stately bird and started my wanderings along the flamingo coast, the coast of the wings of fire.

*Chapter Two*

## HASSELUND AND THE SEALS

THOSE hungry seals in the Flamingo beer-garden led me to make the acquaintance of two unusual characters. One was Herrman Offen of Swakopmund, a huge and prosperous German business man who had taken part successfully in all sorts of ventures from buying a wrecked ship to killing seals. The other was a little sunburnt Swede named August Hasselund, who worked for Offen at his Cape Cross sealing station.

Hasselund was really the more interesting of the two. He had spent most of his life in the salty, white sandy isolation of Cape Cross, that desert headland where the first Portuguese explorer set foot in South West Africa and set up the usual stone *padrao* or cross. Cape Cross is eighty miles north of Swakopmund, and the track when I first drove there was no smooth highway. Hasselund saw little of the delights of Swakopmund, but it was said that he kept a dark harem at a kraal on the Omaruru river. These women also looked after his cattle. I saw Hasselund only at Cape Cross, where he lived alone in a neat cottage surrounded by a white-washed stone wall. Hasselund's hands and arms bore a number of scars, and I asked him whether he had been attacked by seals.

"Yay, eh gort many bites in mein vurk," replied Hasselund in the bubbling, lilting, sing-song rhythm of the Scandinavians. "Eh voss syiprak here long ago, and eh haff kill taooshunns seals—but moss be karful, see." Offen saw that the word "syiprak" had defeated me, and he came in now and again as interpreter.

"He was shipwrecked here at the end of last century, and he found a job as cook—they had a large settlement in those days when an English company was working guano. They pulled out, but Hasselund liked the place and stayed on, making a living out of sealskins. He prefers a quiet life."

I asked Hasselund how he passed the time when he was not slaughtering the seals. His answer was most unexpected. "Eh vurk mit der yong seals—tich dem dricks for der circus," he said with a deep laugh. "Eh hev a skul for seals, yah!" Offen explained in more lucid detail. Animal trainers visited Cape Cross and paid high prices for seals that appeared to be intelligent enough for the sawdust ring. At one time, he said, only sea lions from California and other northern waters were looked upon as suitable for show business. But the Cape Cross seals had shown promise. They had not learnt to juggle with lighted torches without singeing their whiskers. They could not man a seal orchestra, like some American seals, or play a set of horns so that the audience might recognise: "My country, 'tis of thee." It was asking too much to expect a Cape Cross seal to dance a hornpipe wearing wooden shoes, or walk the tightrope. Offen declared than an American seal had been taught to say: "I want my mama." (I accepted this with reserve). The training at Cape Cross was only kindergarten stuff compared with the education a seal received at the Ringling or Barnum circuses.

I went out with Offen and Hasselund to see their recruiting ground for this peculiar form of talent. It was summer, the breeding season, but the shooting of the old males had ended and the noisy seal rookeries were as peaceful as ever they would be. Thousands of Cape fur seals were lying far up on the beaches, snorting and barking and quarrelling happily in the sun. Cow seals were suckling their newborn pups, feeding them with the richest milk in the mammalian world. Great bulls roared over their harems, lunging with menacing jaws at other bulls. Cows threatened other cows which seemed to be rolling too near the delicate pups.

We kept away to avoid causing a stampede, and Offen pointed out the sort of seals that might win frantic applause after proper training. "First the whiskers," began Offen. "A performing seal must have long, thick whiskers curving downwards. The whiskers seem to help them in their balancing acts."

"Also der nose moss be flat," put in Hasselund. "Sharp nose seal iss no goot—can't hold a rubber ball on it, see? All clever seal got blunt nose."

"You have to watch the pups for a long time before you pick one out for training," went on Offen. "See that bunch of pups asleep over there? We call them snoozers. Now a snoozer has a nice, gentle nature, he's easy to handle and there's room for one or two snoozers in a team. But you'll never teach a snoozer the tricks that a barker will learn. Barkers are nervous, active, intelligent seals. See those pups cavorting in the surf? You might find a barker among that lot—the sort of seal that will play a drum or tambourine, do a somersault and answer simple questions by nodding its head. A snoozer will sit up and beg, kiss his trainer, climb a ladder and take its place on a box in the ring. It will toss a rubber ball and catch it, but not many snoozers can spin a ball like a human juggler. When it comes to riding a motor-bike you need a barker. Why, a good barker will lie on its back and balance a smaller seal on its flipper."

Offen led the way to the enclosure where Hasselund kept the four seals he was training. They had a small pool there. Hasselund put his face over the fence, and the seals broke into an expectant: "Honk, honk, honk, honk!" Hasselund put on a pair of thick gloves, for even young seals bite viciously at times. "Tricks first, fish after," announced Hasselund, and the seals appeared to know the rule well enough. By now I could follow Hasselund's strange English as he described the seals and their ways. He picked them from the yearling groups, the milk teeth and coats providing rough indications of age. After a time they ceased whimpering for their mothers and became fond of anyone who threw fish into the pen. "Joost like dogs—sea-dogs," Hasselund declared. "But more brain. Yah, seal got more brain than a monkee. Eh loff der seals an' der seals loff me." Hasselund proved it by skipping over the fence amid barks of pleasure. He fondled each seal in turn with the gloves on and I saw how they craved to be patted, just like dogs. When he neglected a seal it whined with jealousy.

"*Platz!*" called Hasselund firmly, and the four seals took their places on four tubs. He had Swedish names for them —Eugen, Karl, Erik and Oscar. They begged for fish, and when Offen handed Hasselund a parcel of fish the seals rushed forward happily and almost knocked their trainer down. Hasselund watched them fondly until the last scrap had been devoured. Again he shouted: "*Platz!*"

Eugen was a barker, and after a few months in captivity it rolled about the enclosure with a ball on its nose. More fish. All four had learnt to applaud by clapping with their front flippers—a feat enjoyed tremendously by circus audiences. More fish. Karl was a snoozer. Hasselund held up a tennis ball on a string, and Karl put his nose under it. Hasselund let the string go and the ball fell. He repeated the process again and again until Karl balanced the ball for a few seconds. More fish. For half an hour I stared entranced by the seal academy. At last Hasselund distributed the remainder of the fish and climbed out wearily. It seemed that half hour training periods twice a day were all that a man and his seals could stand. Moreover, the insatiable appetites of the seals kept Hasselund busy. The seas that wash Cape Cross are alive with fish; hence the seal population. Hasselund was always fishing. I knew an animal trainer who got some of his seals from Cape Cross, and he was my tutor in the more advanced stages of seal training. Possibly you saw this trainer when he was with Pagel's Circus. He came on in oriental dress with performing elephants. Next he wore a sun-helmet and desert clothes as he led on his unwilling camels. Another quick change and he was in frogged tunic and riding-breeches, with a fine sleek team of circus horses. Finally he became a naval captain, with four trained seals barking at the audience. (All seal trainers are "captains" by courtesy, even if they are unable to row a dinghy). This trainer was a ruddy, middle-aged man when I met him, with curly black hair; easily the most hard-working man in the circus with all those animals to look after. "I prefer bull seals," he told me. "My seals are named Wotan, Dickie, Stumpy and Neptune, and they all came from Cape Cross. Some trainers say that the smaller female seals are gentle and perform better, but my bulls are docile enough now. They are the clowns of the sea, they love a friendly audience, and they are so temperamental that they can tell whether the audience is in a good or bad mood. The great thing in seal training is to watch them closely and encourage them to develop their own tricks. Great exhibitionists, these seals. You can't drive them. They respond to coaxing and they know just what you're saying. Of course it's a slow business, training seals. They won't do a one-flipper stand overnight, but the time comes when your seal will ride an elephant or a pony."

The trainer informed me that seal training had no centuries of tradition behind it, like the circus ring. The first performing seals lolloped into the ring less than a century ago. Captain Webb was one of the pioneers, and his seals delighted Queen Victoria. "I like to get a bull seal aged about eighteen months, with handsome olive-grey fur," said the trainer. "Then I can be fairly sure of having it with me for a long time. Some seals have a working life of sixteen years. You get fond of a friendly seal. Parting with one is like losing a member of the family. But their eyes weaken and in the end they have to go to a zoo. They flourish in the circus. One female Cape fur seal lived for twenty years in the London Zoo."

Of course there are hazards. The trainer said he gave his seals an intensive course of all vitamins every six months to replace the natural vitamins they enjoyed when they lived in the sea. They spent most of their time in a tank van with ledges for resting and sleeping out of the water. He treated the tank water with crystals to give it the same chemical content as sea water. When the circus was at the coast he drove the tank van down to the beach every day and filled up from the ocean. I asked him whether he allowed his seals to swim in the open sea. Some trainers give their seals a regular treat in this way and call them back after the exercise. He shook his head sadly. "They might not come back," he replied. "Then I would be left with only the elephants, the camels and the horses. You can't get fond of elephants and the camels hate everyone. Horses are all right, but the frisky seals are the best companions of the whole lot."

I remembered a seal that entertained untold thousands of people in Table Bay Docks for years. It seemed to enjoy being watched as it dived and twisted and frolicked round the inner basin. Trawlermen threw it pieces of fish, though a seal would never lack nourishment among the shoals of mackerel and *marsbankers* in the dock area. This particular seal would approach an admiring group roaring happily, whiskers fluttering, large round eyes shining, a lithe and sinuous creature of gleaming beauty. One of the harbour officials told me it was a seal that had escaped from a circus and that was the general belief along the waterfront. The trainer was right when he said: "They might not come back." What fools they would be!

The trainer confirmed Offen's incredible story about circus seals learning to talk. "I never had any luck in that way," he admitted. "But there are seals that can sing a little and say a few words distinctly. My seals are better at coughing. They get hoarse like smokers and that makes them cough." I asked him about feeding seals. "It costs a lot when your're away from the coast," he complained. "I give them live fish, mackerel and other cheap fish in Cape Town. Every day upcountry I must have one hundred and twenty pounds of frozen fish. Those four seals have three meals a day, and that's what they get through. Of course they can live on their blubber for weeks provided they have plenty of fresh water, but they will not put on a show unless they are constantly rewarded with fish. If the fish does not arrive I give them chopped liver and hake liver oil. That keep them active until the fish turns up."

Performing seals are given room to swim in a swimming bath whenever this is possible. A trainer told me about a seal that was left overnight in a large glass tank at an aquarium. That seal climbed out and entered tank after tank, feasting on lobsters, squids and the spectacular fish of the world. It was an expensive meal. The hungry seal cleared the aquarium of gold fish, plump rainbow trout and other delicacies. Circus food must have seemed tame after such a varied and memorable banquet.

Sometimes a circus seal caught a cold, but usually they were healthy enough. Trainers have to examine the daily fish rations with great care as hooks were sometimes found in line-caught fish and a hook might kill a seal. Jock, a seal in the Bostock circus, swallowed a rubber ball and died. Barkers and snoozers love a good night's rest. They must have their eight hours' sleep, huddled together and using each other as pillows. Their eyes need washing once a week or scales grow on the eyeballs. Salty water does the trick. All seals became moody at times, but it is possible to talk them out of it. "You have to learn a special palaver for seals," one trainer claimed. "They like being flattered, and they get your meaning far quicker than a dog would. Of course it is the emotion they understand rather than the actual words. If the seal is not fond of you then you can give up."

My friend the trainer said his seals never tried to seize him by the throat and tear his jugular vein out. Only a raw, untrained seal would do that. Their interlocking teeth were ferocious, and a playful, affectionate bite often caused a painful bruise. But they were faithful and affectionate. He had known a blind seal to carry on with its act, walking the tightrope ten years after it had lost its sight.

Cape fur seals have no reason to love the human race. They were massacred by French seamen at Saldanha Bay before the Dutch settlement at Table Bay. Van Riebeeck collected thousands of sealskins and casks of blubber; and his men reported that Dassen Island was "so full of seals that a ship could easily be laden with young ones by just picking them up."

In spite of centuries of persecution the seals have clung to some of their old rookeries from Cape Cross southwards down the flamingo coast. They breed in summer not only on the islands but at several places on the mainland. I have watched them far up on the shore at Wolf Bay, near Luderitz; and I believe there is still a remote beach on the Namaqualand diamond coast where they haul out in hundreds. Saldanha still has its seals, for they have a precarious home on Jacob Rock, north of the entrance. Robbensteen, a reef to the north of Melkbosstrand, is their last retreat in the Table Bay area. They cling to Seal Island in False Bay; Geyser Island on the Bredasdorp coast, a Mossel Bay islet and certain rocks in Algoa Bay. Every year the government sealers kill about six thousand old bulls and thirty thousand yearlings. But the seal herds survive in spite of man, sharks, killer whales and the jackals that prey on young pups left unguarded at the mainland rookeries.

Would you care to adopt a friendly seal? A licence is essential, of course, but once secured you should have no difficulty in selecting an amiable young seal. Old seals, cast out by the herd, have a way of seeking the protection of mankind. They arrive unexpectedly on the stoeps of seaside cottages and beg for food. I saw one at Blaauwberg Strand about ten years ago, a poor old toothless bull that had been pounded against the rocks by the sea. It crept into a yard to the consternation of the fowls and turkeys and came to rest at the front-door of a cottage. After a square meal of fish the seal departed peacefully to die on some more secluded beach.

Perhaps the circus seals are neither the least fortunate nor the happiest of their species. Perhaps the seal that escaped to amuse the people of Table Bay Docks sometimes remembered the applause when it caught the clown hats thrown from the circle on to the stage. It may have missed the warmth of its master's voice when it juggled with a drum or brought off a difficult trick on the trapeze bar. Seals have been described as "slugs in fur coats," but they are really dogs, and like the dogs of the land they become devoted to those humans who are kind and appreciative—and those who satisfy their enormous appetite for fish. They take an interest in their audiences and you may see a seal staring hard at a women in a bright dress taking her seat. It is the colour in motion that holds up the performance. Clapping encourages them enormously and they seek it as hungrily as any other actor. A seal that can balance a glass of water on its nose and roll over without spilling a drop is worth more than a sealskin coat. Now and again the trainer finds a seal that is worth a fortune. The genuine seal comedian is one that says its prayers, gets into bed, pulls up the blankets—and then wakes up and scratches itself. It is a long way from the beaches of Cape Cross to the circus where such talent makes the seal the most popular animal in the show. Old Hasselund never found a seal of that calibre.

*Chapter Three*

## ON THE SWAKOPMUND PLATFORM

On the Swakopmund railway platform some years ago I observed a man staring at an old steam locomotive as others might stand fascinated by the beauty of Mona Lisa. This short, dark man with bristling hair and friendly eyes was Martin Leendertz, a journalist I had often met at Table Bay Docks. Indeed, he was an authority on seafaring matters, with a vast collection of his own drawings and photographs of ships. "I also happen to be interested in trains," Leendertz told me that day. "Thanks to the free pass which a deserving journalist sometimes receives, I have just travelled right across Africa from Lourenco Marques to Swakopmund. It is a form of harmless lunacy which I am unable to explain, but I find a strange pleasure in prowling along railway tracks that I have never seen before. I collect railways as others collect stamps."

We sat on a bench under the Teutonic decorations of the Swakopmund station and I listened to Leendertz rambling happily up and down the main lines, the branch lines and the midget railroads of his life. He was gripped by the rolling-stock of long ago; antiquarian engines like the copper-capped German puffer before us; the coaches of his boyhood and all sorts of curiosities running on steel rails. Leendertz informed me that this handsome terminal at Swakopmund with its clock tower and spire had been built early in the century by the Otavi copper enterprise. A mile away stood the German government station, much less ornate; so that Swakopmund had two stations and two railways of different gauges. "This was not the famous German efficiency," remarked Leendertz with sarcasm. (He had come from Holland as a child, and declared that the Dutch knew more about railway construction than the Germans). It seems that the private line to the mines in

South West Africa was a reproduction of the Festiniog toy railway in Wales, with its two foot gauge and solemn speed of twenty-five miles an hour. The state railway, six inches wider, ran parallel with the copper track as far inland as Karibib; then the "Staatsbahn" trains branched off to Windhuk. Both these pioneer lines have disappeared, but they have left a rich legacy of railway folklore. The tales Leendertz told, the stories they still laugh over in South West Africa, are true.

They shipped a whole German army railway brigade to Swakopmund to build the State line to Windhuk. Hundreds of Italian labourers also sweated in the unfamiliar desert where the copper line was laid. All the coal was brought from Hamburg and all the water had to be distilled from the sea. Each train had a separate tank wagon. Each truck had a native brakeman who acted when the engine-driver whistled. At night the trains stopped, crews made a huge fire and slept round it. Packs of wild dogs attacked railway labourers, leopards were shot on platforms, lions were a constant menace as they visited the newly-built stations in search of water. Every white driver carried a rifle. Springbok and larger game animals loitered in the path of the trains and there was never a shortage of venison. Now and again a tiny locomotive would be derailed by a huge kudu or wildebeest. At first there were only three passenger coaches, with room for eight inside and four on the platform. Those who travelled outside were blinded with dust and smoke. All were jolted constantly and flung about the coaches when they ignored the driver's warning signals. Only the natives enjoyed every minute of these journeys. Sand often covered the tracks. In spite of spark arrestors on the long chimneys the sparks often set the bush on fire. Drivers encountered many hazards and often had trouble with their passengers. They complained that when frantic whistling failed they had to go into wayside bars with their firemen and haul thirsty passengers back to the trains. Leendertz said that the only comfortable coach on the line was a saloon car built for directors and the chief engineer. It had an office, bathroom, kitchen and a sleeping compartment with three beds. I gathered that Leendertz had searched the railway workshops in vain for this museum piece.

Cecil Rhodes was so impressed by the Otavi railway that he planned a link with the German enterprise across Bechuanaland to Rhodesia. The line from Swakopmund to Tsumeb, three hundred and fifty miles, was the longest narrow-gauge line in the world. This was a solid achievement and the engineers had shown what could be done at relatively low cost. Rhodes might have created a fantastic toy railway through the Kalahari but for strong opposition by the Cape Government Railways. When the South African Railways inherited the system early in World War I a number of unwanted narrow-gauge locomotives and coaches were sent up from the Union for the northern railway. Much repair work had to be done, for the Germans had blown up bridges as they retreated. A rail journey from Cape Town to Tsumeb lasted eight and sometimes ten days. Only rail enthusiasts like Martin Leendertz loved the *Schmalspur* trains. Yet more than half a century passed after the German surrender before the last narrow-gauge train was cheered sarcastically down the line. The engine bore a farewell message: "It's too good for words. You'll never see me again. It's truly over. Hurrah!" Among those who saw the first diesel engines arrive on the newly-built three-foot six-inch gauge lines was Mr. R. Pesche, a stationmaster during the German regime, who had retired in 1907 and taken up farming. Mr. Pesche remembered the queer nautical episode which followed the appearance of H.M.S. *Armadale Castle* off Swakopmund early in World War I. A number of lighters, fishing boats and pleasure craft were in use at Swakopmund in those days, and the Germans decided to save this little fleet. The small craft were lifted on to railway trucks and taken inland to Omaruru and Otavi. When the South African invaders crossed the coastal desert they found these ships bottled up in the sand as securely as the Kaiser's other fleet at Kiel.

South African engineers built forty-five miles of new narrow-gauge line through the thorn bush wilderness from

More than half a century passed after the German surrender before the last narrow-gauge train was cheered sarcastically down the line.

Otjiwarongo to Outjo soon after World War I. Old railway officials recall the embarrassing moment at the opening ceremony when a bottle of champagne was suspended on a silken cord across the track at Outjo station. Just before the decorated train arrived the bottle exploded in the heat.

Some hours after the old copper train left Swakopmund the travellers said farewell to the dune country, the mountains of sand in fantastic shapes and colours. Camels met the train at many stations and carried the mails to even more remote outposts. The landscape was decorated with euphorbias, and round the station called Sphinx there was a plain studded with acacias. Usakos was the first important halt, almost one hundred miles from Swakopmund and one thousand miles from De Aar. This square village of German houses grew up round the railway junction, the railway machinery and carpentry shops. Here the Germans repaired boilers and coaches. Hundreds of natives found work here. They were paid in cash and in kind, so that when the South Africans took charge they had to provide their native employees with meat and mealie meal, coffee and sugar, tobacco and carrots, according to the old German custom. Railwaymen at Usakos enjoy a cool sea breeze in the afternoon, and a distant view of the majestic Erongo mountains. They need these compensations. Veld fires are dreaded in this land of tall, dry grass; and for many years Usakos was protected by a tiny fire-engine running about the village on two-foot gauge railway tracks.

North of Usakos the country is transformed. Palms appear, and there are bananas and fruit-trees in wayside gardens. This is a paradise in contrast with the Namib, a tropical land of beef and cream. One lonely monument standing beside the line is the "armistice stone" at Korab, where Botha met Francke under a mimosa tree and the campaign of 1914-15 came to an end. Tsumeb, the malarial northern terminus, remained purely German during many years of South African occupation. Every shop sign was in German from *schlachterei* to *schnapsladen*, and the visitor who could not speak *Krom-Duits* to the servants failed to make himself understood. Shunters marshalling the little copper ore trucks at the Tsumeb mine used bugles, and a number of these German relics have been preserved at the S.A.R. Museum in Johannesburg.

Grootfontein, at the end of another fork in the narrow-gauge line, was entirely different. Here was a meeting-place of Afrikaners, Germans and English-speaking people and the natives of several tribes. Grootfontein had the finest gardens in the country. The magistrate was entitled to employ convict labour and he grew everything from mulberries to dates. Yes, the end of the narrow-gauge line was very different from the seaside station at Swakopmund.

Martin Leendertz told me that by some evil chance he had never been able to travel over a narrow-gauge railway which branched off the Swakopmund-Usakos line about twenty miles from the coast. It ran eastwards through the true desert along the dry Khan river to the Khan copper mine. This private line, about seven miles long, was built a few years before World War I and it was torn up about forty years ago when the mine closed down. Leendertz had followed the old earthworks, noting the spoor of various animals along the abandoned track. Sadly he had arrived at the mine by motor car instead of the romantic, jittering railway. However, he was rewarded by a vision of past grandeur in the midst of stark desolation. Dominating the scene was a watch-tower on a hill, with ramparts like a miniature castle. Just below stood the fine residence where the three mine managers lived. Indeed there were three, and the directors in faraway Germany insisted that every important decision should be put to the vote. You can imagine the arguments in that great house with the double roof and beautiful wrought-iron doors. Those three directors stood on the huge pillared stoep and watched their own railway trucks carrying off thousands of tons of ore. Near the front door there was an inscription:

*Mein Haus ist Meine Welt,*
*Gluck auf Wenn's Drinn Gefallt*

But the Germans had no luck with the Khan mine. They put more than half a million pounds into it, and a great deal of the copper they brought out in 1914 fell into the hands of the South African invaders. Water had to be pumped for seven miles from the Swakop river-bed to the mine. It was a masculine world, with a manager's wife and a cook as the only women. Five years after World War I the mine was abandoned. Crushers stopped, the scorching valley became silent. Green copper ore lay where it had fallen on the last working day. The shafts were dead; all the houses and compounds were deserted; zebra and springbok roamed the railway tracks unafraid. Someone bought the buildings and carried off doors, windows and roofs. Lizards moved into the gutted homes. Only the great house remained untouched, with its motto now a mockery: "My house is my world. Good luck to whoever lives in it. Good luck." Some sardonic visitor wrote another message over the doorway in recent years: "no rain, no wealth, we abandon ye therefore to the sun, the sand and the flies." However, new life reached the ghost town in recent years, blasting is heard again, and the sand no longer encroaches on the old residence up the sweltering hillside. But you must travel there by road, not along the rails of romance.

Follow the narrow-gauge lines and you reach strange places. Martin Leendertz told me the story of the midget locomotive called *Hope* and the railway I had seen in the dunes round Walvis Bay. Ox-wagons set out from the bay last century, crossed the international boundary and trekked on to Windhuk three hundred miles way. When the Germans turned Swakopmund into a port of entry, however, the Walvis Bay trade suffered; and so the Cape Government decided to build a jetty and a railway line to meet the German competition. Oxen had a hard struggle in the sand and it was thought that the railway would provide an easy start for those using the old transport route.

Rails were laid from Walvis eastwards in 1898 to a waterhole called Rooibank. A year later the barque

*Primera* sailed into the bay and offloaded the *Hope* engine and two hundred tons of coal. She also brought a distilling plant, as the locomotive demanded pure water. Service trucks were provided. This was the first two-feet-six gauge railway ever built by the Cape Government Railways. At the end of the eighteen-mile line the freight was dumped at a station called Plum and loaded on to ox-wagons. Mules hauled the two-and-a-half ton trucks until the *Hope* engine made her first run; and the mules were retained for some time in case the pioneer engine broke down. Thus the wretched Walvis Bay village was enriched by a new enterprise and three new wooden buildings: an engine shed, a less elaborate shack for the engine-driver and mule stables.

That driver led a busy life for a time. During the week he took freight to Plum or delivered fresh water (sent up from Cape Town in casks by ship) to the Walvis Bay houses. At week-ends the Walvis residents organised picnics and rode out to Plum in open railway trucks. Unfortunately the Germans boycotted the enterprise, and often the *Hope* locomotive found work only in the Walvis Bay settlement. Then one of the great sandstorms of this century buried almost the entire line so thoroughly that no one felt inclined to uncover the rails. Little *Hope* was laid up and did not run again for years. The engine was resurrected after World War I when the fresh water pipeline was laid between Rooibank and Walvis Bay. Then the line was closed down, though sections of old rails appear and reappear among the dunes at intervals according to the whims of the winds. The *Hope* engine has become an historic monument outside the new Walvis Bay station.

What happens to old narrow-gauge rolling stock when a line closes down? Martin Leendertz and others have enlightened me on this point. The little engines and coaches go to the surviving miniature railways in various parts of Southern Africa. Leendertz, on one of his many journeys, revelled in the railway curiosities of the Avontuur branch line. He knew the coach they called the "Ratcatcher", a self-contained vehicle used by the sanitary inspector and other officials; probably the smallest narrow-gauge coach in Africa, yet equippped with bunks and a galley. Leendertz was delighted to find a station called Kabeljaauw's Siding on this run, and another named Loerie after the bird. He watched the "Bagnall Bustler" haul out on the Port Elizabeth to Walmer run; he noted the Mogul engines and the petrol railcars in his immense diary. Other railway collectors have described to me, with similar affection and wealth of detail, the Port Shepstone-Harding narrow-gauge train which passes through lovely and rugged country, taking a whole day to cover a distance which some motorists rush over in an hour. Natal has other isolated light railways and sugar plantation lines, while in Mozambique there is a ninety-mile run on two feet six track in the Inhambane area.

Favourite items in the vast Leendertz railway collection were the old locomotives built in the eighteen-nineties, engines that had done more than a million miles over South African tracks. He recognised veteran shunting engines that had once hauled famous mail trains between Cape Town and Johannesburg; and always he spoke with such technical accuracy that he might have been taken for a professional railwayman. He could give you details of the fifty-feet wooden coaches, the *Constantia* and *Voorspoed* and others, built in the Salt River workshops before last century ended. A gleam of delight came into his eye when he observed an old coach with fittings for lamps burning colza oil.

Naturally such a determined railway-collector as Leendertz had visited every transport museum from Johannesburg to Lucerne. As a result of his enthusiasm and guidance I found myself recently peering into the superb coaches built for British royalty as far back as Queen Adelaide. I sensed the approving spirit of Martin Leendertz beside me as I inspected the very bathroom once occupied by Queen Victoria on journeys to Scotland. These were indeed aristocrats on wheels. I noted the changing fashions and improvements in upholstering and coachwork; the passing of the rococo and superfluous grandeur; the varnished red mahogony and silver-plated bedsteads and baths in the coaches used by King Edward VII; silk damasks and velvets, golden door handles and maple tables, and the quiet dignity of watered silk. In the same museum at Clapham I walked through early sleeping-cars, and remembered a Leendertz lecture on this pleasant subject. Luxuries on wheels came from the United States, he said; the first sleeping-cars, restaurant cars, lavatories, Pullman cars. Leendertz informed me that train lavatories were first installed only about a century ago, and then only on royal trains. Common travellers had to be content for a long time with chamber-pots. South Africa was not far behind America and Britain in sleeping arrangements, as the distances made bunks and other comforts imperative. I saw sleeping compartments at Clapham that I coveted. Imagine a sleek coach with or without armorial bearings and carving but a splendid coach deposited in a solitude of your own choice. You would have your own bedroom, each cupboard and fitting revealing the work of a master craftsman. Racks and lights and a reading lamp over your head. No screaming whistles, rattling or clanking as you sat down to breakfast with gleaming silver on the table under the clerestory roof of the panelled saloon. Just a compact and self-contained world taken off the noisy rails and left in some peaceful and forgotten corner.

Thanks to Leendertz I indulged in dreams and also became aware of many railway realities. I looked at trains with new eyes, seeing not only grandiose rolling stock but leper coaches, horse-boxes, dog-boxes, mission-coaches, travelling post-offices, flat-cars and box-cars; I saw them all with the fresh interest of a railway collector. Never can I expect to identify the locomotives of the world as Leendertz did; he knew them all from Stephenson's *Rocket* and the old tea-kettles to the modern Garrets and Pacifics and Baldwins. He could talk of queer survivals on the Caminho de Ferro Mocambique and the eight-wheeled tank engines that struggled out from Cape Town with the suburban trains before last century ended. Sometimes when I listened to Leendertz I seemed to be on the footplate of a famous express during the golden age of steam, with the shining rails ahead at one moment, then instantly swallowed up by the dark and rushing abyss of a tunnel. Where will the tunnel open? If you are a railway collector with imagination your trains will range freely from the Gotthard Pass to the Hex River valley.

Martin Leendertz passed on a few years ago. "The finest thing I ever did was to give up daily journalism at the age of forty-five and lead my own free life ever afterwards," he once told me. Ships and railways kept him alive and filled his mind with interest to the age of seventy-nine.

Old railway coaches last much longer than human travellers, but there come a time when a coach must leave the rails and find a niche in a museum, a scrapheap or some other resting-place. I have mentioned my own dream of a sumptuous coach in a wilderness. There are some, more enterprising people than myself, who have realised this ambition in a humble way.

Possibly you have never heard of Wlotzka Beacon. It is a fishing resort on the desert coast to the north of Swakopmund. There you will find the "Villa Schmalspur", a narrow-gauge coach from the Lilliputbahn which was railed to Swakopmund and then transported by lorry to Wlotzka. The chassis and wheels were removed before the railway authorities sold the coach. It cost the new owner fifty pounds, including transport, and it has been fitted up as a holiday bungalow. Major K. R. Thomas, who was once magistrate of Walvis Bay, used his influence with the general manger of railways nearly half a century ago and bought a railway box-car for five pounds. Fishermen at the great angling spot named Rand Rifles, half way between Walvis and Swakopmund, used that box-car as their club-house until a few years ago. Bunks were fitted and many happy parties were held in that shelter while sandstorms raged outside. The old box-car resisted the weather but not the hand of man. Vandals attacked the wooden planking with axes and carried off the timber for their fires.

It seems that a railway collector must guard his coach even in the wilderness.

Now I must travel on to Walvis Bay and hear the views of Major Thomas and others on life in a world of Hottentots and dunes, fish and flamingoes.

*Chapter Four*

## THREE STRANGE HARBOURS

STRANGE harbours appear on the charts of the flamingo coast, three harbours used by the Portuguese explorers and known to the flamingoes long before the first explorers dropped anchor. You have seen Swakopmund, the port that never was a harbour. Now here is Walvis Bay, only twenty miles to the south, the Rostro da Pedra of the old navigators.

Walvis Bay is sheltered by a sandspit five miles long but only three or four feet above sea level. South-west winds change the silhouette of this long peninsula every week; and every day the strong, icy current from the south adds a little (a very little) to the length of the peninsula. Compare the first accurate chart made in 1858 with recent charts and you will find a difference of half a mile. The modern town of Walvis has become a roaring waterfront where the trawlermen of many nations bring their frozen pilchards worth millions. Through the swing-doors of the bars have passed fur-capped Russians, Poles and Bulgarians, polite Japs with toothy grins, volatile Spaniards, prosperous Belgians, even a few Israeli fishermen. When a full moon is reflected in the quiet bay the fish are hard to find and the fishermen swarm on shore and into the saloons and cinemas. Down the long runways of the Walvis airport come not only light aircraft but huge transports. In the new town there are streets of salt and gardens and four-storied buildings. But I knew the wooden Walvis of long ago, a settlement on stilts. That was just after World War I, and the place had not grown appreciably since the opening of the century. It was an odd spot, a grim little outpost; yet people became fond of it, probably because it was small and isolated and they shared unusual experiences.

No doubt the first settlers round this bay, the Strandlopers, were delighted with the fishing, the teeming bird life and the brackish water they found in the Kuiseb river bed. Topnaar Hottentots came later. As they roamed along the river they discovered the remarkable melon, the *narra*, huge fields of nourishing melons. This evergreen creeper goes down forty feet to water and produces a prickly fruit the size of an orange. Do not touch the *narra* until it ripens or the bitter juice will make your mouth bleed. The ripe flesh contains phosphorus and sugar, while the seeds are rich in oil and protein. On this perfect diet the Topnaar grew strong and fat, and the have lived on the *narras* for generations. Years ago the seeds were exported to Cape Town and used in cakes instead of almonds. Hottentots make pancakes and syrup from the *narras*; and they crush the seeds and apply the powder to open wounds. Professor H. H. W. Pearson, the botanist, visited the Topnaars early this century and declared that for four months of the year they could live entirely on *narra* products. Graceful tamarisk trees supplied them with timber for huts and firewood. They had a secret recipe for honey beer; honey, wild raisins and the bark of a tree were the main ingredients. The beer is seldom brewed nowadays, but the *narra* seeds are still gathered eagerly. Narraville, a Walvis suburb for coloured people, is named after the life-giving melon.

Another even greater botanical wonder of the Namib desert is *Welwitschia mirabilis*, discovered by the Austrian botanist Welwitsch a century ago. I have seen acres covered with this plant which has aroused so much interest, plants every professional botanist dreams about and always hopes to see in its natural environment. It is a distant relative of the Californian redwoods and the pines of other lands, yet it is a tree growing underground with only the top showing. It grows only in this sheer desert, sending its roots deep for water and living to a large extent on fog moisture. Sir Joseph Hooker, the English botanist, thought the *Welwitschias* lived for a century. Later students give *Welwitschia* a life of a thousand years or more. Here is Hooker's description of the desert wonder: "The *Welwitschia* is a woody plant with an obconic trunk about two feet long, of which a few inches rise above the soil, presenting the appearance of a flat, two-lobed, depressed mass, sometimes attaining fourteen feet in circumference and looking like a round table. When full-grown it is dark brown, hard and cracked over the whole surface (much like the burnt crust of a loaf of bread); the lower portion forms a stout tap-root, buried in the soil and branching downwards to the end. From deep grooves in the circumference of the depressed mass two enormous leaves are given off, each six feet long when full grown, one corresponding to each lobe: these are quite flat, linear, very leathery, and split to the base into innumerable thongs that lie curling upon the surface or the soil." Yes, it is a remarkable plant, but Walvis residents say they would rather have oak trees.

Early white settlers at Walvis lived in wooden huts with fences of sun-bleached whale skeletons. All the first government offices were wooden buildings standing on stilts to protect them from encroaching dunes, high tides and floods. The wooden church put up by the Rheinischer Mission in the eighteen-eighties has survived. It was moved from the centre of the town after World War I, and it is now the oldest building in Walvis Bay. A wooden post-office came later. This was the traditional refuge of Walvis Bay husbands after a riotous male party. They slept off the effects beneath the post-office and faced their wives in the morning. Brandy, guns and gunpowder, clothing and trinkets were the cargoes the old schooners brought to Walvis, and they carried away ivory and feathers. Cattle often took the place of money in barter deals.

Mr. Frank Guthrie, magistrate at Walvis in the early years of the century, told me that he lived in the large wooden Residency of nineteen rooms. There were twenty other buildings in the township, all raised on stilts or sandbags. No one had dared to attempt any gardening, but they grew mustard and cress on flannel. Most of the food was tinned. They relied on sun-condensers for drinking water. Sloping sheets of glass, pans of seawater and gutters were placed so that the sun's rays struck the salt water and filled the warm air beneath the glass with moisture. When a cool wind blew the moisture condensed on the glass and trickled into the gutters. It was a slow process, and beer gave more satisfaction. However, there were only about twenty white people. Donkeys brought drums of dubious water from the Topnaar settlement at Sandfontein in the Kuiseb river bed, and this was used for washing. Every five weeks the S.S. *Nautilus* arrived with blessed Cape Town water.

One great occasion which the poor Topnaars remembered for years was the feast organised by Mr. Guthrie to celebrate the coronation of King George V. Acting on orders from Cape Town he bought oxen and sweets and summoned the Hottentots to the Walvis settlement. The few white people were invited to lunch at the Residency, toys were obtained for the children, and a shooting competition was to be followed by a smoking concert. The oxen were slaughtered, and that night the delighted Hottentots gathered round their camp fires and awaited the great day. Then a runner arrived from Swakopmund with a cable ordering Guthrie to cancel the festivities as King George V has been taken ill and the coronation had been postponed. Guthrie put the telegram in his pocked and said nothing. Walvis Bay was probably the only "out-post of Empire" to celebrate the event that had not taken place. When all the meat had been eaten, when the Topnaars had danced round their fires and departed, the benevolent Guthrie sent a message stating that the cable had arrived too late. No one ever questioned his action.

Hermits and characters of various types found sanctuary in the Walvis world of sand. The area under the British flag was four hundred square miles, most of it sheer desert. Now and again deserters from the guano islands would struggle along the desert coast to Walvis Bay, arriving more dead than alive. Suspicious and dangerous men drifted in from over the German border; army deserters, criminals and others. They were cropped, shaved, disinfected, hosed with sea water and sent to Cape Town when a British man-o'-war called. Guthrie spoke of a more respectable yet mysterious personality who turned out to be a qualified doctor. Walvis Bay needed a doctor, but the official salary was so tiny that the residents had to collect a sum of money before they could ask the doctor to stay there. The doctor was fond of hunting; this tipped the scale and he was persuaded to remain. His behaviour was eccentric and would not be tolerated nowadays, but the inhabitants preferred a genuine doctor to the rough surgery of various amateurs. Another peculiar early doctor at Walvis hated women and refused to examine them. Naturally there were few who believed in his treatments, and women who could afford the journey travelled to the Roman Catholic hospital at Swakopmund.

Major K. R. Thomas, who was magistrate of Walvis Bay from 1920 to 1925, laid out the present township and watched the wild atmosphere of the old Walvis slowly changing. A rail link with Swakopmund had been built. Major Thomas found a motor-car left by Seitz, the German governor, and had it converted into a rail trolley. For many years certain people lived in Swakopmund and travelled by rail to work in Walvis every day. One driver named Simpson was in charge of a later passenger trolley for eighteen years. They scrapped the trolley when he retired, for no one else could run it regularly along the difficult track through the sand. There was also a local passenger train. The court messenger used this train when he was sent by the Swakopmund magistrate to arrest debtors at Walvis. However, the engine-driver was a sympathetic character. Whenever the court messenger was on board, the driver gave a special whistle signal just before he reached the Walvis station. Anyone who was expecting trouble hid in the locomotive shed until the messenger had left the town.

At this period Walvis Bay had a rather critical local newspaper called the *Messenger*. One issue suggested that the Walvis Bay doctor was not a real doctor. The doctor (who was properly qualified) sued the newspaper and only withdrew the action when the editor promised that he would never bring out another issue. That was the end of the short-lived "Walvis Bay Messenger."

Major Thomas told me the story of a Belgian hermit

who lived at Rooibank twenty miles south of the bay. This man's wife died, and no one could persuade him to leave that remote oasis. He married a Hottentot and stayed there year after year. It was an event when he visited Walvis Bay to see his only friend, the court interpreter. Major Thomas called at Rooibank occasionally and the Belgian always showed him a magnificent coffin which he kept in his bedroom. He impressed on everyone that he was look-king forward to being buried in the coffin; and he made his bed in it every night so that there could be no mistake if he died in his sleep. His wishes were carried out, and the Belgian now rests beneath the dunes of Rooibank in the coffin of his choice.

Close to Rooibank there is a roofless ruin, the old German police station at Ururas. Grim tales are told of the camel patrols that set out from Ururas for the diamond areas at Conception Bay and beyond. Some died of thirst, and their bodies were found long afterwards. The isolation of Ururas proved too much for one or two of the German policemen stationed there; but the last one departed more than half a century ago and the tragedies have faded into vague stories buried in the sand.

Old palm trees near Rooibank are all that remain of the German mission called Scheppmannsdorf, named after a Rhenish missionary who landed at Walvis in the middle of last century. Among these palms stood an abandoned church of timber and mud; but someone chopped up this historic monument for firewood not long ago. Francis Galton, the English explorer, cousin of Charles Darwin, landed at Walvis Bay in 1850 from a schooner loaded with supplies for the mission. One trading store was the only sign of civilisation at the bay. Hottentots came down to the shore and bartered oxen and goats' milk for tobacco and clothes. Galton gave a Hottentot a stick of tobacco and a cotton handkerchiaf as a reward for carrying a message to Scheppmannsdorf, twenty-five miles on foot. Soon afterwards Galton visited this lonely mission in the land still ruled by warring chiefs.

Galton found Bam the missionary and his wife worrying

about a lion. It was a notorious marauder which had killed fifty oxen, three horses, one donkey and many calves and dogs. Galton and Bam set out on horseback to track the lion accompanied by Stewardson, a trader who preferred to ride an ox. A number of Hottentots also followed on oxen and the lion was cornered at last. Galton placed a two-ounce bullet in the lion's rump, and when the Hottentot cavalcade arrived the lion was in a tearing passion. One more shot and the lion fell dead. They found Stewardson's dog in the stomach. Galton described Scheppmannsdorf as a circular settlement built on an island in a bend of the Kuiseb river. A fountain irrigated three acres of gardens, and there was a vlei where wildfowl gathered. Bam and Stewardson had bungalows near the white-washed chapel, and there were thirty wattle huts where the Hottentots lived. It was strange experience, listening to the Hottentots singing hymns in their language of clicks. To the south there was a sea of dunes, to the north stretched the Namib plain. Yet they were content.

This queer country round Walvis Bay has always appealed to lovers of solitude. Some years ago a farmer from the Transvaal cultivated a patch of ground at the far end of the Walvis Bay lagoon and lived there alone for ten years. This hermit managed to grow carrots and pumpkins in the sand, but he relied mainly on a small dairy herd for his income. Donkeys pulled the milk cart to the harbour. The pride of his lonely life was a white stallion he called "Blue Lights," a splendid animal with a long white mane. The previous owner sold it because it was too wild; but the hermit rode it through the dunes, fished on the beaches, rounded up his cows and visited Walvis Bay. "Blue Lights" was his only companion for years. One day the hermit felt that he had a religious mission elsewhere. He abandoned the farm (which he had named "Wortels"); he said farewell to the cows and donkeys and his friend "Blue Lights". Shacks on the farm became ruins. For ten years "Blue Lights" cantered about the dune country like a wild creature. It became known as "the white stallion of the Namib," and some people thought they had encountered a ghost when this apparition passed in the darkness. "Blue Lights" drank at the shallow water-hole dug by the farmer. It was killed at last with tranquillizers, but the legend of the "white stallion" lives on in the Namib.

Deep in the desert, seventy miles up the Kuiseb, you will find hermits of a different sort, the remote men of science. Here is Gobabeb, the desert research station where that fine entomologist Dr. Charles Koch, passes year after year studying the beetles that burrow in the dunes. I once spent a month in the desert with Dr. Koch and other scientists. Koch taught me that the loose dunes which appear dead are really like the sea, teeming with many forms of life. Winds from the interior bring food in the shape of microscopic vegetable matter; the beetles need no water beyond the dew and the moisture found in the sand. Lizards and web-footed geckos prey on the beetles. One tiny gecko contributes loud clicks to the desert chorus, and that is the music which Koch and his assistants love to hear. They find queer specimens swimming in the sand dunes: white dancing spiders, crickets, snouted lizards that dive into sand and vanish. Sidewinding adders lie hidden under the sand with only part of their heads exposed, waiting for victims. But the most remarkable event at Gobabeb was the re-discovery of the golden mole after a century and a quarter. Sir James Alexander, the early Victorian explorer of Damaraland, found the first golden mole of this species; a little golden and olive creature without eyes, eyesockets or ears, but with sensitive whiskers and strong feet like shovels. Alexander's specimen was described and then lost. A century passed, and Dr. Austin Roberts identified a burrow, but the golden mole eluded him. Then, in 1963, Mr. W. Haacke of the Gobabeb staff found tracks of the golden mole, and finally captured several moles alive. They are kept at the research station. Their pelts have been greatly admired, and breeding tests are being carried out with the idea of putting a new fur on the market. Such was one scientific drama of the world of sand where time has stood still for thousands of years. Gobabeb is an outpost of science in the frightening desert solitude. Other people seek life where the earth seems lifeless; they camp in the Kuiseb canyon and collect the succulents that come out after rare showers. Bushmen and animals can smell these plants that resemble stones; they hunt with their noses and refresh themselves with the moist food of the desert.

Most of the Walvis Bay district is a game reserve. Ostriches, zebra, gemsbok and springbok graze in the open when there is grass in the Namib. In the dry river gorges there are klipspringers and leopards. Jackals and brown hyenas join forces and scour the beaches for dead seals, dead fish, dead seabirds, dead crabs. Ravenous hyenas swim off to rocks and feast on mussels.

Close to the Walvis harbour there is the lagoon I have mentioned, five miles long, a paradise for bird-watchers. Here once more are the greater and the lesser flamingoes, the small ones being comparatively rare while the large *ruber* is seen in flocks thousands strong. Pelicans fly overhead in formation, squadrons of hundreds of bulky pelicans. Sometimes the water boils with multitudes of cormorants and black-backed gulls. Sand plovers run among the reeds and green salt bush at the foot of the dunes. Grey herons rear their long white necks out of the marshes. Again and again the eye of the visitor is drawn back to the beauty of the flamingoes. Walvis Bay has its scenes of beauty and it now possesses comforts which would have made the old-timers gasp. Nevertheless the modern town cannot shake off the sands of the desert. They tell the story there of a business man who bought up all the sandpaper in the town and cut it into postcard sizes. He set his staff to work inscribing a corner of each card with the words: "Happy Christmas. This is a picture of Walvis Bay." The whole stock of cards sold out immediately.

Sandwich Harbour, thirty miles to the south of Walvis, is a sandspit harbour in which the sand ran wild and spoilt the anchorage. On the old charts it looks like a replica of Walvis Bay, with the long arm of sand stretching northwards and protecting the bay from the pounding surf.

Men-o'-war and other vessels found perfect shelter there eighty years ago. Then the sandspit turned eastwards, linking up with the coast and blocking the harbour entrance.

Now and again the sandspit is breached by the sea, a narrow channel is formed and small craft may enter the lagoon. But this fine harbour has known better days. There are times when the trapped water becomes stagnant, causing the fish to die and birds seek food elsewhere. Sandwich Harbour still possesses a pool of fresh water; almost a miracle in the world of dunes. For this is part of the Kuiseb estuary. The river rises two hundred and fifty miles from the coast, a hidden river with its course twenty feet underground save in flood seasons. Here at Sandwich Harbour there are a number of fresh-water pools where the river comes to the surface. Thus a place of great desolation has a story, for through the centuries this oasis has lured mammals and birds and human beings.

Portuguese explorers were the first to land there, and it appeared as Port d'Ilheo on their charts. (There are bird islands in the bay). Dutch seamen explored this coast in the sixteen-seventies, and found three huts and a small band of Hottentots at the Sandwich Harbour oasis. The natives were "very greasy and of a yellow colour, with skin clothes, their hair smeared with fat." They drove the Dutch seamen back to their boats, using assegais, bows and arrows. It appeared that other foreigners, possibly slave-traders, had called there. When the Dutch ship *Bode* anchored in Sandwich Harbour seven years later the Hottentots ran for their lives. The purser and second mate walked inland for a couple of miles and found a camp with ostrich egg shells filled with fresh water, seal meat and seal bladders. Next day the Dutch tried to win the confidence of the savages, laying down their guns and putting out strings of beads, tobacco and brandy. After a time the Dutch followed the Hottentots to a settlement of whalebone huts. Attempts at trade ended in a fight, however, the Hottentots sending hundreds of poisoned arrows towards the Dutch sailors. "We found these people were so rash, or rather courageous, that they charged in the face of firearms," reported the Dutch captain. "We doubt very much whether they will come to such close quarters again, seeing they have had a pretty fair experience of muskets and pistols." The poisoned arrows did little harm, as the wounded Dutchmen were shot through their clothes and most of the poison had been wiped off.

French marine surveyors charted the coast of South West Africa in 1733, visited Sandwich Harbour and described the queer sandspit. Whaling vessels must have called there, but they were secretive navigators, leaving few records of their discoveries. De Pass and Spence, the Cape Town fishing and guano firm, set up a station at Sandwich Harbour in the middle of the last century. They were after sharks, hooking the great man-eaters in the bay, turning them into valuable oil. Sandwich became German territory when the colony was proclaimed. Gun-runners sometimes used the harbour during the wars between the Germans and the natives, for the British would not allow arms to be landed at Walvis Bay. Guano has been scraped off the islands in Sandwich Harbour at different times, and for a period the Thesens were gathering one thousand tons a year.

German business men put up a meat-canning factory at Sandwich Harbour in the 'eighties of last century, when word reached Germany of the great herds of Herero cattle. Fuel had to be sent from Germany as there was only driftwood on the spot. Cattle reached the coast in poor condition after the long trek through the desert. Captain von Bruen, first port captain of Swakopmund, retired to take charge of the enterprise, but it was a complete failure. The tins were imperfect, and a great deal of canned meat extract had to be thrown into the sea. Drift sand covered some of the buildings. Yet the weird appeal of Sandwich Harbour gripped Von Bruen's son to such an extent that the young man decided to remain there when the factory closed down. He had a donkey-cart so that he could reach Walvis Bay; but he did not care for shops and streets, and once he allowed five years to go by between visits. With his dinghy and his nets he made large hauls of fish. In the moist ground near the oasis he grew carnations, tomatoes, carrots and parsley. Here the hard working Von Bruen and his wife Anna lived happily with their many children—until Anna died in child birth, aged thirty-six.

All sorts of people called on Von Bruen. The regular visitors were anglers, and there is a house for them; a house said to be haunted by a Portuguese who was drowned in the harbour years ago. Many of the visitors are bird-watchers, for Sandwich Harbour is a meeting-place of land and sea birds, a great avian metropolis. Some birds follow the Kuiseb River bed, finding insects among the *kameeldoring* trees, the wild tobacco and wild fig. Ostriches feed on acacia seeds and green leaves. Doves and sparrows, weavers and starlings drink from the troughs where the Hottentots draw water from their Kuiseb wells. Sandwich Harbour has a marshy area six miles long; fresh water pools fringed with sedge, with bulrushes and reeds growing in the water. Dr. O. P. M. Prozesky of the Transvaal Museum counted eight species of duck round the pools, and a total of more than sixty species of land birds. He saw large flocks of black-necked grebe; white pelicans soaring over the dunes; herons and egrets, a thousand white-bellied storks, marsh harriers, purple gallinules and red-knobbed coot in large numbers. And of course the greater flamingoes were stirring up the mud of the lagoon while the lesser flamingoes fed apart in the smaller pools.

I asked Von Bruen to explain the mysterious old iron ship in the Sandwich Harbour dunes, and mentioned the legend of the Portuguese man-o'-war that entered the harbour and was unable to leave because the entrance closed while she was inside. "The ship was here when I settled at Sandwich Harbour in 1908 and no one could tell me how it got here," replied Von Bruen. "The stern was still afloat in 1914 and the bows were resting on the shore. Sand built up round the hulk and she is now two hundred yards from the water. I believe the old ship was once used as a house. It may have been a German ship as it had a large German eagle on the bows. She was rigged as a four-masted barque."

Sandwich Harbour is the end of the coast where people may move freely without finding the police in pursuit. When you leave that calm lagoon the diamond coast stretches before you, the forbidden coast then runs all the way to the Orange River. However, you may land at Luderitz without a permit, the little harbour known to the old Portuguese as Angra Pequena.

Luderitz bay is not only small but narrow. Master mariners dread these waters in fog, for this is indeed a coast of wrecks. At the northern end of the harbour is Flamingo Island, a sign that the birds are still with us.

I think one feels the Namib landscape as a threatening reality most keenly at Luderitz. The other harbours to the north have some water, and they have known floods. Luderitz is just sun and waterless sand. Even the tombstones have had their inscriptions blasted off in the sandstorms. Roaring winds strain human nerves, strike the face like a whip—and expose the diamonds along the coast. Many an unsuspected pocket of diamonds has been revealed after a south-west gale. This desolate region must once have known a more kindly climate, for the desert round Luderitz has given up not only diamonds but the riches sought by scientists. Here are skulls and shell middens; tools of milky quartz and chalcedony polished by the wind; pottery sherds and ostrich eggshells decorated with geometric patterns; and, most ancient of all, the rolled pebble tools and hand-axes found in the diamond gravels. On the *tafelberg* hills the archeologists have discovered "workshop sites" with artefacts and scrapers.

Dr. Heinrich Vedder, missionary and historian, thought that before the present races came to South West Africa, long before the Bushmen, there was another unknown people. They left engravings totally different from Bushman art, but no other clues. The riddles set twenty thousand years ago remain unsolved. It is possible that the last beachcombers living in the Luderitz area spoke the Nama language and owned cattle. Many secrets still lie buried in the moving *barchan* dunes and the old river valleys swamped with red sand. In Luderitz they showed me the *gipsrosen*, the so-called "Namib roses"; stones like flowers, shaped not by human hands but by the sand and wind. You may well shudder when you imagine living in a desert where even the stones are not hard enough to resist the weather.

Cape Town supplied Luderitz with drinking water for a number of years. Then a sea water distillation plant solved the problem. Steamers had to bring fresh water to Luderitz again, however, when a boiler blew up at the power station and a special water train hauled supplies from Keetmanshoop. The two thousand white inhabitants of Luderitz found that beer was hardly more expensive than water. For some, the water shortage made little difference in the daily routine.

Rain falls so seldom at Luderitz that roofs are not fitted with gutters. The town is without boreholes or gardens. Luderitz is so isolated that convicts go out to work without warders, hemmed in effectively by the desert and the sea.

Within living memory Luderitz was linked with the interior only by horse, donkey or ox-wagon. Of course there were unhappy travellers who walked through the Namib, but I shall never understand how they survived. Wagons with matched teams of fine red Afrikander oxen would draw admiring groups when they reached the sandy streets of Luderitz from Keetmanshoop. I know a man who took weeks on that trek when things went wrong. He flew over his old tracks not long ago, covering the same distance in one hour and twenty minutes. Yet this is still a nightmare country for the pilot who has to make a forced landing. Airmen and many shipwrecked seamen have known the full horror of the Namib, the only true desert in Africa south of the Sahara.

I have met several of the Luderitzbucht pioneers, men who knew the place towards the end of last century when Adolf Luderitz's prefabricated wooden house and store was almost the only building on that sandy shore. Mr. John Burmester, a Cape Town business man, landed at

Luderitz in 1897, when he was twenty.* "My father had a store at Keetmanshoop, and I was on my way to join him," Burmester told me. "Apart from Luderitz's house, taken over by the Deutsche Kolonialgessellschaft, there was only one other white home; that was David Radford's hut. Radford fished for a living and raised a family amid diamonds worth millions. Strandlopers roamed the coast, living on shellfish. It was a weird spot."

Burmester told me how the Diamantberg gained its name. This is a koppie with a fine view of the town. Early settlers left broken bottles, glittering in the sun like diamonds. It was a prophetic name. The great diamond discovery was made years afterwards.

As a young man Burmester often brought cattle from Keetmanshoop to Luderitz for shipment. He decided that Prince of Wales Bay, about forty miles south of Luderitz, would make a better port. There was more water, some grazing and good anchorage for small vessels. So he applied to the German colonial company for rights, including mining rights, from Luderitz to the Orange River. He offered one thousand marks a year. "Money thrown away," declared Scholtz, the company's manager at Luderitz. Six months later the reply came from Berlin, granting Burmester all the rights he wanted except a monopoly of landing rights. Burmester turned it down on that account. Soon afterwards the first diamond was found. He had lost millions.

Burmester was in Kapps Hotel at Luderitz one night during the diamond boom. Some people came on shore from a Woermann liner and one of the women said she would like to see a diamond. An obliging prospector emptied a bag of diamonds on the table, a valuable parcel with one beautiful stone worth thousands of pounds. Next moment the lights went out. When they came on again the large stone had vanished, and the owner never recovered it.

*Mr. Burmester studied geology in Cape Town early this century. His hobbies were painting and prospecting. He died in 1966, shortly after giving this interview. L.G.G.

It was a hard trek through the sand from Luderitz to Keetmanshoop, as I have said, but there was one oasis on the way. This was Naiams on the Fish river, where an Englishman named Wheeler lived with his family in a clay and brick house. They had a fruit garden. Otherwise it was a weary journey, and the oxen suffered greatly from thirst. Burmester saw an opening for camels, wrote to the German consul in the Canary Islands, and imported the first camels from there. They came in the S.S. *Hydaspes*, chartered for the purpose, and the landing of one hundred and fifty camels at Luderitz was an event long remembered by everyone who took part. Later the German Government sent to Arabia for breeding-stock.

Burmester and his father dealt with Hendrik Witbooi and other *kapteins* before the Hottentots went into rebellion. Witbooi had an army of one thousand men on horseback. He raided the Hereros and drove their cattle over the border into the Cape Colony. Scotty Smith, freebooter of the frontier, sold the cattle and supplied Witbooi with guns and ammunition, wagons, saddles and bridles. Scotty dealt with the Burmesters at their store until the Germans put a price on his head; then he remained on his own side of the border. The Burmesters imported strong Pschoor beer for the German garrison at Keetmanshoop; and John Burmester made journey after journey to Luderitz to pick up cargoes. Sometimes he found himself in the path of the springbok migrations. A cloud of dust in the distance was the signal for everyone to take refuge in the wagons, for the thousands of fast-moving buck would have trampled them to death. "They smelt the rainfall far away and made for the young grass like a living wave," said Burmester.

John Burmester was probably the last survivor of the wreck of the S.S. *Eduard Bohlen*, the "ghost ship" of Conception Bay. He left Swakopmund in this German coaster in September 1910, bound for Luderitz. It was a Saturday, and that night the passengers were drinking and singing in the saloon. They ran into fog, and Burmester woke up when the ship bumped on the sand. Everyone was saved. The sand formed up round the trapped ship in such a way that the *Eduard Bohlen* became a ship of the desert, a quarter of a mile from the sea. Labourers on the diamond fields lived on board for years. The "ghost ship" is still there, and has been used by film companies as a realistic background for their dramas.

Round about Luderitz lie the bird islands where the flamingoes pause in their migrations and rest among the gannets and penguins. These strange islands delight the bird-watchers in the same way that the *Welwitschia* grips the botanist. I came to know the islands well some years ago during a voyage in the government steamer *Gamtoos* when the islands were being manned for the guano-collecting season. Recently I found a report on Ichaboe island, which always has the greatest number of birds; it was written in December 1910 by a Mr. W. P. Lowe of the British Museum who was travelling in H.M.S. *Mutine* and collecting specimens. At first the tiny island was a white spot on the blue ocean off the glaring desert coast. Then Lowe saw it was covered with gannets. Sea and air were alive with thousands of birds. Lowe landed and walked up to the huts at the northern end, where a dog chased the birds away from the area reserved for humans. A few men were there, with some dark women and children. The headman said he had been wounded in the face by the formidable beak of a gannet. Lowe found two nests of a rare species of white breasted cormorant on the island. "It was the most marvellous preserve of nesting birds I have ever seen," Lowe declared. "As the sun sank behind the island the sight of the few lonely tombstones appearing against the horizon amid the never-ceasing stream of bird life was a sight weird in the extreme and one which left a lasting impression."

Between Luderitz and the Orange River lies Sinclair's Island, the most southerly of the group. Sinclair's Island was first known as Roast Beef Island, for the British man-o'-war surveying the coast was there at Christmas time, and a neighbouring islet was named Plumpudding. Sealers worked in these waters before the end of the eighteenth century. Captain Benjamin Sinclair came later, a one-eyed man who wore an unsuitable white top-hat and took charge of guano and sealing activities in the eighteen-forties. So many seals were killed by Yankee and other sealers that the herds were almost exterminated. Now the seals have returned to Sinclair's Island and in the breeding season there is little room for birds. Devil's Islet, close to Sinclair's, is a sea-swept rock; yet even here the seals contrive to find shelter when breeding. Plumpudding Island is a penguin rookery, and for some reason the seals never haul up there.

All these isles are in the diamond area. The sea-bed where the bones of pirates and sealers once rested is now being torn open and dredged by ships which are really floating diamond-mines. You can still find the flamingoes on beaches untouched by man, but some of the flamingo coast has been transformed in strange ways since the Portuguese explorers sailed boldly into these unknown waters in their caravels.

*Chapter Five*

# SOUTH TO PORT NOLLOTH

Now we are voyaging southwards along the flamingo coast from Luderitz to Port Nolloth. We steam past the bird islands where the flamingoes visit the penguins and the duikers; past the Orange River mouth, one of the great meeting places for the birds of land and sea, including a flock of flamingoes hundreds strong. This is the diamond coast, but the pink and white strings of flamingoes are more gorgeous than the buried wealth.

Ten miles south of the Orange River mouth I would ask you to stare through the binoculars at the little bay marked on the chart as Homewood Harbour. It lies at the foot of the hills shown as The Twins and it is a boat anchorage rather than harbour. Nevertheless this little bay has its own dramatic story, known to very few people. I discovered it recently through the researches of my old school friend Mr. Ewald Borchers. Mr. Borchers is a descendant of Captain William Homewood, the master mariner who named the bay. Homewood arrived in Cape Town in the thirties of last century at the age of twenty-seven. He stayed at 38 Castle Street, a lodging house run by H. R. Keeve. The young captain married Keeve's daughter Magdalena and took her off to sea with him. They had eleven children, some of them born at sea. Homewood returned to Cape Town in the middle of last century and set up in business as a trader and shipowner. He had a little cutter called *Diving Bell* and he sent her up to Hondeklip Bay in the early days of the Namaqualand copper boom. Homewood bought the farm De Riet near Hondeklip Bay and lived there for some years. He was among the first Justices of the Peace appointed in the new magistracy of Namaqualand.

Homewood gathered on his farm a reckless band of sailors, hunters and adventurers, useful men for his various enterprises but often difficult to handle. The old Cape shipping records mention the wild behaviour of these men; they were charged with refusal to obey orders, assaults and thefts. Captain Homewood lost his *Diving Bell*, and after she was wrecked he appears to have commanded various small craft himself. Among them were the *Beechworth* and *Sarah Jane*, the latter named after one of his daughters. Another vessel called *Northwester* appears in the records with "Homewood and Co." as owners. She traded between the Cape and Natal. Captain Homewood also organised trading expeditions into South West Africa (then known as Great Namaqualand) and he anchored his small craft in Homewood Harbour and disembarked freight for the wagons. His clerk was an educated man, Charles Griffiths, son of a Welsh clergyman. Griffiths was a dangerous character with a criminal record. After a quarrel he poisoned Homewood's tea with strychnine, but the tough captain spat it out and laid a charge against Griffiths. The trial was held in Cape Town and Griffiths was sentenced to five years hard labour.

It was in 1860 that Homewood set out from Homewood Harbour with his wife and nine children on his last trading expedition. The country across the Orange River was still a lawless no-man's-land but Homewood and his family ignored all the risks. Just after crossing the Orange River some buck were sighted among the dunes and Homewood followed them alone. He died as a result of a gun accident. A rogue named Campbell, a member of the expedition, exchanged the trade goods with the Hottentots for cattle worth sixteen hundred pounds. The widow and children found their way back to the farm De Riet and later to Cape Town; but Campbell vanished into the wilds with the cattle he had stolen from the widow. Captain William Homewood was one of those pioneers whose diary (if he had kept one) would have made a great story of adventure. I am glad to find Homewood Harbour on the chart, a tribute to a bold spirit.

Port Nolloth arose after the discovery at Okiep of a copper mine which was at that time the richest in the world. Thanks to an ancient mariner named Samuel Bremer, I always feel that I was present at the birth of Port Nolloth. Bremer was there, and he told me the story. It started in a Portsmouth tavern in 1853, when Bremer saw that "seamen and a good fiddler" were wanted for H.M.S. *Frolic*, which was being commissioned by Captain M. S. Nolloth, R.N. Bremer signed on as signalman, and they sailed for the Cape. Soon afterwards the *Frolic* was ordered to survey the west coast. "When rounding Cape Point we met a sneezer, and I do not believe from that day to this there was ever a vessel so close to the point," Bremer declared. "We thrashed her around with double-reefed topsails, all hands on deck." It was in November 1854 that the *Frolic* anchored off Robbe Bay on the Namaqualand coast. Captain Nolloth waited for suitable weather, then sailed the *Frolic* through the surf, over the bar into the harbour. There he lay for eight days charting the little-known bay. Bremer noticed the remains of a wreck on the beach. The coast was strewn with whalebones. Some of the Hottentots who came from the interior said they had never seen a ship before. A copper-mining company had asked the admiral for a survey of the harbour, and the company had supplied the *Frolic* with what Bremer called "all necessary comforts for the inner man." These consisted of two large casks of dark London beer, and each man received a pint ration every evening. When I met Samuel Bremer in 1921 he was eighty-six years old, and still smacking his lips when he remembered that splendid beer.

Captain Nolloth reported that Robbe Bay was an excellent anchorage for vessels of light draught. Soon afterwards the name was changed to Port Nolloth. Captain Nolloth left the navy and became the first harbourmaster in the employ of the copper company. Port Nolloth grew slowly. The copper company spent £5000 on a wooden jetty, but after ten years there were still only a couple of dozen inhabitants. Governor Sir Henry Barkly noted progress in 1873 when he arrived in the S.S. *Namaqua*. Two barques in the roadstead were dressed for the occasion. A racing gig came out, manned by St. Helena men in duck suits and sailor caps. A salute of seventeen guns was fired as he stepped on shore. The police force of two men saluted. Sir Henry Barkly was shown the wooden church, the residence of the copper company's manager, the hotel with billiard room, wholesale and retail stores, butchery, bakery, forge and carpenter's shop. Railway lines had been laid to the end of the jetty, and the copper ore was tipped into lighters. The governor suffered no hardships, but a housewife who was there told me she would never forget the brack water and the sandstorms. Brack water was brought by railway tank cars from the station called Jules Hoogte, five miles from the port. They made drinkable coffee with this water, but it spoilt their tea. So they hoarded rain-water for tea, or pleaded with masters of visiting ships for Cape Town water. When southerly gales were raging the sand could not be kept out of the houses of those days. Each white home was fitted with a sandproof cupboard where the food was kept. It was impossible to serve food at the table. Each person took a helping from the cupboard and closed the door carefully.

Even in those days little Port Nolloth had three social classes, the Cornishmen, the St. Helena people and the Hottentots. Cornishmen, the "Cousin Jacks" of England's western toe, have left their lovely cobbled villages for centuries to work in distant mines. They brought to Namaqualand a taste for tea and "herby pie", Cornish pasties, clotted cream. Methodists almost to a man, they loved singing hymns and forming brass bands. The coloured St. Helena islanders filled many semi-skilled jobs, and the Hottentots were labourers. Adventurers and other travellers passed through Port Nolloth, for the sea voyage to Cape Town was much quicker and more comfortable than the overland journey by Cape cart or wagon.

Jack Herridge, a trader who had served in the British Army made Port Nolloth his base towards the end of last century. He trekked all over South West Africa by wagon, carrying loads of glass trinkets, cloth, coffee, sugar and tobacco; bringing back live cattle, skins, ostrich plumes ivory and specimens for museums. His wife accompanied him. At the end of one long trip he reached Port Nolloth with a lion in his wagon. Mrs. Herridge played with it like a dog. The lion went by sea to Cape Town, where it was sold and sent to a zoo in England.

Bishop Simon, a French Roman Catholic missionary, travelled to Port Nolloth in the S.S. *Namaqua* during the early eighteen-eighties. He remarked that he had seen ships five times her size on the Rhone. The run lasted three days. The ship's company spent their time catching snoek, which they sold in Port Nolloth. The port was a mining camp in the midst of deep quicksands; shacks, hotels and courthouse all built of corrugated iron. In one street along the waterfront dwelt the aristocrats; behind them lived the carpenters and artisans in smaller, lower houses; and then came the day labourers in huts covered with sacks. Finally there was a slum where the Hottentots tried to exist by selling brushwood for fuel. They were savages with naked children, crouching under bush shelters.

Roman Catholic sisters of the Oblates of St. Frances de Sales started work at Port Nolloth early this century. They opened a school for coloured girls and taught reading, writing, crochet work and music. Every year a coaster brought a Christmas tree to the treeless harbour, bells pealed and the Cornish brass band played in front of the mission. Port Nolloth has had its visions of wealth; fortunes have been made in copper and diamonds and fish; and always there have been the starving or undernourished people whose only happy memories were those of the Christmas treats provided by the sisters.

Much confusion was caused because the three coasting steamers serving Port Nolloth in the eighteen-sixties and after were all named *Namaqua*. The first was German, the second a Union liner, the third owned by William Berry. When the German ship was withdrawn the Union S.S. *Namaqua* became known as the "Big Namaqua" or "Hottentot Packet". She had good passenger accommodation for her size. She was wrecked near Port Nolloth in 1876 without loss of life. A storekeeper bought the hull for five pounds and the cargo (valued at two thousand pounds) for thirty-five pounds and made a huge profit. Berry's *Namaqua* was able to cross the bar at Port Nolloth and moor at the wharf; but in 1889 she, too, was lost on the fogbound coast. Most interesting of all the ships that called regularly at Port Nolloth were the famous Swansea copper ore barques. The ship-lover who described these beauties to me was Mr. George Pilkington, the marine painter. His father was in charge of shipping the copper, and young George spent his school holidays at the desolate harbour. Swansea in Wales held almost a monopoly of the copper carrying and smelting trade all through last century. The barques were specially designed for the task. Small and efficient, they were built of oak, and most were between four hundred and six hundred tons. Thus they were able to enter Port Nolloth and load at the jetty. It was a feat of seamanship, sailing the barques into that difficult harbour, but their masters were superb seaman. Crews were dressed in uniform, blue shirts and white trousers, which the men made at sea. Many sailors wore gold ear-rings. Captains were paid nine pounds ten shillings a month and an able seamen earned two pounds five. Joseph Conrad wrote of the copper-ore trade. "A work, this, for staunch ships, and a great school of staunchness for West Country seamen," he declared. "A whole fleet of copper-bottomed barques, as strong in rib and planking, as well-found in gear, as ever was sent upon the seas, manned by hardy crews and commanded by young masters, was engaged in that now long-defunct trade."

Copper ore was a dangerous cargo on account of its weight and the chance of shifting in heavy weather. One barque, *L'Esperance*, took six months from Port Nolloth to Swansea, reaching her home port battered and short of food, with her crew more dead than alive. Then there was the *Caswell*, with Captain "Bully" Best as master. She made nautical history. Best was murdered by Greeks in the crew, and the ship was brought into port by the carpenter and an apprentice after they had put out a fire. She was lost with all hands at the end of last century. Another of these barques was named *Hondeklip*, after the place where the copper was shipped for some years before Port Nolloth was developed. Now the ore mined in Namaqualand is smelted on the spot and the "blister copper" goes by road to Bitterfontein and by rail to Table Bay Docks. Few alive today can recall the shapely barques that came in with Welsh coal for the mines and carried the ore away. Modern twin-screw coasters tie up at the Port Nolloth jetty nowadays and load frozen fish.

Those old shipmasters must have groaned when they sighted the dreaded, hazardous coastline at Port Nolloth. Fogs and lack of proper shelter caused a long list of shipwrecks. In the very early days of the copper trade a century ago one captain drowned himself when his schooner went on to the rocks. The Swansea barque *Ocean King* was lost at Port Nolloth in the summer of 1881, but all hands were saved. A year passed and the British barque *Gleam* and the Swedish barque *Freda* were wrecked. Port Nolloth had its great gale in February 1886, an event discussed by old-timers for many years afterwards. In the roadstead outside the harbour lay the barque *Veronica*, loaded and ready to sail for Swansea, but with her master on shore paying his bills. The barque *Taunton* was there, taking on copper ore; and also at anchor were the barques *Maxima*, *Marquis of Worcester* and *Esempio*. A heavy south-east gale set in, and it was obvious to everyone that the bar would soon be impassable. The steam tug *Nolloth* hurried out to bring in the lighters. Darkness came and the *Veronica* dragged her anchor. The mate let go a second anchor, but by this time the *Veronica* was sheering wildly across the bows of the *Marquis of Worcester*. A "chopping battle" started, with both ships at the mercy of the gale; the *Marquis of Worcester* striking the *Veronica* violently at every rise and fall of the sea. At last the *Veronica* was seen to be sinking. In spite of the blinding spray and the seas that caused all the anchored ships to plunge and almost stand on end, the captain of the *Marquis of Worcester* managed to launch a boat and rescue the crew of the *Veronica*. When dawn came the people of Port Nolloth saw that the *Veronica* had disappeared, but the other ships were safe. The wreck of the *Veronica* was sold by auction for four pounds, but I doubt whether the buyer recovered anything of value.

Port Nolloth once watched the departure of a shipload of Bushmen, possibly the only occasion when a large band of these little people travelled by sea. They had been at war with the Hottentots in the Kenhardt district, and the Cape Government rounded up the Bushmen and removed them from the scene of conflict. That was in 1884, and it was a rainy March when the unhappy Bushmen were put into camp at Salt River. Farmers called and selected "apprentices": but they soon discovered that the Bushmen could not or would not dig, herd or milk. Very soon the Bushmen disappeared and in small and inconspicuous parties they returned to their desert homeland.

A well-known figure in Port Nolloth during the early years of this century was the Rev. Heinrich Kling, the Rhenish missionary at Steinkopf. Kling had medical experience and was an admirer of Culpepper, the English herbalist. During his years in Namaqualand, Kling studied the herbal lore of the Bushmen and Hottentots, and finally wrote a pamphlet dealing with the medicinal plants of the Cape. He scoured the veld round Port Nolloth for remedies and studied the ways of the local *bossiedokters*. Kling decided that many of them did good work. He saw a woman who appeared to have been cured of a leg affliction after the qualified doctors had failed to help her. Kling also encountered a Bushman who declared that he was immune to the poison of snakes, scorpions and spiders. The Bushman said his father had injected various poisons into his veins to bring about this immunity, and he showed Kling a number of scars. Kling also recorded the failure of a Hottentot "doctor" who had poisoned a number of people with his medicines and had gone to gaol for six months. Hottentots believed that illness was due to the evil actions of enemies. Favourite medicines were herbs, bark, shells of ostrich eggs, dung of animals and the urine of dassies. The "doctor" incised the skin of his patient and injected medicine with the aid of a horn. When a patient died the "doctor" was expected to name the person responsible.

Round about Port Nolloth are many Hottentot graves. Kling and a well-known Customs official, Mr. C. Leo Biden, once watched a burial ceremony. The corpse was sewn up in a kaross after salt had been sprinkled on the chest. Sticks tipped with gemsbok horns were used to dig the grave. Women placed buchu leaves on the body, and then it was lowered into the grave in sitting position. Flat stones were placed over the body so that no sand could fall on it, and the grave was filled in. One long stone was placed upright in the centre of the mound, and one of the gemsbok sticks was left in the sand. It was customary for every Hottentot passing a grave to throw a stone on the mound as a sign of homage to the dead. One huge mass of stones near the Port Nolloth-Okiep railway line was pointed out by Hottentots as the grave of an ancestor who had come from another country. Hottentots at Port Nolloth made horns of the hollow kelp called *Ecklonia buccinalis*, the sea bamboo, or "trumpet grass". Strange music was heard on the dunes of the little harbour when the Hottentot orchestra assembled.

Mrs. Hildegard Mönnig, one of Kling's daughters, talked to me of the Port Nolloth she knew before World War I. She and a number of other school girls travelled between Cape Town and Port Nolloth in the coasting steamers *Ingerid*, *Nautilus* and *Burton Port*. Often they had to wait for days outside the bar at Port Nolloth before it was safe for the coaster to enter the harbour. During one short June holiday the *Nautilus* became lost in fog and had to keep well out to sea. She had no wireless, and there were no aids to navigation. Parents were frantic with anxiety as they thought the ship had been wrecked on the treacherous Namaqualand coast. Every telegraph office from Port Nolloth to Concordia remained open day and night. At last the *Nautilus* reached the wharf safely, days late, but the children had only a short time at home before the holidays ended. Mrs. Mönnig told me that the clothes, dress-materials, shoes and stockings which the mothers of schoolgirls bought in Port Nolloth were greatly admired by the teachers and other girls at boarding-schools in the

Cape. These clothes were different from the lines available in the Cape Town shops and were often better. It appeared that the Cape Copper Company had a clever buyer in England, and their store at Port Nolloth was stocked with goods which were unknown elsewhere in South Africa. "Port Nolloth had a number of charming English families, some of them real aristocrats," said Mrs. Mönnig. "Most of them lived on the copper mines and came to the sea for their holidays."

General Smuts saw the Port Nolloth waterfront in 1902, with a "safe conduct" pass signed by Lieutenant-Colonel Douglas Haig. Smuts had been laying siege to Okiep; but he was needed at peace negotiations. Accompanied by Deneys Reitz he boarded a troopship at Port Nolloth for Cape Town. It was a strong contrast with the hardships of the veld. "Hot baths, soft beds, proper care," noted Reitz.

Gun-runners flitted in and out of Port Nolloth sixty years ago, when the Germans were at war with the Hottentots beyond the Orange River. The police were suspicious but nothing could be proved until a number of Hottentots were rounded up in the Richtersveld and interned. Then the police learnt that two Englishmen named Smith and Huey had buried a quantity of ammunition, which was recovered later and used against the Germans. Smith pretended to be an ordinary *smous*, but he was arrested.

Members of the old Cape Mounted Police usually rode out on patrol in pairs from Port Nolloth. The rule was enforced after a sergeant had lost his way, gone mad with thirst and cut his horse's throat to drink the blood. When a search party found him two days later he was naked and would have died if help had not reached him. The pay he had carried for remote police stations was scattered over the veld. He had to go to a mental hospital for treatment before being invalided out of the service. Many of those patrols called for great endurance as the horses plodded over the sandy plains under the fierce sun. Farms were fifteen to twenty miles apart, and the dwellings were only *matjieshuisies* of reeds and saplings. One police trooper informed me that in spite of many sufferings in heat and cold he was always well; and he thought the brack water contained some mineral which kept everyone in good health. When he returned to civilisation the sweet water tasted insipid.

Passengers for Port Nolloth in 1910 travelled by the S.S. *Hellopes*, and they were slung over the side in a basket and landed by harbour tug. Pot plants on the stoeps of Port Nolloth were the only signs of vegetation. There was a bandstand in the middle of the main street along the waterfront, with the jetty at one end and the makeshift lighthouse at the other; just an oil lamp on a tripod of rails. Heavy ground swells ran in from the ocean, but a strong current scoured out the inner harbour and kept it clear of sand. The port had a wireless station half a century ago, placed there in case the war reached the South African coast. A submarine was reported by a Namaqualand farmer at that period, and a keen look-out was kept for this imaginary menace. Long afterwards I met an old soldier who claimed to be the only man who had ever been sent out on horseback to look for a submarine.

Among the very early residents of Port Nolloth was Captain R. Carstens, a master mariner who was port and shipping manager of the Cape Copper Company. His son William opened a store there, and in 1913 he prospected for diamonds, sent various gravels to Cape Town, and was told that they were "without doubt diamondiferous". Then came the war. Mr. William Carstens had a son Jack, who served on various fronts. While he was in India a fortuneteller told Jack Carstens: "You are going to leave the army and sail to a far-off country. There you are going to dig in the ground and find many shining stones. And you are going to become a very rich man." Jack Carstens never amassed great wealth, but he did find the first diamond in Namaqualand on August 15, 1925. It was a half-carat stone, covered with three feet of earth at a spot six miles south of Port Nolloth. This was not a rich deposit, but it paved the way for the great discovery further up the coast.

Those who, like Martin Leendertz and myself, are fascinated by narrow gauge-railways have never recovered from the shock they experienced when the line from Port Nolloth to Okiep closed down. Construction started almost a century ago, and the tiny engines and quaint matchbox passenger coaches were still jittering over the thirty-inch gauge track after World War II had started. Then the old line (apart from two short sections) was torn up for the sake of the metal and sleepers. You will see the old culverts and embankments, of course, and some of the historic rolling-stock has been preserved. Come back to the beginning of this peculiar venture.

Spooner, the genius behind the Festiniog miniature railway in Wales, inspired this line, one hundred miles long, between Port Nolloth and the copper mines. William Taylor, driver of the pioneer locomotive (named *Miner*) had come from the London underground; a strange contrast in atmosphere. When the governor, Sir Henry Barkly, travelled up the line in 1873 the *Miner* was decorated with rosettes. Proper coaches had not yet arrived, but open trucks had been fitted with canvas roofs, curtains of duck lined with green material and sheepskin carpets. It was early August, the spring flowers were out, and the train stopped often so that the governor and his staff could examine the great display closely. At first the train ran across the sandy coastal plain between the dunes. There were many curves. Someone explained to the visitors that the contractor had been paid one thousand pounds a mile, and naturally made the line as long as possible. At first it was thought that steam locomotives would be put out of action by the sand, but the *Miner* and another little engine called *John King* were imported as an experiment. Each engine weighed about six tons with water and fuel. They were a great success, and soon they replaced the hundreds of mules on the coastal section.

When the governor's train reached Abbevlaak, twenty-two miles from the coast, he was welcomed by a sentry who raised his ancient musket and fired a salute. Twenty miles farther on the governor saw a famous landmark, the first tree, a lone *kameeldoring* twenty feet high. The railway builders had feared that the embankment might give way, but a platelayer named Woodcock had made a name for himself by finding a succulent, the *senecio* or soap-plant, which bound the loose sand perfectly. The train climbed from Anenous to Klipfontein, where the governor spent the night. Next day he watched a copper train, twenty trucks carrying sixty tons, rushing down the hill. This section was then named the Barkly Viaduct. The governor's train went on to Okiep drawn by the Cape Copper Company's finest mules in new harness and rosettes. At Kookfontein (now Steinkopf) the Rhenish missionary had made an archway of evergreens, palms, wild flowers and flags. After another fusillade by a guard-of-honour the governor visited the church and school. The journey to Okiep was completed by Cape cart, as this was faster than the mule train. Okiep had risen on the farm Braakfontein. The visitors thought it looked more like Cornwall than the Cape, with its villas of solid rock. When the mine "roarer" sounded, hot coffee and biscuits were served to all workers free of charge. And a bottle of champagne for the governor.

Mules were still being used on the level section when Bishop Simon arrived nine years later, five hundred mules, each one consuming fifteen pounds of oats, rye and bran a day. The bishop left Port Nolloth in a cold fog at six in the morning. Tiny passenger coaches were provided, each drawn by three mules. Freight cars had six mules. The whole train was made up of thirty little cars. Each car had a conductor with a whip and a brakeman. After the train had covered ten miles fresh relays of mules were attached to the cars. When the train reached the mountains at Anenous the bishop was greatly impressed by the bridges over the ravines, and he thought the scenery resembled the gorges of the Tyrol or Switzerland, with drops of more than two thousand feet. He wondered what would happen if the mules lost their footing, for there were dizzy precipices beside the line. (When the line closed down, officials boasted that there had not been a serious accident during seventy years). Bishop Simon first saw Namaqualand from the railway in the spring, and he remembered the unending flowerbed, yellow on the plains, dark red on the heights.

Everyone travelled free in those days and for years afterwards. Permits were issued in Port Nolloth early this century by Mr. Deane, the copper company's senior official. Passengers quoted a little jingle as they went away with their free passes:

*If you wish to possess*
*The Namaqua Express*
*You call on Deane at the Deanery.*

The line was used by the British Army during the South African War. A famous episode in which General Smuts and Deneys Reitz took part was the capture of one of the small locomotives. The Boers loaded the tender with dynamite and sent it at full speed without a driver along the track leading into beseiged Okiep. However, the engine jumped the points near the mine and rolled over into a ditch without exploding.

Hundreds of troops were rushed up the line early in World War I to cross the Orange River into German South West Africa. The last time men in uniform crowded into the trucks of the "Namaqua Express" was in 1922, during the Bondelswart campaign in the barren, twisted gorges beyond the river.

The exiles of Port Nolloth laid out a cricket field in the dunes outside the settlement. Everyone trudged through the sand to watch the matches, for such events broke the monotony; but it was a grim walk, especially for the women. Then a railwayman had an inspiration. Secretly, and certainly without the knowledge of the directors in London, a branch line was built from the seafront to the cricket pavilion. A special train was run to every match ever afterwards.

Perhaps the item of rolling-stock which made the greatest impression on the primitive Hottentots was Mr. Zebulon Pearce's railway yacht. Pearce, a blacksmith, was fond of hunting. As he had neither horse nor wagon he designed a sail-driven trolley to carry him along the railway line over the veld between Port Nolloth and the mountains. The yacht had a square sail for "running before" and headsails for use when the wind was on the beam. Pearce sometimes reached twenty miles an hour, a speed envied by the engine-drivers on the run. The doctor at Port Nolloth used a "rail bike"; and he, too, had a sail to help him along. This railway curio was still to be seen at Port Nolloth a few years ago, near the pump-house where the camels were once watered. The doctor, by the way, had to cover an area of four thousand square miles; from the port to the Orange River, inland to Anenous, south to the Buffels River. I once saw a letter he wrote: "To any part of this tract of land I am at any time prepared to go," he said, "but I think my salary of £150 a year should be increased."

John Galsworthy the novelist knew Port Nolloth. His father was a London solicitor who acted for the Cape Copper Company and the novelist visited the mines early this century. He trekked through Namaqualand and wrote a little-known murder story based on this experiences. Galsworthy sketched the veld background vividly; the Namaqua partridges flitting to a half-dry water-hole, the springbok drawing together in serried squadrons against a possible attack by stealthy, hungry jackals. He camped under a venerable kokerboom that threw gnarled and fantastic shadows. "That little world of rocks and sand, of scanty brush and tree, held its breath", wrote Galsworthy as the drama moved to its climax.

Port Nolloth is not an earthly paradise, but is has its old families who have been faithful to this weird settlement in the sand. Three generations of Robsons have lived there; the first Robson built the jetty, and his grandson restored a sixty-year-old London locomotive not long ago for shunting trucks along the waterfront. When I close my eyes and think of Port Nolloth I seem to hear the dirge of the bell-buoy, the rumble of surf, the regular explosions of detonators in fog, the seaweed and the sand, the railway whistles, the odour of freshly-boiled crawfish from the factory. Perhaps there are some who have grown fond of this forlorn harbour. As far as I know, Port Nolloth inspired only one poet, the great William Charles Scully:

*Here on the margin of the land's wild waste*
*I sit with eyes set seaward, whilst the sweet*
*Wind from the west, spray-laden, flowing past*
*Bears to the sense faint fragrance, whilst the fleet*
*Foam-bells from each wide-wandering billow cast*
*Over the rocks, are blown about my feet;*
*Far off, a white-winged ship, with straining mast,*
*Bound on her course, close-hauled, with swelling sheet.*

*Chapter Six*

# A CLOUD ON THE HORIZON

In the bad old days of Port Nolloth very early this century the Hottentots knew one brief interlude of delirious happiness. The whole country was depressed after the South African War, many white people were seeking work, and the Hottentots were almost starving. Zebulon Pearce told me the story; a strange episode during the sad and monotonous years of struggle, years of hot east winds, sea winds and fog.

East winds in April brought a swarm of huge moths to the coast. No one remembered seeing moths at Port Nolloth before. They came like a cloud and dropped into the ocean, so that the beaches near the little harbour were piled high with millions of drowned moths. Some were grey, other a dirty white. The phenomenon gave Port Nolloth something to talk about, but a far more serious visitation was on the way. Travellers who came down in the train said that the whole of Namaqualand was talking about locusts. Moths were a nuisance but the locusts were a menace. They were not the red locusts, the Eighth Plague of the Bible, but the small brown desert locusts. Africa had been kind to the locust tribe at that period. No doubt some weather cycle encouraged the swarms, for locusts had been reported over enormous areas; along the fringes of the Sahara, moving resolutely into the more fertile south, spreading right across the continent from Benin to the Sudan. Before long Kenya was invaded, then Tanganyika. The victorious enemies struck into Angola; more eggs hatched out, more *voetgangers* grew up and took to the air. Locusts darkened the skies in German South West Africa and German colonists estimated that one swarm was three hundred miles long. New-planted gardens were devastated in Grootfontein and Windhuk, native crops of mealies and kaffir corn were stripped off; in the south the sheep were robbed of their grasses. Again the locusts halted to make their egg-nests in the Kalahari sands. Old locusts died, but in warm and favourable weather the young locusts hatched out and began to use their powerful legs. Colony joined colony until a new and irresistible army was marching boldly in column of route. Each night the young locusts gathered together for warmth. Each morning they hopped on, guided by mysterious instinct, towards the Orange River and its rich belts of greenery.

No one has ever been able to count these storm-troopers of a locust army. The breeding cycle is so rapid that the progeny of one locust may grow to six million within one year if all goes well. That explains the prodigious swarms hundreds of miles long. So the young and dangerous *voetgangers* moved towards the luscious pastures. They cast their skins, turned black and red, then yellow and brown, their wings growing out. Within a month the babies were becoming adults. But still the ravening horde advanced on foot, in crescendo, with a front of several miles. The whole landscape was alive. Locust millions were marching under the blazing desert sun without shade, without much sustenance, yet without a sign of fatigue. Every grain of sand in the desert seemed to have changed into a locust, such were the numbers. The scanty grass vanished and only the t'samma melons were left untouched through an uncanny respect for the poisonous effects. No leader was to be seen; yet the swarms received signals and answered them. They rested and marched on like a well-drilled army with a strong and faultless sense of direction. Every movement was simultaneous. Some weird locust radio might have been operating throughout the miles of locusts, the millions of locusts. They marched in purposeful columns; the columns merged into a flood; the flood divided when turned from its course by an obstacle; and always the streams flowed round the barrier and merged again into an overwhelming tide. It was a slow advance, one mile an hour perhaps, with such long rests that the whole day's hopping amounted to no more than five miles. Yet it was a noisy progress, with a widespread hissing and rustling and chirruping as they bumped and jostled each other.

Now and again the locust myriads would encounter a fire, started by lightning in the coarse desert grass, or lit by Bushman hunters. Not even fire halted them. Millions of locusts hopped fearlessly into the fire, smothering it with their bodies, giving their lives without a second's hesitation so that the following millions could pass over the blackened area and the scorched bodies of their fellows. Even the beasts and the snakes of the Kalahari avoided the locusts. It is said that a hungry locust army will fling its disciplined might on to the living body of a lion or antelope and devour it with synchronised bites. As a rule a swarm of locusts is no more than a gigantic lawn-mower cutting swathes in the wilderness and the gardens of mankind. The locusts reached those lush gardens when they came, still hopping, to the Orange River. Pioneer settlers were growing oranges and lucerne along the river banks; beans and tobacco and many kinds of fruit. When the army set eyes on this paradise it divided. A cunning leader of the locusts took his followers along the north bank, where his progress was never seriously disputed. Some bolder locust Napoleon led his army into the water to devour the orchards of the south bank. Locust sappers made a bridge with their bodies. Once again numbers were on the side of the invaders. As they had conquered the fires, so they defeated the water barrier, perishing in millions while their comrades hopped with dry legs over the slow-moving narrows of the great river.

There came a day when the hoppers gained the full strength of their wings. Swarms followed the river eastwards and westwards, wings gleaming in the sun like pieces of bright metal. Farmers attacked the swarms furiously when they settled, for they had arsenite of soda even in those days.

But the old native labourers shook their heads and looked hopeless. "We knew the locusts many years before the white man came to this land," declared the natives. "The locusts came in clouds. Pouf! Our crops were finished. Some people died of famine but we could not destroy the locusts."

Such were the stories told by people who reached Port Nolloth from Springbok and Okiep in that dark period. The locusts were everywhere. Upington and Kenhardt were suffering, and all the river settlers were in despair. Hottentots drifted in from the Richtersveld with grim reports of locusts along the lower river, eating the bushes that fed their goats. Flying swarms had settled on the few patches of mountain ground which they cultivated. Grazing in the semi-desert of the Richtersveld was being wiped out. Even the mat-huts were being picked down to the framework by the voracious locusts. It was a tale of disaster from Steinkopf to Lekkersing.

"Anyway, the locusts won't come here," said everyone in Port Nolloth. "Nothing for them to eat here." One morning Port Nolloth awoke to an east wind more annoying and hotter than usual. A coaster was unloading bales of fodder at the wharf, for the Cape Copper Company kept a great number of mules and horses. That green stuff was almost the only refreshing spectacle in Port Nolloth. Some housewives nurtured plants in boxes and tried to grow carrots and turnips, parsnips and celery in sheltered yards; but the east winds shrivelled these pathetic gardens. White people depended on the coasters from Cape Town for their fruit and vegetables, but these items were luxuries at a time when only the higher officials had money to spend. No one knew how the Hottentots existed. They found tiny Hottentot children foraging in rubbish-bins for food, and they were aware of the hardships endured by the ragged population in the huts behind the village. But that was a problem for the government, one of those painful, familiar daily scenes which only the clergy bothered about, and the nuns at the Roman Catholic mission.

As that warm morning wore on the stack of fodder on the wharf grew higher. Zebulon Pearce climbed the arm of a crane to tighten a nut, and as he glanced over the rooftops of the village he noticed a black cloud making a strong contrast with the bright gold of the sunlit sky. The cloud spread like the smoke of an explosion, and Pearce gazed at the horizon in wonder. Soon there were dozens of people on the waterfront, all staring into the heavens. "I'd say it was a forest fire—only there's no forest in these parts," remarked the harbourmaster, his voice puzzled.

Still the cloud grew larger, whirling like dust, forming a curtain between Port Nolloth and the sun. Pearce said that the curtain was never dense enough to cut off the light. It moved towards Port Nolloth with the speed of the east wind, fifteen or twenty miles an hour. When it was about ten miles off, everyone in the village realised that it was an immense swarm of locusts. They were flying high in the grip of the wind, a great dark shape which soon became millions upon millions of silver torpedoes. Hour after hour this frightening procession swirled over the village. Now and again a few locusts in the lower squadrons contrived to defeat the wind and land among the houses. They did not remain on the ground for long. Instinct seemed to compel them to rejoin the stupendous main flight westwards, ever westwards in a suicidal rush to the wastes of the South Atlantic. It was a vast migration dictated by the east wind, and only when a startled Port Nolloth went to lunch did the swarms dwindle and disappear over the ice-cold sea. Then a silence fell over the harbour. At first there had been a distant purring hum. When the main body of locusts approached the coast Pearce said it was like an ominous roar which deepened into a sonorous drone and finally a roaring storm.

"The locusts have no king, yet they go forth by bands," quoted a minister from the Book of Proverbs. "I hope the bands don't come back," replied Pearce loudly, to make himself heard amid the beating and scraping of myriads of wings. People indoors heard another queer sound, for the droppings of the locust horde pattered on the tin roofs of Port Nolloth like a gentle continuous rain. "Then the last of the horde passed over, and we descended from fortissimo to pianissimo," related Pearce. He was one of those musical railwaymen who played in a brass-band.

"A wind brought them, and a wind carried them away,"

said the clergyman thankfully. But he spoke too soon. The east wind dropped, and late that afternoon Port Nolloth watched the return of the locusts from the ocean. The cloud was much lower this time. Pearce declared that when the locusts reached the coast the total effect was like a snowstorm as the rays of the setting sun fell on the countless transparent wings. But the people along the waterfront had little time to admire the strange vision. This time the locusts were landing in millions; landing on the green forage; landing on roofs and in yards; landing on the beaches and in the long waterfront street; landing and invading homes; landing on human beings, striking their faces, clinging to garments tenaciously; hopping on their human victims so that women and children were terrified.

Pearce said the defence of Port Nolloth came too late, and that in any case it would have been useless. They rang the church-bells, hammered pots and pans and lit fires. They beat the locusts down with branches in a futile way, and other locusts descended and ate their fallen brethren. At the railway station a resourceful driver turned a jet of steam on the invaders, but he might as well have tried to empty the ocean with a teaspoon. Along the beaches men dug trenches and buried the thousands of locusts that entered the trenches. They killed thousands of locusts and millions more arrived. Darkness was falling. Locusts are helpless at night, and their unseen leaders had decided to make Port Nolloth their night-stop on their miraculous return from the sea to the inland paradise. It was a night of distress such as Port Nolloth had never gone through before. People complained of the smell of the locust army, little knowing that the smell would soon become a stench. They closed their windows, but their suffocating homes were alive with locusts. It was hard to find all the locusts, difficult to clear them out, for they had only lamps and candles in those days. All night the trapped locusts struggled and thudded noisily as they tried to escape from every room and recess in the village.

Some residents said hopefully that the locusts would fly away at sunrise. The locust leaders took their time about

Locusts are helpless at night and their unseen leaders had decided to make Port Nolloth their night stop.

it, for the east wind had been followed by the traditional mist, and the locust millions had to dry their wings. Port Nolloth cheered soon after daybreak, however, for unexpected help arrived while the locusts were still in possession of the village. Thousands of birds had raced south from the Orange River mouth to feast on their favourite insects. "Heaven alone knows how they heard about the locusts—but birds always do hear that sort of news," went on Pearce. "Never were birds more welcome, all sorts of birds, not only the locust-birds but hawks and kites, guinea fowl, pheasant. Gulls joined in the banquet. They ate greedily." It must have been a relief to watch the brown flocks of *klein sprinkaanvoël* surrounding a horde of locusts and eating the lusty insects with enormous appetites. Neatly the birds severed the wings and legs and gulped the rich flesh. White storks, migrants from Europe, known to farmers as *groot sprinkaanvoël*, joined the smaller birds and gorged until they could hardly fly. And when the harassed locusts rose and departed on an easterly course the insatiable birds followed.

Port Nolloth gasped with relief and licked its wounds. Several of the village drunkards had indeed been wounded, for they had fallen into their usual alcoholic slumber shortly before the locusts arrived and the locusts had settled on them like vultures on carrion. They lurched round to the doctor for treatment and were not well received. Householders found that the locusts, disappointed at the lack of proper foodstuffs, had tried to satisfy their appetities by gnawing wood, cloth, leather and lace curtains. Every home in Port Nolloth had been fouled and damaged.

Each high tide brought drowned locusts to the beaches. Apparently the rearguard of the returning horde had failed to locate the coastline in the darkness and had dropped wearily into the sea. So they lay in long, stinking heaps to the north and south of the port. The magistrate sent parties to set fire to the banks of locusts, but sodden locusts do not burn easily. As time went by the smell drifted farther and farther inland. Train crews arriving at Port Nolloth declared that they first noticed the locust stench miles away. They had other troubles, for locusts had settled on the railway tracks in such numbers that the locomotive wheels slipped. Gangs had to clean the rails near Port Nolloth before the trains could reach the harbour.

Port Nolloth was still groaning under the sickening reek of dead locusts when another blow was delivered. Out at Jules Hoogte the guardian of the wells reported that the locusts had ruined the port's water supply. True, it was brackish water, not to be compared with the delicious water brought up from Cape Town by coaster. But it was water that some drank and others needed for baths and cooking and watering cherished plants; water for the animals and for all those who could not afford a penny a bucket for decent water. Days went by before the wells were cleared of lucusts.

When a coasting steamer crossed the bar soon after the invasion the deckhands were hosing and scrubbing the upperworks. Captain Parow reported that the surface of the water had been so thickly covered with dead locusts that his speed was reduced. He had battened down to prevent the locusts from entering the cabins and engine-room, but a great many had reached the holds through the ventilators. His decks were piled with locusts and the coaster was still in a mess from end to end. Only the fish and the seabirds had welcomed the locust hordes. Captain Parow said that duikers and gulls had flopped down on the coaster exhausted and in agony as a result of eating too many locusts.

When the east wind arose once more it brought to Port Nolloth a strange fragrance from the Hottentot location. Some gargantuan meal was being roasted and very soon the secret was out. During the night of the invasion the Hottentots had gone forth with blankets and sacks, bags and paraffin tins. They alone had welcomed the locusts rapturously, for outside their wretched hovels there had appeared the feast of the century. All next day they had boiled their locusts and dried them in the sun, thus preserving them. Now the thin-ribbed legions of Hottentots were fattening visibly on a generous protein diet. Locusts are really far too rich to form a suitable food without certain additions, such as the Biblical "locusts and wild honey." So the Hottentots mixed their locusts with meal and made locust cakes; they stewed locusts with sheep-fat; they salted their locusts and made a dish that Pearce tasted. "Something like decayed shrimps," he pronounced. "Mind you, I suppose you could serve nice freshly-roasted locusts at a London restaurant and have the customers asking for more." But in Port Nolloth the white people never took to locusts. The smell was too much for them, and only the Hottentots were happy. As the clergyman pointed out to Pearce: "Of these ye may eat, the locust after his kind—Leviticus."

"You're right this time reverend," answered Pearce. "But what a pity the Hottentots couldn't have eaten the whole lot." He held his nose significantly, a gesture seen on all sides in Port Nolloth at that time, except among the merry bloated Hottentots.

*Chapter Seven*

# RIDDLE OF THE PANS

ALL down the flamingo coast run the pans. You find them within reach of the sea, like the Cape Cross pans with their millions of tons of almost pure rock salt. As you go southwards to Port Nolloth there are many more salt pans, dazzling the beholder with their white crusts; and these thin deposits are worked eagerly by poor fishermen. Other pans with clay or sand or limestone floors are strung out inland, far into the interior, perpetual riddles for the geologists and all thoughtful travellers.

Pans, the mysterious pans of Southern Africa, are most common in dry and remote places. In the western Kalahari region surveyors have counted nine thousand pans. Through the northern Cape runs the Panneveld, where the country is speckled with innumerable pans for hundreds of miles. Some maps show pans as blue circles; but pans are not ponds and all too seldom nowadays are they filled with water. What is a pan? The name suggests a shallow basin and indeed they are depressions in the landscape, usually egg-shaped. Some are like dumb-bells, the result of two pans becoming linked; while very large pans have irregular edges. Pans do not slope gradually to a central point like ponds and lakes. The bottom of a pan is flat. There is also the *vloer* formation of the North West Cape; the very devil in wet seasons as I found when I lost my way in the Brandvlei district years ago. The *vloer* has a very gradual fall. It may be related in some way to the pan formation, but here again the geologists are baffled. Often it is hard to distinguish between a pan, a *vloer* and a *vlei*.

Large pans are so spectacular that they aroused the interest of scientific travellers long ago. They can be dangerous, too, owing to mirages. Mr. E. J. Dunn, the official Cape geologist almost a century ago, met a farmer who had attempted the crossing of a huge pan by Cape cart in the Zak River area in summer. After driving for miles he outspanned and went to sleep in the shade of his cart. When he awoke there seemed to be horses everywhere; but as he approached them he found only shadows. At last, tired and thirsty, he abandoned his cart and followed the wheel-marks back to the farm he had left. He was more fortunate than some people who lost their heads when they lost their way, and perished. Many pans are so hard that you need the eyesight of a Bushman to observe marks on the surface. Apart from the mockery of the mirage, dust-devils whirl over the brown expanse, heatwaves rise and fall and a man needs strong nerves, a keen sense of direction, or a compass.

Verneuk Pan gained its name because of the mirage, and this was the pan I came to know only too well when Malcolm Campbell was racing there. Verneuk Pan has an area of about one hundred square miles. I climbed the dolerite hill called Zwartkop at the southern end one day and looked out over the vast stretch of yellowish sandy mud, dry as the little flints that menaced Campbell's tyres. Old maps show a village called Zwartkop; but a local farmer told me there was never a village at the pan. A solitary native once lived there in a hut, and this sign of man, so rare in that wilderness, must have been mistaken for a village. I cannot imagine why the man lived there. Dr. A. W. Rogers, that fine old Cape geologist, examined Verneuk Pan early this century. He found that the eastern end was crossed by two rivers which flooded the pan at intervals. The origin of such a wide tract of flat country as Verneuk Pan puzzled Rogers and many later geologists. Rogers thought that river action might have been responsible. Sand dunes at the southern end could have arisen when sand from the pan was deposited there by the floods. "Great flat surfaces practically devoid of vegetation may be primarily due in this region to the extremely low grade reached by streams behind bars of hard rock," Rogers declared. "Then the conditions for plant growth would be unfavourable owing to the increasing brackness of the soil. Finally there would be the scope given to the wind to remove dust and sand from the bare ground."

Mr. E. G. Bryant, farmer and scholar who lived in the North West Cape for many years, was fascinated by the riddle of the pans. "They seem to represent the last retreat of the water in a drying lake," Bryant once told me. "Yet one looks in vain for signs that the pans were once larger. Old farmers in this area say that the pans once held rainwater for most of the year, but that is a rarity now. The days are gone when pans were surrounded by reeds and bush and grass above a horse's head. This part of South Africa is drying up. The parched surfaces of the pans are signs of a dying land." Bryant was convinced that there was a direct relationship between pans and diamonds. The era when the diamond pipes were formed was intensely volcanic. Were the pans relics of an old drainage system disturbed by the upheavals which produced the diamond pipes? The great Pretoria soda pan was regarded by many geologists as the crater of a great volcano. Near this pan are several diamond mines.

Most ingenious of the pan origin theories was that put forward by Mr. M. S. Alison, a well-known geologist at the end of last century. He pointed out that many pans have springs near their edges. Farmers in the pan country always dig for water at the edge of a pan, and water sometimes reaches the surface of the well. Alison declared that the depressions now called pans were made by the hooves of wild animals going to and from the springs to drink. "Not so long ago the plains were swarming with springbok, hartebees, wildebees and quaggas," Alison argued. "The springs were not strong enough to feed a river, so a marsh was formed and this became the nucleus of a pan. Thousands of animals carried the mud away on their hooves and stamped it off on the surrounding plains. If each animal removed only a quarter of a pound of mud you can see how the process started. As the pans became larger they held more water and thus attracted more animals. This slow excavation went on as long as the water lasted—and as long as the animals were there. Sometimes the gradual deepening continued down to bedrock and afterwards spread out to increase the area of the pan. Antelopes preferred drinking in the open on the pans as lions often lurked in the marshes. It is clear that since the game has been exterminated the pans are filling in again."

Alison's theory was greeted with approval by his fellow geologists, and he was hailed as a man with an original idea which had escaped previous students of the mystery. Mr. David Draper, F.G.S., agreed that animals would transport tons of mud from a pan every rainy season. At one period about one and a half million animals were shot every year for their skins; and Draper supported the statement that the pans had silted after the disappearance of the animals. Dr. Paul Range and Passarge, both eminent foreign geologists, came to the same conclusion. Mr. J. P. Johnson went over the whole problem in 1912 and decided that vast herds of game pulverised the shale, and the dust was removed by the wind. He said the process was still in operation. South Africa once possessed a more generous rainfall, summed up Mr. Johnson, but the pans were formed only after arid conditions had set in.

Rival theorists soon appeared. They congratulated Alison on his bold views and then pointed out that many pans were to be seen in places which the great herds of game never visited. For example there was a large pan on Platberg, a table mountain near Harrismith in the Orange Free State. Panfontein near Krugersdorp was cited as another inaccessible pan. O'Reilly's Pan, to the northwest of Vryburg, is a vast depression which the geologist Alexander du Toit regarded as the site of an old glaciated rock basin. He thought the hollow had been produced by the erosion of the soft boulder clay by the prevailing northerly winds. Water which covered the pan for months every year would aid the process. Du Toit also described the peculiar salt pan known as Groot Chwaing in the same area. Wells put down round the edge of this pan yielded abundant fresh water, yet the pan gave an inexhaustibel supply of brine.

Dr. Rogers made a study of the Kalahari pan called

Haakskein Vlei, the largest pan in the Gordonia district. Fourteen miles long and six miles wide, it is without a scrap of vegetation. Storm water invades the pan on the rare occasions when floods occur in the desert. Rautenbach a farmer who had lived near the pan for many years, informed Rogers that the pan had changed during the previous two decades. Patches of bare rock had appeared on the pan floor. Rogers crossed Haakskein on a windy day, when the fine dust blotted out conspicuous objects three hundred yards away. He had no doubt that wind action had been responsible for the pan. Rogers could not explain a queer sight he encountered during that journey; a pan with millions of dead locusts and beetles, all neatly arranged in separate belts. The *vloer* formations, according to Rogers, were probably due to flooding when blown sand obstructed the occasional rivers. Floods tended to distribute the silt over wide areas, thus levelling up those river valleys which had a very gradual fall.

Rogers admitted that it was hard to discover the origin of the coastal pans. These pans were usually low and separated from the sea by a belt of sand dunes. He visited a number of coastal pans on the west coast to the north of the Olifants River mouth, and noted that rain water collected in the pans. This water did not drain away but evaporated slowly, leaving a thin crust of common salt. The salt, blown from the sea as spray, was collected by the rainwater as it seeped through the surrounding sand. This low-lying coast, said Rogers, must once have been under the sea. But the salt pans far inland could not have derived their salt from the ocean; the salt must come from the surrounding rocks. Dr. Paul Range said these salt pans resembled frozen lakes covered with snow. Round many salt pans are beds of gypsum, which is worked for the cement factories. Geologists look upon the gypsum as proof of the great age of the salt pans, for gypsum crystallizes out very slowly compared with salt.

I think the intelligent modern geologist admits the animal theory as one of a number of possible causes, and refuses to be dogmatic on the subject. Half a century ago the prospector Fred Cornell reminded the scientists that pans differed so greatly that one theory would not account for all the pans. In the Kalahari he found circular pans in the midst of concentric rings of dunes, suggesting old volcanic action. Some pans were soft, others were hard, with red, sun-baked mud. He saw green clay pans, with black volcanic mud below. One pan composed of blue shale and surrounded by sandhills looked just like a lake. The pans that lured Cornell into the desert were filled with blueground, with indications of diamonds. Cornell noticed that the Kalahari pans were marked by high dunes, up to one hundred feet high, usually at their southern ends.

Bryant, too, emphasised that there were many pans, some of them very large, and that wind action could not have been the primary cause. Some of the large pans were still connected with various river channels; others had been connected in the past. When probed by drills, no bottom was found at eighty or one hundred feet. The pans had been filled in during a long period, not blasted out suddenly. Pan and *vloer* formation did not coincide with the surrounding geological formations; but they did correspond roughly with the distribution of the diamond pipes. Pans occur in all sort of rocks, and some of the largest are found in the Karoo shales. In the Kenhardt district hundreds of small pans (up to five hundred yards across) are in granite and quartz rocks. Some of these pans are ploughed up after rain and sown with wheat. Bryant also spoke of the Prieska commonage pan, where shrimp-like creatures appear in rainy seasons. They are known locally as "water-fleas," and they lie dormant in the mud for years.

Chemical action may have been responsible for some pans. Vegetation growing on the mineral material formed acids which brought about decomposition. Sinkage of the underlying dolomite has been mentioned as a cause. Professor Prister said that the pans belonged mainly to the undulating country peculiar to South Africa. These undulations formed a river-bed where there was an outlet; but a pan might come into being where no outlet was found.

The rainfall in Europe was so evenly distributed that it formed rivers. In South Africa the intermittent rainfall helped the pan formation. Prister found the influence of the wind self-evident, and agreed that the animals might have widened and deepened the pans.

Draper suggested that the origin of some pans might be found in a shrinkage of the strata, but this was rare. Hall said the pans were due to general physical and climatic conditions. Where the watercourses were feebly defined, pans were abundant. He saw a direct link between a poor drainage system and the pans. Professor Fritz Jaeger of Basle University spent five years in South West Africa studying the geology of the country. He defined a pan as "a flat surface below the level of the surrounding country without a stream-bed leading from it." Jaeger decided that pans which were hollows in the bed-rock were caused by earth movements or volcanic action. Others were due to ice-bound erosion, wind and water erosion. He gave the Etosha and the Makarikari and Pretoria salt pans as examples of volcanic origin, while the Panneveld and Lake Chrissie pans were relics of the ice age. Evaporation and flat ground encouraged pan formation, and for those reasons pans were also found in Australia. Jaeger declared that the animal theory had been greatly exaggerated. More recently Mr. G. W. P. Geyser has denied the animal theory and stated: "Pans must be regarded as temporary formations which originated in a transition period between one drainage system and another." Alexander du Toit favoured wind erosion, as did L. C. King; and these are weighty opinions. "Whirlwinds carry away the disintegrating products in the dry season," King declared. "In the course of thousands of years the pans have grown in depth and area." King admitted, however, that factors other than wind erosion had to be sought at Etosha and Makarikari. The *vloer* he thought, came about owing to the growth and coalescence of pans. Lake Chrissie was a pan formed by an ancient drainage system, when flat channels were blocked by sand and developed into pans.

Mr. R. G. Shuttleworth, an authority on salt, declared

that the coastal salt pans were once arms of the sea. Rietfontein pan to the north of the Olifants River, the Bethelsdorp mission pan and others near Port Elizabeth all derived their salt from marine sediments. The valuable inland salt pans were created when underground waters found their way to the surface and deposited the salt.

Stone Age man knew the pans. Implements have been found in many pans; other relics come to light in great profusion at the springs on the edges of the pans. It is clear that the Bushmen and the forerunners of the Bushmen wandered from pan to pan, from spring to spring, living on the game, the bulbs and roots. Those primitive clans knew the pans great and small, muddy pans and salt pans. But I doubt whether it ever entered their heads to discuss this geological mystery which has caused so much speculation among the scientists. Pans were just part of the South African landscape in the days of the Bushmen.

*Chapter Eight*

# THE NAMAQUAS

NAMAQUALAND is still the home of Namaqua remnants. The interesting clans of Hottentots who gave the land its name favoured the coastal regions. They knew the beaches and river mouths and pans and the taste of flamingo meat. Their origin is still a mystery and the migration routes which brought them to Southern Africa are controversial. They call themselves Khoi Khoin, "excellent people".

William Threlfall, the Methodist missionary, spent some time among the Namaquas at Leliefontein in the eighteen-twenties. He praised their singing in one of his last letters before he travelled on across the Orange River to his death. "As a tribe they have probably the finest voices and best ears in the world, especially the females," he wrote. "They know nothing of music as a science, but after getting the air of a tune they, as if by a sort of instinct, find various chords for every note and so modify their voices that a stranger who could not see them would take their full strains for a fine-tuned organ under the hand of a skilful musician, but so soft and pure and smooth and flowing and easy and simple that one hymn tune sung by them is more gratifying to my ear than all the oratorios I ever heard."

Leliefontein, the mission five thousand feet up in the Kamiesberg range, has been a Namaqua reserve for more than a century. There they have nearly half a million acres of sunbaked earth with some grazing and a little ground for sowing and gardens; but life is hard for the last of the Hottentots, there and in the other reserves in the Richtersveld and at Steinkopf, Concordia and Komaggas. At each oasis there are fine old white churches, beautiful trees of species rare in Namaqualand, and other relics of bygone missionaries. When the Rev. Barnabas Shaw and his wife sowed lettuce, peas and onions at Leliefontein early last century the Hottentots gazed in wonder as the plants came up. The Hottentots were hunters, sheep-owners and root-gatherers. They had never seen a plough. These nomads lived then, as they do now, in mat huts which were carried on oxen down to the coastal plains when the cold of winter came to the Kamiesberg.

Many of the surviving Namaquas have never seen a city. Two elderly members of the Leliefontein congregation, Abraham Boyes and Joseph Cloete, were taken to Cape Town in October 1966 to take part in a Methodist missionary exhibition. They brought a mat hut and some of their primitive implements with them; stones for grinding corn, drill sticks and dry grass for making fire. The high buildings frightened them and they were terrified in a lift. Cape Town held no lasting charm for these contented, illiterate Namaquas. They returned thankfully to Leliefontein, saying in Afrikaans to each well-wisher: "It has been a privilege and an honour to meet you."

Namaquas closely resembled the other Hottentot clans in appearance and habits, though some early writers said that the Namaquas were taller than the little five-footers of the Cape clans and that they had Chinese eyes, like slits. Apparently the Hottentots were never a very numerous race. George W. Stow the ethnologist estimated a total of forty thousand in Van Riebeeck's day.

Pieter Cruijthoff led the company sent out by Van Riebeeck in search of the Namaquas, and he found a circle of seventy-three huts beyond the Olifant's river. There were three hundred able-bodied men and four hundred women and children. Van Cruijthoff admired their garb, beautiful leopard and dassie skins, "excellently cured and adorned magnificently with copper beads." On their arms they wore copper and ivory rings. The chief of the kraal owned four thousand head of cattle and three thousand sheep. Their household utensils consisted of large wooden vessels with narrow necks hollowed out of a piece of solid wood. They also had calabashes for storing milk. They churned butter and ate with tortoise-shell spoons. Milk was an important item in the diet of the Namaquas; butter was used mainly for rubbing on the body.

Van Meerhoff the explorer met the most southerly Namaquas where Clanwilliam now stands, but their stronghold was in the Kamiesberg range. What was their origin? They arrived in South Africa before the Bantu, but long after the Bushmen. Hottentots and Bushmen belong to the same racial stock. They are Khoisan people with the same anatomical peculiarities, especially among the women. Some authorities think the Hottentots are Bushmen who mingled with a Hamitic race; others favour a cross between Bushman and Bantu. There is a record of a body of Egyptian soldiers who deserted about the year 600 A.D. They travelled south beyond Ethiopia and settled among the Bushman, taking wives and losing their identity in an ocean of savage blood. Philologists have discovered affinities in the Egyptian, Bushman and Hottentot languages. Some scientists claim to have detected Mongoloid features in the physical structure of Hottentot and Bushmen. More recent research suggests that the Hottentots, Bushmen and African negroid peoples all sprang from a common stock. Then they broke away and migrated and evolved in different ways in separate environments.

The late Professor T. F. Dreyer of Bloemfontein examined skeletons from primitive graves near Kakamas on the Orange River, and identified skulls which were clearly Hottentot, yet with characteristics unknown in modern Hottentot skulls. Thus a theory arose that the Kakamas people were the pure Hottentots, members of a race which had not yet mingled with the Bushman race. These people may have arrived on the Orange River seven centuries ago. Professor Dreyer noted Hamitic influences in the skulls. His theory was followed up by other ethnologists. One expedition visited Angola in the hope of finding links in a migration that ended at Kakamas. An unusual yellow man living in the Kalahari was thought to be a "pure Hottentot"; but his mother was traced and she was a Masarwa hybrid. A remote burial ground in Zambia has revealed a Hottentot type skeleton interred with golden ornaments; something unknown in the study of Hottentot origins. There appears to be some relationship, however, between the people who made their beaten gold ornaments at Mapungubwe in the Limpopo Valley and the Namaquas living north and south of the Orange River. Skeletons and pottery form the evidence. Possibly the ancient Hottentots were of a higher order of humanity than the scientists have imagined.

How did these migrants reach Southern Africa? Some ethnologists believe they came by way of the Great Lakes and the Zambesi river. Others think the coast of South West Africa provided a route. Stow declared firmly: "It is quite evident that when the Hottentot race commenced its southern migration along the western coast about the end of the fourteenth century, the tribes did not move onward in a dense body, but, as in every other native migration we have been able to trace, one tribe or group of clans followed the other in a straggling, scattered manner, some lingering in the rear while others were pushing on in front like the advance guard of the main body."

Dr. Heinrich Vedder the historian was inclined to accept the Hamitic-Bushman mingling as the origin of the Hottentots. It was their Hamitic blood which made the Hottentots cling to their fat-tailed sheep; while the Bushman strain explained their fondness for hunting. Hottentots who were mainly hunters came first. That migration may have taken place a thousand years ago or earlier. After the hunters came the Hottentots stock farmers. They spoke different dialects of the same language but they understood one another easily. The early Dutch settlers often spoke of wild and tame Hottentots, the hunters and the herdsmen. Vedder had an open mind on the enigma of the Hottentots. He suggested two migration routes, one from the north-west, the other from the north-east. The ancient African people described by Herodotus was, in Vedder's opinion, the Hottentot race. They spoke a wonderful click language like no other tongue on earth and at times they made hissing sounds and noises like the squeakings of bats.

According to their own traditions the Hottentots wandered down Africa from the north-east, always facing the setting sun until they came at last to the "great waters" (the South Atlantic). Then they turned southwards down the coast and arrived in South Africa.

Mr. E. J. Dunn the geologist, a keen observer of native types, studied the Namaquas during his travels in the eighteen-seventies. He declared that no Bushman or Hottentot with a trace of black colour in his skin could be called a pure Bushman or pure Hottentot; and he encountered many hybrids. The eyes of the Hottentot were not deeply sunk, as in the Bushman. Often the Hottentot wore an expression which looked like a self-satisfied smirk. The nose of the Hottentot was better-formed than the Bushman's nose, and not so flat and broad; the ear was better shaped and had a distinct lobe; the hair was profuse, longer and intensely black. Dunn pointed out that the Hottentot was not a pygmy, as he was over five feet in height. Steatopygia reached its utmost limits in Hottentot women. The Namaquas were taller than the Hottentots he met farther south in the Cape. While the Hottentots were much higher in culture than the Bushmen, they lacked artistic instinct. He saw large gatherings of Namaquas, as many were employed on the copper mines. Along the Orange River he was present when two or three hundred Hottentots assembled to drink honey beer. Throughout the Cape Colony in the 'seventies there were thousands of pure-bred Hottentots. "I saw many Bushmen and Hottentots, and the differences between the two were so great that in the flesh, with rare exceptions, there was no mistaking the one for the other," summed up Dunn.

Once the Namaquas lived mainly on meat and milk. In recent years they have changed to bread and tea, making a dramatic break with the old diet.

Namaquas of the original stock may often be identified by their short peppercorn hair. Others of mixed Hottentot stock who came up from the Cape and joined the Namaquas are known as Basters. Some of these later arrivals have a certain amount of white blood owing to men from the Netherlands, Engelbrecht, Cloete and others, settling in Namaqualand early in the eighteenth century. Engelbrecht was a trader who married a Namaqua woman; he exchanged tobacco, coffee and sugar for giraffe and gemsbok karosses.

Magic has not yet vanished among the Namaquas and both the *towenaar* or evil sorcerer and the more useful *bossiedokter* or herbalist are still to be found. The *towenaar* prefers strong-smelling and revolting medicines such as jackal kidneys. However, it is possible to defeat a *towenaar* if you have a supply of the rare dried gecko skin. Namaquas share with other African races a belief in lycanthropy, the transformation of human beings into animals.

Animals have provided clues to the wanderings of many nations over the earth's surface. It is clear that the Hottentots brought with them long-horned cattle of the species still found in Somaliland; fat-tailed sheep such as the Hamites owned; and the mongrel ancestors of the present aristocratic ridgeback dogs. One flock of pure-bred Namaqua sheep has survived though the Hottentot breed as a whole is in no danger of extinction. These are remarkable sheep indeed and it is fascinating to follow them through the centuries. Herodotus, the first historian, described them well: "In Arabia there are marvellous sheep. One kind has tails three ells long, so that men attach them to a little trolley to prevent them from trailing along the ground and so contracting sores. The other sort have tails more than an ell broad."

Sheep must have been domesticated where wild sheep were available for the purpose. Africa had no wild sheep. Urials, the wild sheep of the Himalayas, may have been the ultimate ancestors of the fat-tailed and fat-rumped sheep. Whole herds were tamed (like the reindeer elsewhere) when the wild creatures learned that human beings were protecting them from beasts of prey. So the tame sheep were driven westwards until they came into the possession of the Israelites and entered Africa with their owners. Dr. H. Epstein, the veterinary scientist, has declared that the domestic animals of the Hottentots were Semitic rather than Hamitic, and thus the Hottentots may be of Semitic origin.

It was a long trek for the sheep down Africa. One may imagine their escapes and losses when lions and other carnivora discovered this grand new meat. Only after they reached the Cape of Good Hope do we hear of them again, when Portuguese explorers mentioned the sheep. Sir James Lancaster, the British navigator, also gave a description after calling at Table Bay near the end of the sixteenth century: "The sheep are very big and very good meat, they have no wool on their backs but hair, and have great tails like the sheep in Syria." Lancaster smacked his lips over the "fat and pleasant, remarkably good meat". Van Riebeeck coveted the Hottentot sheep, as everyone knows. The sheep had large bodies, long heads, small eyes and various tail structures. The hair was short and coarse, though some had thick woolly fleeces. Colours ranged from dirty white to dark brown.

Paterson and Gordon encountered the other type of Hottentot sheep during their journey to the Orange River. "Their sheep are very different from those near the Cape, these having much longer tails," they reported. "They are covered with hair instead of wool, which at a distance gives them more the appearance of dogs than sheep." Sir John Barrow discussed the two distinct types of indigenous sheep early last century. "The broad-tailed breed of the Cape seems to be of a very inferior kind to those of Siberia and Tartary," wrote Barrow. "They are long-legged, small in the body, remarkably thin in the fore-quarters and across the ribs. They have very little intestine or no fat, the whole of this seems to be collected upon the hind part of the thigh and upon the tail; this is short, broad, flat, naked on the underside and weighs in general five or six pounds; sometimes it exceeds a dozen pounds in weight. The sheep of the Cape are marked with every shade of colour; some are black, some brown and others bay; but the greatest number are spotted. Their necks are small and extended and their ears long and pendulous. They weigh from sixty to seventy pounds each when taken from their pasture. The wool of the sheep is little better than a strong frizzled hair."

Barrow then moved on to the land of the Namaquas and dealt with the sheep he saw there: "The sheep were totally different from the breed usually met with in the colony. Instead of the short, broad and curling tails, the Namaqua sheep have long and round tails like the common English sheep. The rams had small straight horns. The covering was short, straight, shining hair in general, spotted bay and white. These in all probability were the indigenous sheep of the country, the broad-tailed ones having been brought into the colony from the northward." (Barrow, of course, did not realise that all the sheep at the Cape had come down from the north). According to Barrow, the Namaquas spoke a language which the Cape Hottentots could not understand. They were isolated in the desolate areas of the west coast. Dr. J. S. Starke of the agricultural research institute, Pretoria thought it was possible that the Namaqua sheep were of a somewhat different type from other sheep owned by the Cape Hottentots even before the first white settlers arrived. Proof that the Namaquas were a race apart is found in their possession of goats. Goats were unknown among the Cape Hottentot tribes. The Xosa had neither sheep nor goats, only cattle and dogs.

Shipments of Dutch rams and woolled sheep arrived from Holland in Van Riebeeck's time, and ten Bengal sheep were imported. William Adriaan van der Stel ordered rams and ewes from Persia. These were crossed with the Cape sheep, which then began to disappear as a breed. Spanish sheep also arrived, but were unpopular. The colonists loved the fat-tailed sheep, as they used the fat instead of butter. Dr. Starke declared: "It would appear that the early importations of sheep, although limited in number, must have had some influence on the Cape Hottentot or Afrikaner sheep in the possession of the Dutch settlers."

Many observers noted that strange resemblance between the Hottentots and Bushmen and the fat-tailed sheep. Here were human beings storing up fat in the buttocks exactly like the animals; and it was argued that this was a reserve for seasons of hunger. Many years ago Mr. J. B. Evans, a Graaff-Reinet farmer, met a Bushman with shrunken buttocks; and the Bushman assured him that he had lost his fat during the long drought. Modern scientists are not entirely satisfied with this explanation. They say the Hottentot's buttocks are small, but seem prominent owing to the inward curvature of the spine.

Mr. H. A. Bryden, farmer and naturalist, had a friend who cut off the tails of his lambs when they were very young. As the animals matured, the lower parts of the back became clothed in fat; more so than is usual with tailed sheep. This flock carried more flesh and sold for higher prices than the average fat-tailed sheep. To sum up, human anatomists and animal husbandry experts have never solved the mystery of the Hottentots' rumps and the fat-tailed sheep. As one authority on natural history phrased it recently: "The over-developed tail is now generally regarded as an inexplicable side-effect of domestication. It has no particular value either to its owner or to mankind, except to provide grease for lamps and cooking."

People in Namaqualand and other wide areas have found many other uses for this tail-fat. When you feel a typical tail it is like a skin-bag full of soft jelly. Arabs have been melting this fat since the days of the Bible, and eating the browned skin; and the *kaiings* of Afrikaans cookery are exactly the same thing. All sorts of dishes from mealie-bread to pumpkin fritters are fried in sheep's tail-fat; and many a newcomer to the Cape has looked askance at mutton-chops afloat in a sea of the same fat. Tail-fat was an essential ingredient of many old-fashioned ointments and veld medicines. Those fat-tailed sheep roamed in enormous herds in the Cape districts. The climate suited them. In the hot summer months they grazed on mountain pastures and found succulent and saline plants. Their shepherds, mainly Hottentots, relied on fierce dogs to keep the lions and leopards away. In the autumn they returned to the plains. Ships calling at the "Tavern of the Seas" bought fat-tailed sheep to feed their crews; and some carried live Cape sheep to New Zealand and far Tahiti.

Throughout this period the remote Namaquas remained in possession of their pure, unique sheep. The broad-tailed Cape sheep were probably an inproved type, influenced by the Persian breed, and they became known as Afrikaner sheep. Only when the traveller crossed the Olifants river did he encounter the Namaqua sheep in great numbers. The true Namaqua sheep were found in the dry, western area, where they had adapted themselves to semi-desert conditions, with a rainfall varying from nothing to five inches. They flourished because they had inner and outer coats of hair; a fine white inner coat and an outer protective coat which they shed in the burning summer. Creamy white in colour, the sheep sometimes had brown patches on their heads. Their excessively long, fat tails had queer shapes; hence the Afrikaans terms *sweepstert*, *draaistert* and *wipstert*. They are leggy animals with remarkable depth of body. At first glance they may appear scraggy, but they are extremely vigorous, with well-developed hind legs. The ears are pendulous, the stamp (according to Charles Darwin) of long domestication. Long legs and an easy gait enable the Namaqua sheep to cover wide areas in search of grazing. They move fast, in close formation with the flock instinct highly developed, and this is regarded as a sign of the primitive strain. They do not suffer from thirst and soon move on when water has been provided. Rams weigh up to one hundred and forty pounds alive, ewes up to one hundred. Authorities regard the Namaqua sheep as a supreme example of natural selection under most adverse conditions. The great merit of the sheep lies in the ability to live in harmony with grim surroundings and produce a ninety per cent lamb crop in great extremes of temperature. Lambs grow quickly. The meat is coarse-grained and not to be compared with the mutton of other breeds.

Until recent years the Namaqua breed retained its purity for it was the only sheep that could survive in Namaland and Bushmanland. When the karakuls reached those areas in the nineteen-thirties, however, it was found that they could stand up to the same hard conditons as the

Namaqua sheep. More and more bore-holes were drilled in the semi-desert areas. So the Merinos came in and heavy losses were avoided when water became available. The pioneer breed of Namaqua sheep mingled with the newcomers and dwindled almost to the point of extinction. Fortunately the experts realised that a breed which was able to thrive under devastating conditions should be preserved and studied. Valuable breeding material woud be lost for ever if the Namaqua sheep died out.

Only one pure flock remained in Namaqualand in 1950, when a committee of experts toured the country in search of genuine Namaquas. This was the Maas flock. The first Maas settled in Namaqualand more than a century ago, and generation after generation farmed with pure Namaqua sheep. The government experts bought two hundred ewes and six rams, and these were placed under the supervision of sheep and wool officers at the Upington experimental station. Qualities peculiar to the Namaqua are being studied, and it is hoped that the results will show how much has been gained by retaining a breeding nucleus which might have disappeared completely. These sheep have the traditional long, narrow tails which may reach a weight of fifteen pounds. At that point the tail sometimes breaks away where it joins the body.

Skins of these sheep are known as "Cape glovers"; they have a high market value as they make excellent glove leather. Years ago the skin blanket or *velkombers* of Namaqualand was famous. Nowadays there are few craftsmen able to prepare the skins. One of the last families still curing the skins are the Bassons of Nieuwoudtville. A wild lettuce plant is used in the traditional process. The fat inside the skin is removed and then the glossy hair is combed, washed and combed again. Eleven skins go to a kaross, and they are sewn together with the back sinews of a sheep. After stitching, the kaross is lined with cloth.

Cape Town ate thousands of Namaqua sheep every year at the end of last century. Buyers left Cape Town by cart and horse in the spring and sought out the Namaqualand trekboers who owned the sheep. After days of trekking and haggling the sheep were branded and sent to posts in charge of Hottentot shepherds. When a flock of about two thousand sheep had been gathered together the journey to Cape Town started; and by some process born of long experience the band of shepherds kept the sheep together and lost very few on the way. The *kaptein* of the shepherds knew exactly where to find water and suitable veld. Great cavalcades of sheep crossed the drifts, converging on the old Compagnie's Drift over the Olifants river south of Klaver. Most flocks then followed the coastal route through the Sandveld, crossing the Berg river at the Melck's farm at Kersefontein, and then passing along the recognised trek paths past Hopefield and Darling to Cape Town. Such a trek usually lasted four weeks, and the sheep reached the market in good condition. Trekboers never sold their lambs. The sheep were four years old. Legs, loins and chops were sold at sixpence a pound retail in 1898, and people loved the taste of Namaqua sheep. Lamb was a luxury in town. If it had been easily obtainable, the coarse Namaqua meat would not have been so popular.

Centuries ago the Hottentots of Namaqualand drove their sheep through the flames and smoke of their camp-fires, believing that this ritual would protect them from wild dogs and other predators. Possibly the odour of smoke kept these raiders away. Hottentot bridegrooms sprinkled the sheep with water. These were little ceremonies which must have been observed during the long migration down Africa; all sorts of magic with origins lost in the darkness of antiquity.

Sheep and goats appear to have been derived from a common ancestor, and they are probably the oldest of all domesticated animals with the exception of the dog. Namaqualand is the last stronghold of old secrets of men and animals, secrets which had been forgotten by the Namaquas even before the first Dutch explorers set eyes on the Hottentots and their sheep.

*Chapter Nine*

# LAND OF THE DONKEY

*The tattered outlaw of the earth,*
*Of ancient crooked will;*
*Starve, scrourge, deride me: I am dumb,*
*I keep my secret still.*

G. K. CHESTERTON

NAMAQUALAND is the land of the donkey. I became aware of the essential donkey when I entered the country on my first visit, at a time when there were more donkeys on the road than motor-cars. That was more than forty years ago.

As I passed through Clanwilliam they told me that the Doorn river bridge was down, washed away by floods that seemed remote under the burning sun. I drove northwards hopefully, anxious to reach Vanrhynsdorp before dark; and the unknown road was filled with such interest for me that I forgot all about that bridge. Then I reached the ruins left by the winter floods. It was a broad river and there was an expanse of glaring white sand to cross before entering the shallow water. I wondered how any motor-car could reach the far side. Then out of nothing a boy appeared, a small bare-footed white boy wearing a limp felt hat. He stared with admiration at my woeful old car; admitted sorrowfully that he had never been away from his father's farm; shared my lunch of tinned salmon and biscuits; and finally waved his arms vigorously. Looking into the sun-dazzle ahead I saw that the boy's signal had brought a team of donkeys.

I had taken a photograph of the young Namaqualander. When the father panted up with the donkeys the boy told him of this new experience. It seemed that the father, too, had never faced a camera. I must take a picture of the whole family. Cameras were common enough forty years ago, and I realised that I had come into a far corner when the click of a shutter could produce such excitement. "Tow my car safely across the river, and it shall be done," I promised.

So father and son hitched chains to my front axle and with loud cries they urged the donkeys forward. Sometimes the father ran back yelling for the help of the engine. The wheels, with the hard tyres of forty years ago, sank deep into the heavy sand, the donkeys strained, the water covered the running-boards. I had previously crossed the Limpopo (where Beit bridge now stands) in exactly the same way. This, too, was an anxious episode. The donkeys faltered on the steep north bank and I imagined the whole cavalcade toppling backwards into the river. Then I saw the donkeys straightening out and we halted at the farmhouse. Geese and goats lounged about the mud walls and from a low doorway the family emerged. The father changed into his best clothes, snatched the young baby from his wife and reminded me of my promise. I wanted to include the donkeys in the picture for I felt they were the real heroes of a precarious crossing. But no, they were not proud of the donkeys. That team must have brought a small fortune to the farmer at the Doorn river before the bridge was rebuilt; but they were not even allowed in the background. Ten minutes later I had departed and the brown homestead with its corrugated iron roof was a speck on the veld. Into the aching distance stretched the dusty Namaqualand road. The donkeys had brought me safely over the border. They were not the last of their kind I was to see during that journey.

There was a time, I was told, when there were more donkeys than human beings in Namaqualand. Governor Simon van der Stel had eight donkeys in his cavalcade three centuries ago, and they were the pioneers. When the white settlers moved into Namaqualand, donkeys trekked with them. The old-fashioned *perdemeul* was more of a donkey-mill in those parts, the tireless donkeys walking round and grinding the wheat. That was great bread, made with the home-ground flour, rising surely and making a loaf full of flavour such as city bakers never achieve.

Many families in Namaqualand still own only a *donkie-karretjie* or *donkiewaentjie*. Of course the rubber tyre has made a difference. The modern type of donkey-cart made by cutting a motor-car in two and fitting a pole has added to the comfort of donkey travel. But the plain donkey, with or without a saddle, has been the link between farm and school ever since the first schools were opened in that wide area. Donkeys are used for ploughing, but only the poorest of the poor would think of going to church with their donkeys. Mules and horses are status symbols and they must be used for the journey to the dorp on Sunday. The donkey has lost its dignity, but it was not always so.

Donkeys first came to the Cape in Van Riebeeck's day. Ships of the Dutch East India Company called at the Cape Verde islands and picked up donkeys and goats. They were fine animals, the Portuguese donkeys. Governor Jan de la Fontaine, nicknamed "the man with the smiling face", kept splendid donkeys to carry fish from Fish Hoek to the Castle and corn from Klapmuts. Paarden Island was reserved as their grazing ground. In later years, however, the donkey fell into disrepute. A fine breed soon deteriorates when underfed and otherwise ill-treated. Nevertheless, it was the donkey that pulled Namaqualand and many parts of South Africa out of stagnation when rinderpest and other diseases wiped out oxen, horses and mules.

Afrikaner dealers flocked to Ireland towards the end of last century and bought thousands of donkeys to make good the ravages of the rinderpest. Some of the Irish donkeys went to Rhodesia, where the *tsetse* fly was killing off the horses. Thousands of pounds were spent in Limerick and Tipperary. The motor-car was still a great rarity. Ireland exported two hundred thousand donkeys a year to England; poor, stunted beasts without breeding, yet with good health and endurance.

It was in Namaqualand on my first journey that I met a man who had studied the whole horse tribe and had gained a special affection for the donkey. He was employed as a sheep inspector, but he told me that when one served the government it was not always possible to find the work of one's dreams. This expert had a streak of poetry in him, and I still remember some of his phrases. "Namaqualand folklore resounds to the gentle tapping of the donkey's hooves," he remarked. "It has borne every load from heavy copper to mat-huts, a beast of burden which carries on with little water and miserable fodder. No wonder it sometimes looks dejected in spite of its noble origin."

"Noble?" I queried.

"Noble," he repeated firmly. "The donkey is one of Africa's aristocrats. Horses are of dubious origin but the donkey is clearly the African wild ass, tamed and domesticated. It has served mankind for thousands of years and man has not always treated it with compassion."

The donkey, he said, was the only African equine which had been domesticated. Experiments with zebras were rarely successful. The quagga had been exterminated. But the donkey had become man's faithful companion. He said this was due to the fact that wild horses ran in large herds and liked company. The wild ass grazed in two and threes and developed a loud bray and large ears so that it could talk to its scattered friends some way away. Horses would return to the wild if they were given the chance. A donkey would find its way back to its owner like a cat.

I learned from this expert how the Egyptians rode donkeys long before they saddled a horse. Rock paintings in the Atlas mountains show an extinct species of wild ass which may have supplied the people of the Nile valley with some of their donkeys; but there is in Abyssinia and Somaliland a wild race which differs little in colour and markings from the tame donkey. Of course the wild ass, roaming warily in small herds, possesses grace and dignity and courage seldom found in the donkey. Galloping over the desert sands with the speed of a horse, the wild ass is indeed a creature of beauty. Egyptian tombs have revealed pictures of domesticated asses nearly three thousand years years before Christ. In the Old Testament there are many favourable references to the ass. Pharoah presented Abraham with "sheep and oxen, and he-asses and men-servants, and maidservants and she-asses, and camels". The importance of this animal was stressed in the tenth commandment: "Thou shall not covet thy neighbour's ass . . ." It has a long and honourable history, and my friend the donkey-lover reminded me of Balaam's journey, the angel and the ass that was given the power of speech. Nor did he omit to mention Christ's ride to Jesuralem on an ass. It is on Palm Sunday, of course, that the donkey comes into its own and takes part in many processions. Only this animal bears the mark of the cross on its withers and shoulders. This cross is really a link with the zebra's stripes, and nearly every donkey has it. The hair of the cross has a different texture from the rest of the donkey's coat. I have seen white donkeys in Egypt with the cross in pale grey.

Malta, Italy, France and Spain acquired the donkey long before the first of the breed reached England. Donkeys flourished in Southern Europe, and the Poitou, the Sicilian and the Catalonian were bred almost to the size of horses and weighing nine hundred pounds. The ordinaary donkey is about one-third of that weight. But the finest of all donkeys are American, where enormous donkey stallions are kept for mule-breeding. My friend the expert objected to the terms "jack" and "jackass" as being too vague. He said that young male donkeys were colts and foals, and they became "entires" at five years of age. When a donkey stallion (a male kept at stud for breeding purposes) was operated upon it became a gelding. Female donkeys started out in life as fillies; then they became mares. Donkey stallions hated mules and had been known to go for their throats like bulldogs and fight savagely. It is said that the mating of the donkey stallion and the mare was man's greatest discovery in the field of genetics. For some unknown reason the stallion and the donkey mare do not produce such a useful animal as the mule.

South Africa imported some fine stud donkeys from Catalonia between the wars, but the Spanish Civil War put an end to the trade. In 1937 the United States sent to South Africa a donkey stallion named Joe Louis standing fifteen and a half hands in height, weighing twelve hundred pounds, price five hundred pounds. Joe Louis was selected on account of its bone and muscle. Roman noses are liked by breeders, and they also look for alert ears, deep bodies and broad chests. As I have said, America has the finest stock, built up on the Poitou of France and the Spanish breeds. The world's best mules are also found in the United States. Mules are faster than the ox and stronger than the donkey for draught purposes, and they are healthier than horses. When the wheat districts of the Western Cape were developed late in the eighteenth century mule-breeding became a necessity. Mules played a great part in the growth of South Africa last century, before the railways and the motor-car, for they were used in coach and transport services. And without the donkey there would have been no mules.

Donkeys fetched twenty shillings apiece for years in Namaqualand between the wars. In times of drought they were sold from the pound at sixpence each, and eaten greedily. Of course the flesh of the donkey cannot be compared with the highly-prized meat of the wild ass. I believe the Nubian wild ass became extinct because of the demand for the flesh. Wild asses live on desert succulents, hence the superior flavour. I have never tasted it, but it is akin to zebra, which I ate often enough in a distant corner of South West Africa when there was nothing else for the pot. France consumes great quantities of horsemeat and donkeymeat, so possibly I have tasted these equine dishes without knowing it. André L. Simon, that wise gastronome, assures us that the meat is "most acceptable for the hungry, wholesome and nutrituous". It is like mutton in colour, firm and savoury. As for the milk of asses, that is used as a medicine in Namaqualand and elsewhere. The milk has more sugar and less cheese, and resembles human milk. Invalids can take it when cow's milk causes indigestion. It is used in the treatment of lung, liver, gall-bladder and kidney ailments, and this is no mere superstition. Cleopatra bathed in asses' milk, and some believe that it promotes a white complexion. Donkey skin, by the way, also has its uses. Parchment and shagreen leather are made from it, and you can cover a drum with this resonant material.

"Donkey should really be pronounced to rhyme with monkey," declared the expert, "You see, the coat is dun-coloured, hence the name." Next he dealt with the dwindling of the donkey from the magnificent wild creature to a pathetic slave no larger than a dog. "It was brought about mainly by coarse, unpalatable fodder," he said. "Donkeys are popular because they eat only half as much as horses; but they become stunted on a low nutritive diet. The donkey is the poor man's slave, and ill-treatment brings about a drastic change. It loses the handsome coat of the wild species just as it loses its spirit. Yet the tame, despised little donkey still retains certain inherited wild traits. It brays like the ass of the desert. Transverse stripes on the legs, a mark of the wild, keep reappearing. It rolls in the dust like a desert ass. And because of its desert origin it is still rather cautious about crossing a stream."

Donkeys do not return to the primitive form when they are left to their own resources. I have watched the wild horses in Namaqualand near the Orange River mouth but never have I set eyes on a wild donkey. The first beast of burden tamed by man has, however, assumed some queer shapes as a result of selective breeding. India has donkeys no larger than sheep. In a circus I have seen a midget mule, progeny of a tiny Maltese donkey stallion and a Shetland mare. African wild asses are grey; the donkey ranges from white to grey, brown and black.

Horses are delicate and short-lived animals in comparison with the donkey. Twenty-five is a great age for a horse, though I believe the record is sixty-three years. All we can say about the donkey is that its natural life-span is longer than the horse; possibly half as long again. The donkey may suffer from lice, ticks and ringworm, urticaria and warts; but it avoids poisonous plants instinctively, it is not accident-prone and is immune to certain horse-diseases. Charles Dickens had the longivity of the donkey in mind when his character Sam Weller remarked: "And there's another thing no man will ever see, and that's a dead donkey."

Is the donkey stupid? My friend the expert declared rather boldly that it was intellectually inferior only to man. If it chose to look like an idiot that was merely a sign of cunning. The wisdom of the donkey lay in its pathetic appearance. But a man who loved donkeys, a man who could interpret the meaning of its different braying calls, would find it as friendly as a dog. Properly treated, the donkey is good-tempered and clever. It has far more personality than a pony.The donkey might sometimes lay its ears back, swish its tail, kick or bite; but there were not many bad-tempered donkeys. It liked to know what was going on. You could trust a donkey with children. If it was not always energetic, that was merely a sign of intelligence. The soft-eyed donkey carried the harvests of ancient Egypt under suns that would have crumpled any horse. No wonder the King of Egypt presented Abraham with he-asses and she-asses; they were valuable gifts. And when I rode across the desert of the Pharoahs to the pyramids of Sakkara in wartime it was on a trotting donkey, as I have good reason to remember. H. M. Stanley and many other exploreres used donkeys. Livingstone was lifted from his donkey to die in prayer near Bangweulu. You find the velvet-nosed donkey treading the alleys of Tangier with panniers of fruit; clattering through the narrow streets of Zanzibar with cloves; bearing incredible loads in the heat of the tropics; hauling the wagons of white and Hottentot in Namaqualand, through the bush of the Sandveld, past the mountains of naked rock, over the foothills of the Kamiesberg and up to the Leliefontein heights. The animal man adopted when the world was young still bears a heavy share of the world's trade on its shoulders.

You saw me being drawn through the sands of the Doorn river by donkeys. That first journey into Namaqualand ended in complete break down. Somewhere to the south of Garies I waited with the patience of a donkey for help to arrive, and when it came it took the shape of a donkey-wagon. Yes, I was thankful for the donkeys of

Namaqualand that day as I was towed slowly towards Garies. The aroma of Namaqualand is a queer blend. They use the manure from sheep kraals in their fires, and this gives out a veld odour, not at all unpleasant, but unmistakable. Add to this the equine odour of a team of donkeys and the long road up into the Kamiesberg rises once again before me.

*Chapter Ten*

# ELEPHANT RIVER

If you are a navigator then you must know the "Africa Pilot", that safe guide to oceans, coasts and harbours. We are sailing along the coast of Namaqualand, south from Port Nolloth, picking out the landmarks from the "Pilot" lying open beside the chart. Each little bay is mentioned, with breakers across the entrance when the south-wester blows. Here are grass-covered hills; cliffs of sand; a few river mouths that can be entered by small boats in the rainy season; a stone beacon here and there; the flag-staffs and houses of Hondeklip Bay with its granite "dog stone"; red sandstone cliffs and long, desolate ridges; sunken rocks and breakers; a coast which makes the weary navigator long for a safe harbour.

About two hundred miles from Port Nolloth you come to a river, the Olifants river, which might have answered thousands of seamen's prayers. Portuguese explorers called it the Rio do Infante. Now listen to one old navigator's description of the river entrance: "As the westerly swell is constantly heaving in on this coast there are generally heavy breakers on the bar. But within this bar there is plenty of water for a large ship for two miles up the river to a village where several Dutch farmers reside. *If there could be a passage cut through the bar at the mouth of the river it would be the finest harbour on the west coast of Africa.*"

I call the Olifant's river the unknown river of South Africa. Many travellers know the upper stretches flowing past Citrusdal and Clanwilliam; but the lower parts and the mouth are remote. This is indeed a river of strange tales, and perhaps the most unusual dramas of all were played round the river mouth.

Jan Danckaert, a seasoned traveller and man of some

education, led the expedition which discovered the Olifants river. That was three centuries ago. Pieter van Meerhoff the Dane was in the party. They marched for nine days, found a route over the mountains with the aid of Bushman guides, and beheld a large river flowing northwards. Beyond the river was a herd of two to three hundred elephants, and for this reason the Olifants river gained its Dutch name. But to the Hottentots it was always Tharakama, the "rugged river". Governor Simon van der Stel passed that way some years later and made these remarks: "The river has its source in the mountains which lay east of us and it runs with many bends towards the west, finally discharging its waters into the sea. It takes its name from the elephants which are often found in large numbers along its course. On its banks grow willows, also thorn trees which bear a fruit like Turkish beans, but wild and disagreeable." Van der Stel noted the fish, like the barbel of the rivers in Holland. He gave his men permission to shoot the hippo, rhino and eland. Along the river he saw a scorpion "as large as a Rhine crawfish, green, with long hair on its claws, very venomous and savage". He visited the Olifants river mouth on the return journey; and he landed on the seal islet nearby and sounded the channel.

Let us start the journey at the source of the Olifants river on a high plateau between the Witzenburg and Schurfteberg ranges ten miles north of Ceres. If you follow the river on foot in these parts you must find the old cattle paths known only to the farmers and mountaineers. At times the river cuts through deep fissures. You will swim often, and jump from rock to rock, and burn your feet in hot sand. This is the adventurous way, of course, but I found it easier to trace the upper river from the air. However, I would rather view the great mountain ranges from the ground, the Olifants river mountains to the west, the Cold Bokkeveld peaks to the east; for this huge spectacular kloof is not an aerodrome.

Northwards flows the river without many bends to the farm Keerom, and here I would ask you to halt for a while. Keerom stands in a secluded glen where three kloofs meet.

There is a cattle track and then a road from the farm to Citrusdal; but this is one of the most isolated farms in the Cape, a place where only a lover of solitude would have settled. Someone built the homestead early last century, and planted oaks, a quince hedge, pear and orange trees, guavas and figs. Under a lemon tree is the old stone baking-oven, near the threshing-floor. A mountaineer who visited the farm long after it had been abandoned told me that the farmer had been defeated by wild beasts. Leopards took his calves, jackals preyed on the lambs, wild cats killed his fowls and the baboons raided the mealie-fields and orchards. Floods damaged the water furrows. Man departed and a roofless farmhouse stood under the rock towers. Yet the beauty of Keerom remained unchanged beside the deep pools of the lonely river and called for a new lover of solitude.

So you come out of this glen to find the Warmwatersberg above the left bank. Here is a famous mineral spring and the old buildings of Warmbaths; a double-storied house and a gabled building with casement windows. Some of these walls may have been built in 1742, when the farm was first occupied. The timber expert will detect not only cedar in the old homes of this valley, but also the orangewood furniture that resembles yellow wood. Now you approach Citrusdal and travel on again through white sand and green bush until the river widens into the Clanwilliam dam. Here it is joined by the Jan Dissel's River; and the contrast between rich crops and barren surroundings are astonishing. Once the hippo grunted in these reeds and cooled themselves in the pools. Burchell the botanist studied the flowers here; the vlei lilies and chinkerinchees, ixias and sorrel. Here are wild fig trees, wild olives, the *sandolyf* with leaves used as medicine for chest ailments. Seventeen miles to the north of Clanwilliam is the Bulshoek weir and the canal system that has brought water to ten thousand morgen. When the Doorn river comes in you can see the miles of *melkbos* and *kraalbos* that are sure signs of good soil. White farmers settled in this area in 1725, and the first farms were given out a quarter of a century later. Dutch explorers had returned with accounts of the land. Simon van der Stel's journal spoke of the "wild horses" encountered near the Olifants river; either Hartmann's zebra or the Cape mountain zebra. Lions and rhino and elephant were there, too, and thousands of red hartebeest. Now only the small antelope and ostriches remain.

The river turns north-west into a land of hot summer winds and pleasant winters; a land where the pepper bush, the *volstruisbos* the *porcelainbos* and other plants of the barren spaces have given way to neat little irrigated holdings where lucerne and grapes, citrus and tomatoes flourish. White farmers have lived along the lower Olifants river for nearly two and a half centuries. The best farms, Windhoek, Vredendal and Melkboom were occupied in the middle of the eighteenth century. By that time the most dangerous bands of Bushman raiders had been defeated, but it was still lonely country and the settlers had to go all the way to Tulbagh to church. Hail never troubles these Olifants river settlers; there are no frosts, no insect pests. Mr. F. E. Kanthack, the irrigation engineer, reached Vredendal by motor-car (a difficult feat) in 1910 and described the climate as similar to southern California. Vredendal village was laid out on the farm Bankrotskraal. Not far away is Dolfkloof, where the Hottentot leader Dolf was shot during a fight and buried. Walk among the gardens of Trawal, and you will discover peace and plenty. Trawal means "with difficulty" in Afrikaans, but to all outward appearance it seems that those hard times were experienced long ago. I entered Trawal by chance, having lost my way, and knew at once that I had come unexpectedly to the tranquil atmosphere which makes city life seem futile. The early name for the farm where Trawal stands was De Melkboom aan de Kompagniesdrift. Irish settlers of 1820, the Fosters and Shaws, settled there; and Gerrit Nieuwoudt followed. There was a cloudburst in this dry area in 1870, and the farm was wrecked.

An old guide book in my collection, written nearly eighty years ago, describes the lower Olifants river, for there were little irrigated farms in those days, with pioneer water schemes carried out by the farmers themselves. "The farms are small but good and there is plenty of cultivation, the lands being mostly irrigated and all cereals doing well," reported my guide book. "Not much stock is kept, but there are splendid vineyards, orchards and orangeries. There are now several steam pumps along the river and large extents of country are being irrigated. The yield of produce is over one hundred-fold. In fact the soil is so rich that wheat has to be sown sparingly or else it is destroyed by rust. Stone fruit is extremely abundant and great quantities are dried. The cherry, apple, pear, peach, apricot, plum, nectarine, walnut and almond grow as fine here as do the *nartjies* and oranges. Vineyards produce the finest grapes and raisins. In other parts the banana, guava and loquat do remarkably well."

These remote people were not pampered by the government. Their first district postal service was organised a century ago. There was so little education early this century that two-thirds of the children of school-going age were still illiterate.

John Gamble the hydraulic engineer drew up an irrigation scheme at that period, but it was not adopted. Only in 1908 was the river surveyed for the present scheme, and fifteen more years passed before the Bulshoek barrage was completed. Now one morgen may produce a tomato crop worth one thousand rands. Those farmers of last century depended largely on the Olifants river overflowing its banks. Ordinary floods rose from ten to twelve feet above the bed; and these were the results of winter rains supplying the upper tributaries. You can imagine how anxiously the people watched the river, for their bread was at stake. Early last century the overflows could be relied upon every year. During the 1822 flood the water rose thirty feet. Half a century later the Olifant's river had so deepened its bed and eroded its banks that the area of the waterway became much greater and overflows became rare.

This is dry country, down near the Olifants mouth, yet the soil is the most fertile in South Africa under irrigation. Light showers fall in winter but they hardly lay the dust.

When the south-easter blows continuously the people look out hopefully for the dense, watery clouds that roll sluggishly over the thirsty veld. All too often the clouds pass on to dash against the buttresses of the Cedarberg and precipitate showers on the eastern slopes far inland. In the mountains the rainfall is forty inches; by the time the Olifants river has reached the coast it has dropped to five inches.

Last of the irrigation settlements is Ebenezer, the old Rhenish mission twenty miles by river from the mouth. Hottentots were living there in 1837 when the Rhenish missionaries secured a grant of eleven thousand morgen; and this included nearly one thousand morgen of rich ground along the river. Mr. P. Fletcher, a civil engineer who described the mission about twenty years later, said the Hottentots had oxen, cows, sheep, goats and horses; but at certain seasons many of them were reduced to a diet of dried pumpkins. Ants were eaten with enjoyment. When the people were able to hunt wild ostriches they lived on the meat for months. Their dwellings were *matjieshuisies*. Their church seated two hundred people, and they had a school. Another visitor declared that the missionaries had failed, for the Hottentots were half-starved.

When the river has run its course of two hundred miles you come at last to the mouth and sense the dramas this lonely place has known. Sergeant Pieter Everaert was the first of the Dutch explorers to reach the mouth by land. It was in 1661, and though Everaert had travelled along the river on previous journeys he had not noticed the ebb and flow. Now he was impressed by this fact; and that night he heard a noise which sounded like the sea. He travelled south-west and reached the end of the river.

One of the first wrecks near the river mouth was the Dutch hooker *Meteren*. She ran aground not in fog or heavy weather or as a result of human folly but simply because her whole crew went down with scurvy. They were all too ill to handle her, and she drifted on to the beach. Nine sick men reached safety. All the rest were drowned. That was in 1723, and in 1963 a party of diamond prospectors dug up four of her cannon, two bronze, two iron. They bore the Dutch East India Company's monogram. One of the iron cannon still held its gunpowder and a cannon ball.

Francois le Vaillant pitched a tent on the beach at the Olifants mouth during his journey to the Orange River late in the eighteenth century. It was winter,the river was in flood, and the French bird collector was kept awake by the sharp ocean breeze and the crying of the gulls. Vultures were there, too, in great numbers, and Le Vaillant's companions told him the birds had been feasting on a dead elephant. Le Vaillant examined the decaying meat on the shore and found it was a sperm whale. It appeared to have been stranded by a great wave and as it lay dying the birds and polecats and beetles attacked the mighty carcase. Polecats scampered away as Le Vaillant approached, and most of the birds took to flight. The crows remained, hovering over the flesh, croaking frightfully. Le Vaillant counted fourteen species of beetle. His band of Hottentots made bags of antelope skin and carried away quantities of sperm oil.

Le Vaillant was a poor swimmer, and he declared that he was nearly drowned at the Olifants mouth. His servants found a suitable "swimming log" and hauled him across the stream by this well-known Hottentot method. They took with them his "powder flasks and artillery". In midstream the flood was so strong that the whole party was almost swept out to sea. Fortunately the wind helped them to reach the far bank, and there Le Vaillant revived his men with a calabash of brandy.

Sir John Barrow was at the Olifants mouth not long after Le Vaillant. He noted the "excellent farms" on the banks, "the large heavy grain, white as snow, attracting the birds." Barrow said the river never dried up, for it was fed from the great northern chain of mountains. The mouth was seldom safe enough to be entered by boats, but once inside a boat could proceed for thirty miles through "wild uninhabited country".

Charts of the river mouth show a slight curve to the

north called Elizabeth Bay. I am glad the ship *Elizabeth* left her name there, for this is the last, faint echo of a desperate adventure that ended in a deep mystery. It was in November 1817 that the *Elizabeth* was lying off Murray's whaling station on Robben Island, loading barrels of oil. One night the convicts were mustered and locked up as usual; but a military sentry released eleven of them and gave them muskets and ammunition. They seized a boat, rowed out to the *Elizabeth* and boarded her. Someone fired a musket. Captain White, the master, surrendered and the ship was taken. Coogan, a convict who had served in the navy, took charge. He gave orders to make sail and cut the cable; and soon the *Elizabeth* was at sea and steering northwest. The convicts forced the captain to hand over his keys. There was talk of murdering the captain and crew; but Coogan finally decided to send them off in the long boat with provisions and water. The convicts had a fair start, but when the news reached Simonstown the admiral sent H.M.S. *Mosquito* in pursuit. She never caught the *Elizabeth*. Weeks later news reached Cape Town of a wreck at the Olifants river mouth. It was the *Elizabeth*, but she had been abandoned. What happened to the convicts? I have searched the records in vain. This is one of the mysteries which appears to have been swallowed up by the river of strange tales. All I found was this advertisement in the "Cape Town Gazette":

I am authorised by Lloyd's and the parties concerned to offer for sale the wreck of the *Elizabeth* as she now lies stranded, with a few casks of whale oil, empty casks, planks, beams, rope, masts, rigging and iron.

*A. V. Bergh, Jnr.*

It seems that the convicts escaped into the wilderness of Namaqualand as other runaways had done before them. One such fugitive, Hendrik Wikar returned to civilisation with a narrative of exploration which has become a South African classic. I wish the convicts of the *Elizabeth* had been able to tell their story, though it may have been a wretched one. One imagines that if they had survived for long, some word or legend would have come down through the years.

Official visits to the Olifants river mouth started early last century. Mr. P. S. Buissinne, sent by the colonial secretary, reported that the river was navigable from the mouth for fifty miles, within seventeen miles of Clanwilliam. Towards the entrance it spread out like a lake. "Violent surf on the bar defies the art of navigation," Buissinne declared. Nevertheless, there was an old Swede named Pieter Nielsen who rowed out often and visited a seal rock. He was in danger of drowning and no one dared to accompany him. Captain Roberts of H.M.S. *Shearwater* surveyed the Olifants mouth early in February 1821. There was a heavy swell, and the rollers broke in thirteen fathoms. "I do not think a boat can land with safety," Captain Roberts wrote. "The sea beat tremendously on the bar." All these reports, expert and otherwise, become interesting when you hear of the exploits of certain dare-devils at this frightening river entrance.

Sir James Alexander, soldier and explorer, was the first traveller to put forward the idea of a harbour at the Olifants river mouth. He was making the pioneer overland journey from the Cape to Walvis Bay in the eighteen-thirties when he studied the difficult entrance. Alexander pointed out that wheat fetched low prices in the Bokkeveld owing to the transport problem and often remained unsold for years. If the river mouth could be opened far more wheat would be grown. The river valley was flat; much karoo mud was carried down with the floods; and when this was sown with wheat the yield was one hundred-fold.

Alexander observed the river dividing itself into branches round an island (now called Bird Island) and then flowing into the South Atlantic through one mouth. Just inside the river, beyond the white foam, there was a depth of twelve feet. Gulls, sea swallow and flamingoes haunted the still waters of the estuary. At the mouth Alexander found a mat hut, a wagon, and old Hendrik van Zyl with his fine blue-eyed son. They were splitting, salting and drying harders and springers they had caught in the estuary. After a meal of fried fish Alexander set off in a boat rowed by a Frenchman, an old soldier who had fought in Napoleon's army at Austerlitz and Jena. Another character Alexander met was a Hottentot woman, a rival of the "Hottentot Venus". He said that for a trifle of money or tobacco she would allow a cloth to be spread behind, on which four plates might be laid. Alexander regarded the Olifants river as the boundary of civilisation. He had left houses behind and entered a wild region where he felt a glorious liberty, where he could dress as he liked, sing aloud or keep silent and eat with keen appetite. Possibly the convicts from the *Elizabeth* had shared that feeling.

Mr. P. Fletcher, a civil engineer, studied the Olifants mouth carefully for sixty-four days about a century ago. He noted a ridge like a miniature Lion's Rump on the north bank; the bird island which altered its shape after heavy floods; the fishing hamlet called Papendorp near the salt pan on the south bank; and the Viswater farm two miles upstream. Fish spawned in the river, he said, and the fishermen netted harders. There were days in summer when an ordinary boat might slip out of the river safely. Fletcher met a fine old seaman named William Love, who had a whaleboat and a daring crew. They used a rocky side channel, not the main entrance, and thus they were able to visit Elephant Rock, the seal island three miles up the coast. Love never lost his boat or crew. Others made the hazardous crossing of the bar. One of my old Cape directories states that the American whalers anchored in Elizabeth Bay and sent their boats up the river for water and provisions.

Among the happiest men ever to set eyes on the lonely mouth of the Olifants River were the tired Transvalers of the commando serving under General Smuts late in the South African War. They were twenty-five miles from the coast, and Smuts passed the word round that all the men who had never seen the sea were to join him. Sixty of them rode by way of Ebenezer mission. Deneys Reitz said it was amusing to watch the expression on the men's faces when the great expanse of ocean burst into view. Many had seen nothing larger than a farm dam before. They galloped towards the beach shouting: "The sea! The sea!" They threw off their clothes. Some rode into the surf and were in danger of being swept out to sea. General Smuts ordered Reitz to visit the fishermen's huts and find out whether the British had been at the river mouth. When they learnt that the area was clear of British troops they had a seaside holiday, sleeping among the dunes round great fires of driftwood. Smuts and his men spent two more days at the Olifants mouth, boating in the estuary and helping the fishermen to haul their nets.

Fishing has always flourished along the Olifants river. Danckaert the discoverer hooked what he described as "the finest fish in the world, and that in great abundance". Van Meerhoff reported "beautiful carp". Simon van der Stel noted in his diary "a fish resembling in shape the carp of Holland, in taste the salmon, and of the size of a cod fish". This, I imagine, was the Clanwilliam yellowfish, one of the finest Cape fresh water fish. However, the most remarkable Olifants river denizen of all was described to Van Meerhoff by some Bushmen. This was an amphibious monster with three legs which devoured human beings. Many sea fish enter the Olifants river as fry and grow to maturity there. Harders remain close to the mouth; but other species of mullet swim up the river to fresh water. White steenbras are also found in the estuary, forty-pounders among them. Dr. S. A. Hey has pointed out a peculiarity of this fish; it thrives as well in fresh water as in salt if the feeding is equal.

Nowadays a thousand fishing boats are at work in the rich seas off the Cape west coast. For more than a century the hard-pressed fishermen have longed for a harbour at the Olifants river mouth. Between the wars I saw a decked motor fishing cutter at anchor in the river. Some dare devil had seized his chance and rushed her through the surf and into the river in defiance of expert opinion. One day, perhaps, the words of the old navigator I mentioned will come true. A passage will be cut through the bar and the fishermen will find shelter in the Olifants river at last.

*Chapter Eleven*

# THE CAVE OF DREAMS

THIRTY miles from the Olifants river mouth (on the wings of a flamingo) there is a cool rock shelter filled with the atmosphere of old adventure. Here explorers and many famous travellers linger in the shadows while you stare at their names on the north wall. Nearly two hundred men carved or painted their names or initials and dates on the hard quartzite.

Someone named the place Heerenlogement in the late seventeenth or early eighteenth century, for it provided them with a spring of clear drinking water, grazing for their animals and shade for their tired eyes. In the wilderness of the route to Namaqualand this was indeed a "gentlemen's lodging", great luxury after the hot, loose sand of the aching plains. Heerenlogement is a cavern open to the west. It is about fifty feet wide and thirty feet deep, so that men who had been riding all day were able to rest out of the sun and wind. As a camping place it ranked high in the memories of Dutch East India Company's soldiers and those bold traders, prospectors, botanists and other fearless travellers who came later. South Africa has no other historic place so rich in inscriptions. Portuguese explorers left a few interesting pillars along the coast; captains of later merchant ships hacked out the letter stones they left beside the Table Valley stream; and the name of Piet Retief the voortrekker has survived since 1837, when his daughter painted it on Retief Rock. But these Heerenlogement names go back for nearly three centuries. Some have vanished. Those that remain are worth driving through the Sandveld to gaze upon in wonder.

Heerenlogement is more than a rock shelter nowadays. It is a tiny hamlet that remains in the mind as a peaceful, well-watered and lovely corner of a dry Cape district; a

Someone named the place Heerenlogement, for it provided them with a spring of clean drinking water, grazing for their animals and shade for their tired eyes.

group of old houses, some under thatch; gardens and trees, a shop and postal agency. Oldest of the present buildings is the farm homestead with walls several feet thick; rooms with yellowwood beams and peachstone floors; an enormous hearth with its pot racks; and a *solderkamer* reached from the outside. On a beam in the front room stands the date 1820, but parts of the homestead may be older. Many of the nineteenth century names in the shelter were those of people who spent a night in the homestead as guests of John Foster, the Nieuwoudts and other early owners of the building. As a farm, of course, Heerenlogement is much older than any of the houses. Jacob Cloete, an ancestor of President Paul Kruger, secured grazing rights there as far back as 1732. His widow gave up this lonely cattle post thirty years later. Then came J. A. Meyer and his widow, and later Gerrit Nieuwoudt. No doubt some of these people and many trekboers camped in the cave for long periods at a time when ox-wagons outnumbered permanent homes in the Sandveld.

Now I return to the travellers who reached the Heerenlogement spring and slaked their huge thirsts gratefully during the years before the first settlers arrived. They came this way, along the Sandveld track running parallel with the coast, to avoid the steep mountain passes leading into the Olifant's river valley. Railway engineers chose the route pioneered by Van Riebeeck's men for the same reason. Only after Grey's Pass had been built was road traffic diverted to the river valley. To this day the old Sandveld wagon track can be followed in many areas, and from the air I have seen it as clearly as though it was still in use. So here are the old knights in armour, the men seeking Monomotapa, the Dutch treasure hunters and prospectors and cattle traders; a parched, sunburnt procession, weary yet still eager to penetrate the unknown; brave men who needed all their strength and courage to face the hardships awaiting them in Namaqualand.

Earliest of all the names still visible in the cave are K. J. Slotsbo and Caspar Hemery 1712. Captain Slotsbo was on his way to find out whether thousands of Namaqua

Hottentots had invaded the Sandveld. Hemery, his companion, carved a lively elephant with upraised tusks. There is no doubt, however, that many travellers visited the cave decades before Slotsbo and Hemery. Jan Danckaert, an engineer and fine leader, was probably there in 1660 with Van Meerhoff and George Frederick Wreede as his companions. Wreede was an educated German who was compiling a Hottentot vocabulary. Pieter Cruythoff and Pieter Everaert were in the neighbourhood not long afterwards, and must have needed the water of the Heerenlogement spring. Olof Bergh certainly drank at the spring, but in 1682 he chose to leave his name and the year on a rock at another spring which he named after himself, Berghfontein, six miles to the south. Bergh gave Heerenlogement its first Dutch name, Dassenbergh's Fontein, "because we saw some coneys amongst the rocks." He spent the night there on his way north, and called again while returning from Namaqualand to the Cape. Olof Bergh was an intelligent Swede and a grand explorer, a friend of both Van der Stels and a trusted servant of the company. He recovered a fortune in specie from the wrecked English ship *Johanna* near Agulhas; but he stole valuable jewels from a later wreck, the Portuguese *Nossa Senhora dos Milagros*, and went to Robben Island as a convict for three years. This remarkable man then served with such distinction in Ceylon that he was able to return to the Cape as captain of the Castle. During his exploring years Olof Bergh carved his initials in a cave called the Ziekenhuis beyond Caledon, but apparently he saw no reason to leave his mark at Heerenlogement.

Isaac Schryver (who named Schryver's Hoek at the southern end of Saldanha Bay) must have passed by on his way to the Kamiesberg in 1684, but if he inscribed his name it is not there now. A year later came the greatest cavalcade ever seen at that quiet spot during the seventeenth century; a coach drawn by six horses, riding horses, field-guns, eight carts (one carrying a boat), nearly three hundred draught and pack oxen, six burghers in their own wagons, and more than fifty other white men. This was

Governor Simon van der Stel's expedition to Namaqualand. He refreshed his men and animals at both springs, and described the Heerenlogement mountain: "It is full of holes and caves, closely resembling some old, dilapidated building. We had to camp at the foot of the mountain because we had this day traversed routes deep in sand, which had greatly exhausted our draught oxen so that they were unable to cross the great height which confronted us. At this camp there was exceptionally good grass, and it was watered by various running streams containing very fresh and agreeable water. The mountain was also abundantly supplied with fuel."

On the Heerenlogement mountain Van der Stel shot a *klipspringer* and also a hare with a large tail, a *blouhaas* that puzzled the zoologists for many years. According to the governor's journal it had a muzzle like a jackal and a tail like a fox. It was "white of flesh and agreeable to the taste". A picture of this hare appeared in the journal, and it was clear that this was not any common hare. Possibly it was a rare form that has been exterminated. According to local tradition, Van der Stel left a huge iron cooking pot near the cave. It was so large that long afterwards a farmer used it for dipping his sheep. Then it was broken, but fragments were preserved and were still to be seen in recent years.

Simon van der Stel waited until he had reached Namaqualand before carving his name anywhere. Professor Percival R. Kirby, who made a close examination of the cave, thinks that Van der Stel would have mentioned inscriptions at Heerenlogement if there had been any there at the time of his visits; but the silence of the governor suggests that the cave was still decorated only with Bushman paintings. Slotsbo, the first carver, had one hundred and eighty-one men in his column, but Hemery and one I. Sersein were the only members to record their presence. Next came Ensign I. T. Rhenius in 1721, a son-in-law of Olof Bergh, bound for the north on a cattle-buying expedition. Jan Philip Giebeler, who carved his name in 1739, was on his way to the Namaqualand coast in search of a wreck.

I can find no record of a west coast wreck at that period; and so this may be a lost chapter in the book of adventure. Jacob Cloete, the grazier I have mentioned, added his name in 1747, and his guest Jacob Breedt followed his example. Captain Hendrik Hop came in 1761 with a large expedition which crossed the Orange River and reached the Karas mountains. Hendrik Kruger, one of Hop's men, was a great-great-grandfather of President Paul Kruger, but he did not leave his name in the cave. Another interesting personality in Hop's party was the German gardener J. A. Auge, first of a number of famous botanists to see the cave. Auge transformed the company's garden in Cape Town from a vegetable patch into a fine collection of plants and trees. It has been suggested that Hop gave the cavern the name Heerenlogement, but there is no definite evidence. Possibly the visit of Governor Simon van der Stel may have led to the use of such an aristocratic name.

Charles Peter Thunberg, the Swedish botanist, described the cave twelve years after Hop's visit, but he was too tired to carve his name. "I found a scarce and long-sought-for plant, viz: the *Codon Royené*, but did not see more than one shrub of it which, however, I think I shall never forget," Thunberg wrote. "It was one of the hottest days in summer and the heat was so intolerable that we were afraid that our beasts would grow faint and drop down quite exhausted. By this insufferable and tormenting heat our bodies were swelled up, as it were, and our pores opened in the highest degree. The bushes we met with were covered all over with white and transparent prickles which, when my fellow-traveller and I suddenly fell upon them and strove which should pluck the most flowers with our naked hands, scratched them in such a terrible manner that for several days we experienced great pain and inconvenience. At length we arrived quite exhausted to the Gentlemen's Hotel, which was a vale between the mountains with a pretty high hill . . . This place, which is pleasant being ornamented with a small wood and a rivulet of fresh water, is called the Gentlemen's Hotel because on one side of the mountain there is a large cavern to the westward like a hall, formed by two rocks which were hollowed out by the hand of time. I climbed up to it and found the names of several travellers written on the sides. Near this was another hollow vault, but somewhat less. In the former of these caves there was a small fissure in which a tree, probably a *Sideroxylon*, had taken root and stood in a very flourishing condition being above eight feet in height; although it had no more water for its nourishment and support than the trifling quantity that was retained by the fissure in the rainy season."

You will hear more of that tree; it is still there. Thunberg's companion, of course, was Francis Masson, the English gardener from Kew, the man who gave the first description of the springbok. As you have heard, Masson's hands were sore and he did not leave his name for posterity. Four years after Thunberg, the Scottish plant collector William Paterson rested in the cave, and he halted there again during later journeys. Once he found a "peasant" at the spring. Paterson observed that this man had many Hottentots and a number of guns in his wagon; he was trekking to the Orange River to join Colonel Robert Gordon. It is not clear whether Gordon ever visited the cave, though he must have passed by.

Now watch the approach of the most vivid of the eighteenth century travellers—Francois le Vaillant, the French naturalist. In spite of all his braggadocio and exaggerated claims, Le Vaillant was a man of great achievements. He was obviously in a bad mood when he rode up to Heerenlogement in July 1783; nevertheless he made the first drawings of the place and his description is memorable: "I was now only a day's journey from the 'master's residence' where I should find, I was told, a very abundant spring of water, a most agreeable retreat, and groves and grottoes covered with inscriptions and figures . . . It appeared as if a second Angelica, or a Hottentot Medor, had visited and embellished this scene of enchantment. I banished, however, from my mind all this improbable romance, and indulged only in the hope of finding the fountain. My wants were urgent. I looked forward to it therefore with longing and expectation and resolved if possible to reach it before night . . . I arrived, I found it . . . Its waters were soon rendered turbid by my Hottentots and cattle. With regard to the grotto, the inscriptions and creeping shrubs hanging in festoons, all these like a dream vanished on our approach. I saw only a large cavern which served to shelter me and my caravan. It was spacious and lofty, and being open we were covered without being shut up in it. Situated upon a small mound, it overlooked on one side my camp and the plain which, by the uniform and dreary prospect it presented, filled me with melancholy and discouragement; and on the other was joined to an immense chain of dry mountains, extending in the form of an amphitheatre, the nakedness of which, and the different tints of ochre, grey and white, exhibited a view at once terrifying and majestic. The remains of a habitation, now fallen into ruins, attested that the proprietor had been long forced to abandon this wild and unproductive waste. I made preparations for passing the night in the grotto, but was obliged to share it with jackdaws and wood-pigeons which repaired to it at the close of day. They perched in hundreds on a tree, the roots of which were implanted in an enormous crevice, while one of its branches overspread the floor of this natural hall. The figures and inscriptions consisted only of a few caricatures of the elephant and ostrich, with the names of three or four travellers who had probably stopped here formerly to refresh themselves."

I tried in vain to trace the ostrich mentioned by Le Vaillant. Probably this was a Bushman painting, obliterated by later travellers who carved their names in the days when cave art was treated with contempt. (Unfortunately this attitude has never died out.) An engraving, like Hemery's trumpeting elephant, would probably have survived because of the difficulties of cutting a name over a previous design on the rock. The mystery of the Le Vaillant signature at Heerenlogement is the spelling, for there is only one "l" in Vaillant. It has been suggested that the disappointed naturalist left this monotonous task to some ignorant person who spelt the name wrong. Le Vaillant wound up his account of the visit as follows: "Six weeks only had elapsed since I quitted the Cape, yet my oxen were as much fatigued as they had been during my first journey after a march of six months. To give them time to rest themselves and recover their strength I remained at Heerenlogement seven whole days, during which our table occasioned such a consumption of *dassen* or damans that even my Hottentots began to loathe them. At length, however, on the fourth of July, the war we had declared against those poor animals ceased and I quitted the place, after having left my name and the date of my arrival in the grotto, according to the custom of preceding travellers."

First of many missionaries to leave their names in the cave were Abraham and Christian Albrecht, the German brothers who were sent by the London Mission Society to settle in South West Africa. They visited Heerenlogement in 1805. In 1809 the Wesleyan missionary Farquhar added his name, and four years later in September the celebrated Rev. Barnabas Shaw joined the signatories. He was bound for the Kamiesberg to set up the Leliefontein mission. His wife was with him, but she left no record. Indeed, the shelter is very much a "Gentleman's Lodging", for there are not more than about half a dozen feminine names or initials to be seen. Shaw left these details: "We reached this place about midnight. Our cattle having had no water during the day and the sand being very deep, the croaking of frogs was to all a joyful sound. Here we halted some days to rest our oxen, during which the people were engaged in making bullets for the guns. The fissure in the rock described by Vaillant was visited, and the tree which he mentions still spreads its branches over the floor of the so-called *kliphuis*. The names of many travellers are to be seen carved on the rock, some of whom visited the place in 1712. Where are these travellers now?"

Robert Moffat was the next missionary to pass Heerenlogement, but he did not mention a visit in his writings. Then, in June 1828, came the versatile Scottish military surgeon Andrew Smith, explorer and ornithologist and botanist, first superintendent of the South African

Museum; later Sir Andrew Smith, director of army medical services in the Crimea. He made a detailed investigation of the cave, listed twenty-seven names, and carved his own name below Le Vaillant. (It was seen there fifteen years later, but some vandal hacked it off.) Smith was on his way to the Orange River, telling everyone that his mission was scientific. In fact, his main purpose was to gather confidential information about the Bushmen on the frontier for the acting governor at the Cape. Dr. Smith spent some days round about Heerenlogement mountain collecting birds. Karl Zeyher, botanist and hunter, cut his name soon after Smith's visit; and in 1830 the little-known Johann Drege came to the spring, but did not join the gallery of names. Drege was an indefatigable and meticulous plant collector, the pioneer in describing the Cape botanical regions; but the biographers have discovered nothing about the man himself. According to Drege's diary, Heerenlogement was a cattle post in his day. Edward Cook the Wesleyan missionary followed Drege; then came an unidentified person D. Callaghan, and L. M. Greeff, assistant field cornet of the Clanwilliam district.

Sir James Alexander, soldier and explorer, left only his initials J.E.A. on the wall in 1836, but he was one of the most interesting of all the travellers who passed that way. He was making the first overland journey from Cape Town to Walvis Bay when he visited the cave. His narrative mentions the excellent ox-wagon he used, complete with chests and water-kegs, for which he paid sixty pounds. His span of handsome black and white oxen cost another thirty pounds. So it is possible to visualise him loading his wagon with guns and powder-horns, trade knives, beads and tobacco, food and a medicine chest, violin and tambourine; everything necessary for a year in the South African wilderness. He left Government House in Cape Town early enough to have breakfast and a stirrup-cup at the Royal Observatory; then the wagon left the shores of Table Bay. It was spring and brilliant wild flowers covered the green face of the land. Alexander passed through Malmesbury, the *broodkamer* of the colony even in those days. He found the Berg River filled from "bank to brae" and flowing through a flat and fertile country. So strong was the current that the pont was unable to cross, and twenty wagons had been held up on the far side. Van der Merwe, the pont owner, invited Alexander to a supper of mutton and peaches. The waters subsided and the explorer passed on. He left his wagon for a time, forded the Olifants River on horseback, and visited Clanwilliam. At a farm house he enjoyed cakes made with flour and mountain honey. He described an old cedar with a girth of thirty-six feet which provided one thousand feet of sawn planks. Alexander saw Bushman caves, one with a fine painting of a flock of sheep in red ochre. People in Clanwilliam complained that they had twice lost their post owing to the lack of a pont or boat on the Olifants River; and on the second occasion the postman had been drowned. Alexander was also shocked when he found that between Cape Town and a mission far beyond Clanwilliam there was not a single doctor. No one could set a limb or heal a wound, so that sufferers had to travel four hundred miles. Now here is Alexander's description of Heerenlogement:

"We journeyed onwards through flower-decked coppices (the season was rainy) with a range of mountains on our right. We arrived at Heerenlogement, where was a pool of water, under a hill, some distance up which there is a large and open cave or *kliphuis*. A small tree grows out of the fissure of the rock above, and partly overshadows the floor of the cave; whilst, on the north side, is carved the names of travellers and hunters from the year 1712 to recent periods. Among others, conspicuous, is that of the renowned F. Vaillant 1783. Looking from the cave in a westerly direction the eye ranges over a wide extent of plain on which bushes are scattered . . . Elephants have long since disappeared from this locality; the only traces of them being the name of the river and the rude figure of one I had seen carved in the *kliphuis* at Heerenlogement."

Names which appeared on the wall during the eighteen-thirties were Wesleyan missionaries J. Jackson and Joseph Tindall. Mrs. Tindall accompanied her husband to the mission at Warmbad, across the Orange River. The Rev. James Backhouse, also Wesleyan, called in 1840 on his way back to the Cape from Leliefontein, but did not leave his name. He provided this impression of the scene: "Before five in the morning we again set forward; as we descended the Knagersberg the beams of the moon were distinctly to be seen glittering on the sea near the mouth of the Olifants River. At eight o'clock we reached the rugged, isolated sandstone hills of the Heerenlogement, where there is a slender spring supplying some pools of water. At this place there is a cavernous opening with perpendicular sides among the rocks on the ascent of a lofty hill; on the sides of the cave the names of several persons were inscribed; among them were Casp. Hem. 1712 with the figure of an elephant underneath, and F. Vaillant 1783. Elephants are not now met with in this part of Africa, nor on the western side much to the south of the Tropic of Capricorn. A wild fig-tree hangs into the top of this cave and gives it a pretty appearance. The adjacent country is so destitute of water that a wagon which was here from Clanwillian, going to a ship lying near the mouth of the Olifants River, and which left this place after noon today, would reach its destination tomorrow morning. It would load during the day, and return the following morning without the oxen having the opportunity of drinking till they should again reach this place. The trader was taking some casks of water with him for the use of the merchant at the ship."

Yet another Wesleyan missionary left impressions of his Heerenlogement visit during a December in the eighteen-forties. He was the Rev. Benjamin Ridsdale, travelling with his wife and Tindall. Ridsdale enriched the literature of the cave with this piece: "About midnight we arrived at Heerenlogement extremely fatigued with long journeying through deep and heavy sand and with the intense heat of the day. But though the day had been so hot we were now quite nipped by the strong keen wind that was blowing. Having arrived so late, the men and oxen being jaded, we took no morning stage on Thursday the fourteenth, but after breakfast went on an expedition to the famous 'Logement' or cavernous chamber, from which the place takes its name. After ascending a steep hillside thickly overgrown with bushes at about one hundred feet above the plain we came to a large cavern in the side of the rock, forming a tolerably spacious apartment. Through a fissure in the rock's roof a wild fig-tree sends its spreading branches, giving a pretty effect. On one side of this cavern, full open to the daylight, the names of many travellers and missionaries were cut. And here I spent some time chiselling my name into the hard face of the rock, a process which I found required much patience . . . The only instruments available were a hammer and an old blunt screw-driver. I succeeded quite to my own satisfaction, considering the sorry tools at my command, and left my name, as Brother Tindall said, 'in superfine London type'."

Among the many signatories of the eighteen-forties were James Foster, sheriff's officer at Clanwilliam, member of an Irish family which arrived with the 1820 settlers; P. C. van Ellewee, field cornet at Clanwilliam; F. C. Bain possibly a relative of the famous Andrew Geddes Bain who signed during the next decade; and R. Harry, a Wesleyan missionary. William Mann the astronomer described the cave during this period. "Visited a kind of cave at the foot of the mountain, upon the sides of which were inscribed numerous names and devices, the handiwork of the scores of travellers who have passed this spot. Why such great affection should be shown for this particular place I am at a loss to conceive, but since what everybody does must be right and proper I followed the good example and left my mark there also." Mann's name has since disappeared. He was on his way to assist his chief, Sir Thomas Maclear, in verifying and extending La Caille's arc of meridian. Maclear and Mann spent many hard years on this task, and both men suffered in health as a result. Maclear, a doctor before he became an astronomer, was called upon in emergencies by the farmers of the Clanwilliam district; and once, when he had climbed a high peak in the Cedarberg, he returned exhausted to find two wagon-loads of sick women waiting for him. Hot summers and the winter snows brought on rheumatic fever, and Maclear was crippled for life. William Mann was Maclear's son-in-law. He was first assistant at the observatory for thirty-two years, and was also a capable artist. Often he went on foot with one Hottentot servant. They carried a bag of rusks,maps and instruments; and it was usually a long way between water sources. Mann had to fill his mouth with pebbles to keep it moist. The years of field work caused chest trouble and Mann died at the age of fifty-five.

Two fellow-travellers who signed in 1849 were L. Leygonie and J. P. Philip. Leygonie had been one of Napoleon's staff officers on St. Helena. He and Philip started to carve the words "Vive la France", but gave up. Albert von Schlicht, a successful prospector and Namaqualand copper pioneer, signed at that period. (More than a century later Von Schlicht's nonagenarian daughter Henrietta gave me a first-hand account of trekking with her parents in horse-wagons, twelve days from the Cape to the Concordia mine.) Thomas Fannin, another man who helped to open up the copper deposits, cut his surname only. I have seen a letter he wrote describing the ox-wagon journey with his wife and family. Each wagon was loaded with gunpowder. "We used to stop at Dutch farmhouses sometimes," Fannin said. "I remember their stewed mutton and sweet brown bread, made from wheat grown by themselves. It was dry, desert country inhabited only by Namaquas. They were friendly enough, and the women brought goats'-milk to sell for the children, but the boys were not allowed to go far from the camp as the Bushmen were wild little creatures using poisoned arrows," Fannin became a farmer in Natal. His grandson was Dr. Austin Roberts, author of "The Birds of South Africa."

Baron Carel von Ludwig, founder of the Kloof Street garden in Cape Town, was also a copper pioneer; and in 1853 his son W. F. J. von Ludwig left his name. Other visitors in the middle of last century were J. J. Turpin, carpenter, and J. Southgate, omnibus proprietor, both from Cape Town. Andrew Geddes Bain has been mentioned; in 1854 this great road engineer wrote his name in white paint, and this has survived marvellously. Four members of the Fryer family carved a castellated tower and signed within the walls: Mrs. Fryer 23rd February 1861, A. Fryer, E. Fryer, M. Fryer. They were 1820 settlers at Clanwilliam who moved on to the farm Groot Toren in the Calvinia district; hence the tower. These daring people trekked even farther north long before the Orange River became safe for white farmers. Fryer's Fontein appeared on an early map of South West Africa. Dr. George H. B. Fisk, a Cape Town medico who lived in Buitencingel, visited the cave in the eighteen-seventies. One of the undated names is that of A. de Pass (Aaron), wealthy owner of guano ships, uncle of the art collector who left many valuable paintings to South African galleries. Aaron de Pass usually travelled by sea, and I can only imagine that he was trekking overland to the bird island at Lambert Bay or the seal rock to the north of the Olifants river mouth. P. S. Krige, who signed in 1902, was a brother-in-law of General Smuts, and served in Smut's commando.

All sorts of men sheltered in this cave and some left their names there, as you have seen. Some met sudden, violent or shameful deaths. Van Meerhoff, the Danish surgeon, one of the greatest adventurers of them all, survived the hazards of Namaqualand only to die on a beach in Madagascar when the natives massacred the Dutch landing party. Pieter Roman, a companion of Everaert, was killed by an elephant near where Porterville now stands. Cornelis de Cretser was captured by pirates and disappeared. Wreede was drowned at Mauritius. Auge lived to ninety, blind and poverty-stricken, ending his days miserably on a lonely Cape farm. But the most haunting of those carved names is one that appears near the ground: L. J. Colyn 1882. Lambert Colyn was a farmer with a flowing beard. He was forty-five when he joined Commandant Bouwer's commando in 1902 during the invasion of the Cape by General Smuts. Colyn told the men of the commando that the English had put him in gaol in Clanwilliam, but he had escaped over the wall and had come to take up arms. He was given a rifle. In fact, Colyn was a spy. He deserted from the commando, and soon afterwards he appeared at the head of a body of British cavalry which rode into the commando's camp, leaving seventeen Boers dead or wounded. Colyn was captured by Smuts a week later. Smuts himself presided at the court-martial on the farm Atties, and finally gave the order: "Take him out and shoot him". Deneys Reitz, who was present, said that Colyn showed no sign of fear while the evidence was being given, but when he heard the death sentence his nerve deserted him. He fell on his knees and begged for mercy. The women of the farm left the room in tears. A grave was dug near the homestead while a minister of the Dutch Reformed Church named Kriel tried to comfort the condemned man. Colyn told Reitz that he had taken the blood money for the sake of his wife and children, who were starving. Then the firing party assembled and after praying for some time Kriel spoke to Colyn: "Brother, be a man, your time has come." Colyn asked for a final interview with Smuts but the request was not granted. It was evening. Colyn was blindfolded and Kriel said a last prayer. When he uttered the word "Amen" the firing party raised their rifles and Colyn fell dead.

Naturally the names inscribed in other centuries are more interesting than recent additions. I am not prepared to lay down a deadline between valuable historic relics and moddern vandalism, however, as I feel that there are names of our own times which deserve a niche in the crowded north wall of Heerenlogement. For example, Professor H. H. W. Pearson, founder of Kirstenbosch, might well have carved a place for himself in this strange and varied collection when he examined the cave in 1911 on his way to Namaqualand. Pearson knew a great deal about the men who had passed that way before him. Among the old families of Namaqualand he found people whose ancestors had known Drege and other travellers of the early nineteenth century. The father of a man still living in 1911 had provided Sir James Alexander with oxen. In remote homesteads Pearson met farmers who had hardly felt the influence of events in the greater world beyond their own horizons.

Pearson found that the Heerenlogement cave was being used a cattle kraal. Inscriptions in the friable sandstone were being worn down by the cattle; some had been almost obliterated. Pearson called the cave "Le Vaillant's grotto", and he was deeply interested in the tree which Le Vaillant and others had described. The earlier records enabled him to trace the very slow growth of this Namaqualand fig-tree, *Ficus cordata*. Yes, I would like to have seen Pearson's name there. Another candidate for this posthumous honour would be Dr. E. E. Mossop, who traced the routes of the old explorers, climbed mountains in search of history, and used his influence so that the precious heritage of Heerenlogement became a national monument. A third name that should be hammered out high up on the north wall would be that of Professor Percival R. Kirby, musician and Africana enthusiast, whose research at Heerenlogement was both thorough and enlightening. These names might well replace certain rude, fairly recent daubs which are without interest or artistic value.

I have mentioned the early owners of the Heerenlogement farm. Dutch East India Company maps showed it as a loan farm of more than two thousand morgen. After the British occupation the Nieuwoudts applied for owner's rights, and in 1837 three of them received "perpetual quitrent" from Governor Sir Benjamin D'Urban. The annual rent was reasonable enough, four guineas for an area of nearly twenty thousand morgen. Two years later Heremias Nieuwoudt paid thirty three pounds and became sole owner. It appears that J. A. Nieuwoudt, *heemraad* of Clanwilliam in 1823, was the first of the line to carve his name in the cave. Nine members of the De Villiers family appear on the cave wall, the first in 1868, the last in 1922. For thirty-five years the farm belonged to P. J. A. de Villiers, a second cousin of Lord de Villiers. Among the sights of the farm is a *perdemeul*, the old-fashioned device for grinding wheat. On the mountainside is a *wolwehok* with a stone door, a trap which must have caught generations of hyenas. A corrugated-iron fort built by British troops during the South African War has also been preserved.

Professor Kirby's son John excavated part of the cave floor and found stone implements, various fragments, ostrich egg, shell beads and teeth of animals no longer found in the district. Professor van Riet Lowe identified these as Late Stone Age relics. The cave has also yielded an old-fashioned round bullet used for elephant hunting, and the button of a dragoon. Somehow an iron box has found its way to the cave and is preserved there. It is four feet long, and it was discovered on the farm of that remarkable Hottentot, Kaptein Hendrik Witbooi, after he had left the Cape for South West Africa. Local tradition maintains that the box was found near the Olifants river mouth, and that it came from a wrecked ship.

"Only foolish men and boors scribble names on glass and doors," so they say. Yet the names of Heerenlogement are part of South Africa's past, and I only hope the barbed wire and the locked gate will preserve this secluded corner with its historic north wall from the mischievous hand of man. Le Vaillant's tree is still there; so are the handsome Namaqua doves calling *wooo-hooo* round Le Vaillant's grotto. If you have only a grain of imagination, look outwards from that cave and you must see in the rocky frame a burning landscape brought to life by all those old retinues of horsemen and wagons struggling into the north; the unknown north, the little-known north, the north that was mapped at last but remained hot and cruel. And surely when you turn to the north wall you must see ghosts in daylight. Perhaps you, too, will remember the psalm that rang in the mind of Barnabas Shaw the missionary when he thought of the travellers who had paused in that cave before him:

*Time is like an ever-rolling stream*
*Bears all its sons away;*
*They fly forgotten as a dream*
*Dies at the opening day.*

*Chapter Twelve*

# IN THE LEIPOLDT COUNTRY

FIRST of the Cape mountains to appear on the charts of the Portuguese explorers were the Cedarberg, for they sighted these peaks while sailing close inshore along the flamingo coast towards Table Bay. Vasco de Gama marked them on his parchment about forty miles eastwards of the vague coastline, and named them "Mountains of the Three Magi Kings".

I would like to have set eyes on the fastnesses of the virgin Cedarberg in those days, four centuries ago; before the Bushmen and the great beasts had been disturbed by the first Dutch expeditions. True, there are still Cedarberg landscapes which remain untouched by the hand of man. I have wandered in the wild veld there among the fantastic rock formations; and nearly forty years ago I looked at the Cedarberg from the cold, open cockpit of a single-engined biplane. The fuel-pipe had been giving trouble, and I was nervous. Yet even in that threatening situation I could admire the great parallel ranges beyond the shuddering wingtips. Eastwards lay the highest peaks, Sneeuberg and Tafelberg, both well over six thousand feet. It was a dark and massive chain, more than thirty miles of peaks and long, deep kloofs; the village and orange groves of Citrusdal below me and the larger village of Clanwilliam away to the north. Mountaineers love the Cedarberg, and with good reason. The weathered sandstone is never treacherous. Many of the secluded valleys give the impression that no one has ever been there before. Frightening mountain passes were built years ago for carts and pack-donkeys, but only in fairly recent years have motor-cars gone through. Footpaths made by foresters and buchu-gatherers wind past huge monoliths and cedar plantations and masses of tumbled rock. Stone huts and caves with crystal pools nearby are used by climbers for their assaults on the great snow peaks. And when they reach those summits they gaze in rapture westwards to the golden South Atlantic, northwards to snowfields tinted with rose, south to a tiny Table Mountain more than a hundred miles away. In these remote mountains there are charming and unexpected corners. I remember that great climber Kenneth Cameron describing a deserted farm called Hoogvertoon in the heart of the Cedarberg, a little plateau four thousand feet above sea level where some bold spirit had planted oak and pear trees and laid out a flower garden. Daffodils were flourishing there although the farm had been abandoned for many years. My old friend Denis Woods, another mountaineer who was claimed by the Cedarberg many years ago, told me of the block houses he found there. They were solidly built of local stone and clay, neatly embrasured, inaccessible except on foot, along a track which did not seem to have been used since the South African War. Probably the isolated soldiers never fired a shot except at the leopard and buck, but they were built to stop General Smuts when he invaded the Cape Colony.

Glance at the animal place names on the maps of the Cedarberg and you realise that this was once a wonderland of wild life. Cape mountain zebra, first of the zebra tribe to be seen by white men, survived in these mountains almost until the end of last century. Now such names as Perdefontein, Paardekloof and Perdekop bring visions of these splendid creatures, their stripes blending perfectly with the sunlight and shadows of their terrain. Mountaineers still follow the tracks they made, especially in the Uitkyk Pass area. The mountain zebra might be there to this day if only they had not been forced down from the safety of the heights in times of drought. Ordinary zebra and the quagga living on the plains to the east of the Cedarberg were exterminated long before the mountain zebra.

Rheboksvallei and Rheboksfontein remind us of the *vaalribbok*, happily still abundant. You would not think these antelope belonged to the same family as the *rooiribbok* or mountain reedbuck as the *vaalribbok* is small and slender compared to other reedbuck, and has woolly hair and upright horns. Farmers have told me that the mountain reedbuck further to the east were wiped out because they were good to eat, whereas the *vaalribbok* often harbour botfly eggs under the skin and the flesh is dry and unpalatable. However, the *vaalribbok* is shot now and then by a farmer who has had the unhappy experience of these buck running amok and killing his sheep and goats.

Buffelshoek is a reminder that buffalo once wallowed in the Cedarberg pools, though they were far more common in the eastern parts of the Cape. The absence of giraffe names (such as Kameelfontein and Kameelvlei, often found to the north) confirms the reports of early Dutch explorers, who encountered giraffe only when they reached the Kamiesberg. Lion names are fairly common, and there were still a few lions in the Cedarberg early last century. Herds of elephant roamed the west coast until the white hunters arrived; but Olifantsdam in the Clanwilliam district has not seen an elephant since the latter half of the eighteenth century. Elandsfontein and Elandskloof saw the last eland at about the same period that the elephant vanished; for eland lived on the plains, they were easily shot and their meat was excellent. Duikerfontein, on the other hand, may still slake the thirst of this artful buck. A duiker knows how to find cover when hunted, and it has never been exterminated. Duiker skins were prized by the old Cedarberg farmers, for the stout *riempies* they provided were used for making chairs and stools and sewing on the soles of *velskoene*. A goatskin *riempie* is not in the same class. Rhinoceros names are rare in the Clanwilliam distict, for these blundering beasts preferred the inland plains. Now and again they came through the gaps in the mountains, but along the west coast they were killed off about two centuries ago. Tierhoek and Tierkloof, Jakkalsvlei and Patrysberg commemorate birds and beasts that still find sanctuary in the Cedarberg.

Though much wild life has vanished the botanist still finds rarities and plants of great fascination in these mountains. Once the people of the district regarded the unique cedar trees as ordinary timber for every sort of furniture from cradles to coffins. You find cedar doors and window-frames in the homesteads, cedar seats in the churches. Yet some of the gnarled wild trees have been watered by the snows of centuries and lived through the dreaded fires. Only the dying and the gaunt dead cedars are cut down nowadays, and plantations of young cedars have been laid out. No longer are the mountains covered thickly as they were early last century in the mist belt above three thousand feet. As far back as 1805 an official commission reported that "the manner in which the forest is worked at present can only lead to its early destruction". Those words almost came true. Sheep and goats devoured the seedlings while the woodcutters swung their axes. Yet protection came in time and the cedars have been saved.

Many botanists regard the Clanwilliam cedars as South Africa's most interesting trees. No one knows why they should have become established on these hot mountains, for they really belong to the cold northern hemisphere. Like the silver trees of Table Mountain, the cedars are found only in limited areas. (The *gifboom* of the Gifberge and the Cape box-tree of East London are other examples). The mystery of the cedars remains unsolved. They may have grown on the Cedarberg since primeval times; but it would be surprising to find an indigenous tree in such an unsuitable area. Possibly the cones were carried thousands of miles by birds from the Atlas Mountains of North Africa.

Proteas are the most spectacular of the Cedarberg flowers. You find the dramatic king protea with its flowers twelve inches wide; the little Cedarberg protea, wine-coloured; the rare nodding protea and the rocket pincushion with scarlet flowers. In the snows of the great peaks grow the *sneeublom* and the rainbow pincushion. The *waboom* is a protea, the famous tree that has provided so much firewood, so much bark for tanning, so many wagon-wheels; so, too, is the wild almond with a fruit containing prussic acid, the fruit that is soaked in water and roasted as a coffee substitute. Monarch of the range in the protea family is the woolly-bearded protea in glorious shades of pink and cream.

In the Cedarberg you are in the bush tea country. Although bush tea has been described as the stepchild of South African beverages it has a flavour which might well stand up to a blindfold test. Only the expert, however, would be able to name the different types of *rooibos* from the Cedarberg range; the reddish liquid brewed from the leaves from high altitudes, the black tea of the plains and so on. This drink is made from a legume and not from any plant of the tea family. Early this century is was an entirely wild product, known to the Cedarberg people under such queer names as *springkaan* and *naaltjie*. Coloured people and some farmers brewed it. Bush tea was then almost unknown outside the Clanwilliam district, the only place in the world where it grows. Then a Russian named Benjamin Ginsberg came on the scene. Ginsberg's great-uncle was a Popoff, a favourite of the Tsar, who held a tea monopoly and brought tea from China to Moscow. Ginsberg was soon planning to fill the samovars and tea-pots of the world with this scented mountain growth. Only in recent years, however, has the export of bush tea become a reality, but the flavour is now appreciated in many parts of Southern Africa. It contains very little tannin and no alkaloids, so that it does not keep anyone awake or upset the stomach. I have heard that bush tea is regarded as a cure for rheumatism, for it has a high vitamin C content, and is also rich in potash, phosphates, calcium and iron. This is essentially a poor man's drink, half the price of genuine tea.

Bush tea is tasted at its best, I think, when it is iced and served with lemon. In a long glass the tawny colour and the bouquet may be appreciated. Some say that it should be spiced with gin. The crop is enormous nowadays; three million pounds or more a year. Each pound of *rooibos* yields three times as many cups as a pound of India or Ceylon tea. It is exported as "red tea", and the growers have found buyers as far away as France and the United States.

Cattle farmers crossed the ranges and settled in the shadow of the Cedarberg early in the eighteenth century. Some of the pioneers found land near the present Citrusdal; yet it was not until 1916 that Citrusdal village was laid out.

Clanwilliam is much older. Dr. C. Louis Leipoldt, greatest of Clanwilliam's sons, tried for years to discover the origin of this settlement in the elbow of the Jan Dissel's and the Olifants rivers. He ended in a mist of legend. It seems that one Koenraad Fiet, alias Dierman, founded the place; a murderer who buried disobedient slaves alive, baked others in a red-hot oven, and cracked the skulls of wayfarers for the sake of their money. No one heard of those crimes, for his nearest neighbour was fifty miles away. Koenraad Fiet was still there when Daniel van Ryneveld was appointed assistant landdrost early last century; and before he died the murderer cursed the new village and its people. Because of the curse (runs the legend) Clanwilliam remained a small village all through last century.

Clanwilliam is an Irish name and among the early Clanwilliam villagers were O'Shaughnessys and Shaws, O'Callaghans and Fosters, O'Dwyers, O'Kennedys and Fryers and other members of an Irish 1820 Settler group. Most of them moved on but several artisans remained. Their descendants are still there, and though the brogue has given way to English and Afrikaans, the Irish origin is plain to see. Their cottages in the Cedarberg, thatched and surrounded by cows and goats, are like the dwellings of Connemara crofters; and the Irish features are still unmistakable. German missionaries arrived, the Leipoldts and Wagenaars, Budlers and Fismers. Afrikaner farmers looking for large farms entered the area, the Berghs and Burgers and Van Wyks. Dr. Leipoldt declared that this unusual blend gave Clanwilliam an entirely different atmosphere from other Cape villages. It was, for almost the whole of last century, "a paradise without politics".

I found an old official document giving details of the Clanwilliam district towards the middle of last century.

The area was enormous although the district had been separated from Tulbagh. Mr. J. van Ryneveld was resident magistrate at a salary of three hundred pounds a year, with free house, wagon and horses. Mr. A. H. C. van Zyl, field cornet at the Olifants river mouth, received only ten pounds a year. A horseman setting out from Cape Town for Clanwilliam reached Mostert's farm in the Koeberg in four hours, and another three hours brought him to Malmesbury. The next halt was Jordaan's farm at Riebeek Kasteel, a ride of ninety minutes; then a four hour ride to Onderste Poort; three and a half hours to Oberholster at Twenty-four Rivers; three and a half hours to Baviaan's Kloof; five and a half hours to Klaver Vallei; and then Clanwilliam was reached after a total of twenty-seven and a half hours in the saddle.

Tobacco and rice were among the crops in those days. The rice yield was two hundred to one in that hot climate. Cattle and horses flourished. Two hatters were at work. My document explained that "ostrich wool", the soft down lying under the feathers, was used for hat-making as beaver was seldom procurable. Clanwilliam had become the centre for the eighteen farmers along the upper Olifants river and the twenty-nine farms between the village and Lambert Bay salt pan. About forty miles to the east of Clanwilliam was the Bidouw, a group of thirty-one farms where sheep and horses were reared. "The horses are of a good, strong race, able to bear much fatigue," runs the document. "They are sent to the Cedar Mountains when horse-sickness appears, and they are safe." Clanwilliam also administered Wupperthal, the mission village which I shall visit later; the Onder Bokkeveld with its forty-eight sheep farms; the Hantam, purely a grazing area inhabited by trekboers; the Onder Roggeveld, also a grazing area; the Renoster river, more than two hundred miles away, karoo veld "where the inhabitants seldom see a stranger"; and the lower Olifants river, which the writer of the document expected to become "the Nile of South Africa". The magistrate at Clanwilliam was also responsible for the Hardeveld, land of trekboers, the Kamiesberg and the whole of Namaqualand. There were only twenty white farmers in all Namaqualand at that period.

Bishop Robert Gray, that great traveller, set out in 1857 for Clanwilliam, "the first clergyman to visit the old English settlers for thirty-three years". Gray had to swim for his life when he crossed the flooded Olifants river. When he reached Clanwilliam he found that some of the English settlers had joined the Dutch Reformed Church. Later that year he appointed a rector.

Leipoldt lived in Clanwilliam during the last two decades of last century. "A miniature paradise with the tree of knowledge left out", was one of his descriptions of the place. He loved the main street with its wild rose hedges, the white blooms in summer, the pomegranates, the oranges and blue gums, the willows and reeds along the rivers. Scents he remembered were jasmine and a white orchid. One of the Fryers had a famous garden in the village, filled with guavas from Japan and strange fruits imported from Madagascar and Mauritius, Java and Florida. All this beauty was encircled by the mountains, the peaks and sandstone battlements and the blue range to the south capped by snow in winter. This was the scene which inspired one of Leipoldt's finest poems:

*Dit is die maand Oktober*
*Ek dink die mense vier*
*Vir ewig in die hemel*
*Oktobermaand soos hier.*

Clanwilliam lost some of its fine old homes in the great fire of 1901, but the rectory (built in or about 1840) was not touched. It stands in Main Street, a house with Georgian windows and dormer gables. Park Street has the oldest houses, homes of Drostdy officials going back to the 1820 Settler period. Each house has its irrigated garden running down to the river. Patrysvlei, two miles from Clanwilliam, has an 1840 homestead with a *stoepkamer*. Out on the Lambert Bay road is Groendam, nicknamed "Die Trein" because the homestead and the outbuildings are all joined and have one roof. The unbroken facade, two hundred feet long, is unique. Groendam was built about 1825 by one of the Engelbrechts.

Leipoldt said there was a remarkable standard of culture in the remote Clanwilliam of his day. As the Anglican clergyman was the schoolmaster, the children were taught in English; but they spoke Afrikaans and English among themselves without effort. Book salesman went round the district and farmers had libraries. Clanwilliam has maintained this tradition, and there is a Leipoldt room in the memorial library; eleven thousand books and the reading lamp and stool used by the poet. Leipoldt gained his lifelong interest in medicine during his Clanwilliam years. Outa Klaas, a witchdoctor, was his teacher. Outa Klaas showed him where to find the healing plants of the veld, the remedies for snakebite, the love potions, the bulbs that cure a sore throat, the euphorbia which relieves the pain caused by tarantula poison, the lebechia seeds for gastritis. "Outa Klaas possessed a storehouse of unknown knowledge," declared Leipoldt long afterwards. "Perhaps there was a spark of truth in his magic." Outa Klaas also smoked dagga; not the dangerous *cannabis sativa* with its narcotic, habit-forming properties, but the *leonotis* or *wilde dagga* which grew as a weed in the gardens of the village. Leipoldt always argued that *wilde dagga* was harmless. This was regarded as one of Leipoldt's many eccentric views, but later research has tended to confirm his opinion.

Although the Clanwilliam climate includes extremes of temperature, Leipoldt said it would restore health to many a dying man. Everyone who has ever known Clanwilliam in summer recalls the intense heat. A great water-furrow runs through the village. Before water was piped to the buildings many homes had small bath-houses which drew water from the furrow. During unbearable summer nights people lay in their baths with the water flowing over them in an attempt to defeat the heat. Clanwilliam's high temperatures are due to bare mountain slopes and river dunes acting as reflectors. One hotel proprietor halved his coal bill when he set up a solar heater in the back yard. It gave water of such high temperature that the cold tap had to be turned on before the bath was safe.

Clanwilliam is ravaged at intervals by high winds, and in 1925 part of the village was wrecked by a tornado. Augsburg farm across the bridge suffered most heavily. This is now a famous agricultural school with a fine Jersey stud. Karakul farming is taught more skilfully here, it is said, than anywhere else in the world.

Fifty miles from Clanwilliam is another unusual place, the mission village of Wupperthal in the Cedarberg. It was founded by the Rev. Johann Gottlieb Leipoldt, grandfather of the poet and a most remarkable man.

No doubt J. G. Leipoldt would be surprised if he could read some of the modern impressions of the village he founded nearly a century and a half ago. It has been described as a mountain oasis in a bleak rocky amphitheatre; a Spanish village of snow-white houses against the reddish slopes; the most picturesque village in the Cape; a toy village in an awe-inspiring hollow in the earth; an unknown mission in an almost impenetrable pocket of the Cedarberg; a slice of Ireland with typical crofters' cabins in the Cape mountains; and finally, a paradise on earth.

There is some accuracy in all these descriptions. Wupperthal certainly has atmosphere, the tranquillity which is found in all the Cape mission villages; but in Wupperthal this peace on earth is heightened by the remoteness of the settlement. When I first drove there thirty years ago the last section of road was a dangerous track safe only for pack-donkeys. Now the loose and narrow road with its hairpin bends has been improved; though the last ten miles still offer the precipitous views which I dislike. When the first missionaries arrived, Leipoldt and Baron von Wurmb, they came from the south, from Ceres, with ox-wagons, over a far more frightening pass than the present motor-road. The trek from Cape Town had lasted a fortnight. They saw the Tra-tra river, soil that seemed promising, and an abandoned farmhouse. In this inaccessible corner they decided to stay. Leipoldt had a firm idea that a mission should be self-supporting. They bought the farm of three thousand morgen for eight hundred pounds. Both men had come from Elberfeld on the Wupper river in Germany; hence this Wupperthal. Von Wurmb and his wife lived in the half-ruined homestead. Leipoldt, who was twenty-six and a bachelor, camped in the smithy. It was on New Year's Day 1830 that the farm came into their hands. They started work immediately. Scores of degraded coloured people and Hottentots, poverty-stricken groups living in the mountains, had already come under Christian influence. A Cedarberg farmer named Kok had held Sunday services for these people. Kok went to the North West Cape as a missionary early last century and was murdered; but his good work was remembered when the Rhenish missionaries settled at Wupperthal, and the leaderless coloured people gathered there under Leipoldt and Von Wurmb. Many of them fancied they would find an easy life. Leipoldt, a tremendous worker, soon disillusioned them. He gave each family a garden thirty-five feet square and saw that they planted and sowed. Before long there were a hundred people at the mission. A few owned pack-oxen and simple possessions; most were half-naked, dressed in animal skins. This was indeed the simple life. The missionaries set out benches under the pear trees in the farm garden and held their services there. When winter came they built the first little church. Leipoldt also designed and built a grain mill with a huge water-wheel in the Tra-tra stream. He was a trained shoe-maker, and he put up a tannery and shoe factory. I have before me the report Leipoldt wrote after two years' work: "By the help of God we have come so far that the Hottentots send their children to school regularly. We have already sixty scholars of whom sixteen can read the New Testament and an equal number can write. Of the one hundred and fifty inhabitants on the station with whom we have daily contact we can say that the word of God is beginning to bear fruit in their lives. Not only is there less gross sin among them, but we hear them discussing the Word which they heard and we also hear them singing and praying."

Von Wurmb, a restless spirit, returned to Germany at this period, Leipoldt married Caroline Lind, daughter of the Simonstown magistrate, and laboured at Wupperthal for forty-two years, until he died. He was a firm ruler, though his punishments were not really severe when you consider the time and the isolation of the place. His followers were hardly aware of the meaning of law and order. Leipoldt's diary shows that Old Augustus was fined sixpence for trespassing; while Sarah Moses, a thief, had to sit at the *strafpaal* (literally "punishment stake") outside the church during Sunday services for four months with an account of her crime on a placard round her neck.

Leipoldt never deceived himself about his flock. Only after five years did he consider that the first two men were ready to be baptized. Their wives were not allowed to attend the ceremony "because one has a slanderous tongue and the other cloaks herself with a garment of self-righteousness". In that year, 1835, the permanent church was dedicated; the lovely thatched white church in the Cape Dutch style with fanlights over the doorway and windows. This monument to Leipoldt's work, with its two large bells and old-fashioned organ, serves the larger congregation of today. The choral singing tradition, which began under the pear trees, grew up in this church. Wupperthal has four choirs; the "old choir", devoted to the traditional hymns, the male-voice choir, youth choir and *basuin* (or trumpet) choir. At Christmas and on other special occasions the choirs gather at Singkop near the village and the splendid voices reverberate through the valley as they did in Leipoldt's day. After all these years the Wupperthal people sing and speak with the German-Afrikaans accent which their forefathers acquired from the Rhenish missionaries long ago.

My 1843 directory mentions Wupperthal as a flourishing mission, and states that the people felled the cedar trees and dragged the sawn planks on sledges into the Cedarberg villages. There the precious timber was sold at about sixpence a foot. "Care ought to be taken to preserve these trees by planting," added the directory. Even in those days the Wupperthal tannery was producing excellent leather, boots, shoes and harness. The girls were learning needlework. Apples, pears and cherries were the main fruit crops. Good wine was made at Wupperthal but this was never sold in the settlement. Those old missionaries understood the use and abuse of wine.

Wupperthal had twenty-two thousand morgen of land before the middle of last century. Tobacco became an important crop. Freed slaves joined the congregation. Oaks and poplars grew high with the years and shaded rows of thatched, white-plastered cottages. Leipoldt's sons grew with the village, went to Germany and returned as missionaries. One of them, Christian Frederick, served the Wupperthal congregation for five years as his father's assistant. Other missionaries helped to raise the Wupperthal people from ignorance and poverty to a good standard of behaviour and comfort; Schroder and Knab, Gerdener, Luckhoff, Weich, Strassberger, Dittmer, Esslinger; but the Leipoldts made Wupperthal and left their mark on the serene village in the mountains.

When the first Leipoldt held his first service under the pear tree there were seven coloured families in his congregation. Now there are more than two thousand people in the Wupperthal area. The old factory, a picturesque thatched barn, still turns out the *Wupperthalvelskoene*, similar to those Leipoldt designed, and hand-sewn shoes of various types. Apart from the strong odour of tanning, there are several aromas that mingle with the honey-suckle and speak of Wupperthal's industries. Tobacco, the strong tobacco, rich in nicotine, grown and rolled at Wupperthal, is typical of the mission, and the flavour is known and enjoyed far beyond the Cedarberg range. You can smell the *rooibos* tea when it is bruised and sprayed with water and fermented under the sun. Watered by the Tra-tra river, thousands of peach and pear trees give out their scents in summer. And there are the fragrant vineyards that the Leipoldts first planted, though this was not the Rhineland and here they had to lock up their wine. The pass into Wupperthal from the south is no more than a jeep-track. You can still see the store built in the 'thirties of last century; the cottages in rows, on terraces, with worn stone steps and vines over the stoeps. Wupperthal has almost escaped the twentieth century. Here indeed is a "lost world" in the Cedarberg, this village of craftsmen and smallholders flourishing under the dry slopes of the Vaalheuningsberg, the mountain of dark honey.

I have described Dr. C. Louis Leipoldt as Clanwilliam's greatest son, for he always claimed Clanwilliam as his home town. However, he was not born there, and there is a curious mystery about Leipoldt's birth-place which I shall attempt to explain.

Louis Leipoldt's father married a sister of Advocate Ewald Esselen, K.C. In the eighteen-seventies he took his wife to Sumatra, where he worked as a missionary. He returned to the Cape, joined the Dutch Reformed Church and in 1884 he found himself back in the Cedarberg as minister at Clanwilliam. Many writers who have dealt with Louis Leipoldt's life have stated that he was born on December 28, 1880 at Worcester. This is probably correct. Yet it is also on record that Dr. Louis Leipoldt informed his friend Mr. "Swart" Andries Nieuwoudt of Clanwilliam that he was born on Krakatoa, the volcanic island between Java and Sumatra, which blew up in 1883. Louis Leipoldt was a mystic, a member of a Javanese sect, and I think he was probably referring to a spiritual experience when he spoke to his friend Nieuwoudt about Krakatoa as his birthplace. You will hear more of this side of Leipoldt's strange nature.

Louis Leipoldt never went to school. His parents taught him at home, where German was the home language. Of course he spoke the "Cape Dutch" of those days, and this he turned into the most perfect Afrikaans ever written. He spoke and wrote English fluently and with sensitive feeling. Hottentots in the location taught him Nama. Latin and Greek formed part of his lessons at the *pastorie*. His interest in botany, aroused by the witchdoctor Outa Klaas, was enlarged when he accompanied a qualified botanist named Rudolp Schleuther on Cedarberg expeditions. Leipoldt came to know all the creatures of veld and vlei; they are all in his writings and poems, from the flamingo to the *sandkruiper*, the carp that travels overland between mudholes when the rivers dry up. He found time to investigate the farm names of the district, and found inspiration for his poems in the legends of old murders. Douwenis baffled him, though he discovered that a farmer had poisoned his wife there long ago. This dreamer of the mountains was also a practical man; and when a surveyor named De Smidt found a diamond in the Doorn river bed, Louis Leipoldt and his elder brother Johann went out prospecting. They never found a diamond, and the traces of gold they located in the Cedarberg were never payable.

Louis Leipoldt was a promising journalist before he was twenty. Early this century he went to Europe and travelled widely. Then he became a medical student at Guy's Hospital, London; and after qualifying he studied the diseases of children and then gained a Fellowship of the Royal College of Surgeons.

Leipoldt and his father always corresponded in German, and the father always opened his letters with "Lieber Chris". (The son preferred the name Louis, but his full name was Christian Frederick Louis Leipoldt.) When the father was on his death-bed he started to write a letter to his son, but after an intimate passage he laid down his pen and died. Mr. Imker Hoogenhout of Optenhorst, Wellington, vouched for a sequel which is as strange a tale as any told of Louis Leipoldt the mystic. Louis Leipoldt voyaged to the Dutch East Indies for health reasons in 1911, and while he was in Java he arranged a meeting with a famous mystic, the head of a sect. The mystic stared at Leipoldt as he entered the room and then spoke in German. "Lieber Chris", he began, and quoted Leopoldt senior's last letter; not only the passage Louis Leopoldt had received, but the whole letter. I include this episode not as a psychic experience but more as a sidelight on the brilliant imagination of the Afrikaans poet. No doubt Louis Leipoldt came away from his interview with the Javanese mystic with some such impression in his mind.

Louis Leipoldt's greatest friend in Clanwilliam was Dr. Peter le Fras Nortier, a medical colleague who settled there towards the end of World War I. Nortier, a Nortje of Willowmore, changed the name back to the original Huguenot form. Peter Nortier was a student at Stellenbosch when he gained the distinction, in 1905, of becoming one of the first Rhodes Scholars at Oxford. There and at Liverpool he secured his medical degrees and revealed his talent for research. Nortier and Leipoldt both served as army doctors in World War I. Both these highly intelligent men loved the soil, and when Nortier rooted himself at Clanwilliam he remembered the words of Jonathan Swift: "That whoever could make two ears of corn or two blades of grass to grow upon a spot where only one grew before would deserve better of minkind . . . than the whole race of politicians put together". Nortier not only saved lives as he rode about the district on horseback or Cape cart or his Ford Model-T car. He also tackled soil erosion problems in the Sandveld and started an experimental farm on the banks of the Olifants river to the north of Clanwilliam. There he evolved by bud selection a seedless seedling orange that brought prosperity to many growers. He grew mangoes, avocado pears, paw-paw, pecan nuts and enormous grapefruit, and showed the farmers how to cultivate *rooibos* tea. His grateful patients gave him a new motor-car and Stellenbosch University made him an honorary doctor of agriculture. When you drive through the Nortier Reserve beyond Lambert Bay, gaze upon the veld, the grass and bushes and blue Afrikaners, the wild ostriches and steenbok, and remember this country doctor, the great Peter Nortier.

Leipoldt and Nortier began their friendship during World War I, and it lasted through three decades. They sought the rare plants together and opened many a good bottle of wine. Nortier knew Leipoldt better than any other man in South Africa. It was a memorable day when by chance I found these two fine characters together and listened reverently while they discussed a subject close to my own heart.

*Chapter Thirteen*

## LEIPOLDT THE CHEF

*"Remember that every man who has been worth a fig in this world as poet, painter or musician, has had a good appetite, and a good taste."*

WILLIAM MAKEPEACE THACKERAY.

I FOUND Leipoldt and Nortier at the "O. M. Bergh Garden". That was the name of Nortier's small farm outside Clanwilliam, and the two doctors were bending over the succulents when I arrived. Leipoldt was a tall, intellectual, clean-shaven man with a wide smile that reflected his peculiar sense of humour. It was too friendly to be mischievous, though Leipoldt delighted in leading pompous and opinionated people into carefully-devised traps. Nortier was shorter and rather stout, but there was no mistaking the brain in the fine head, with its broad forehead, grey eyes and grey hair brushed back. His deep tan spoke of long years under the strong Clanwilliam sun.

I had come to ask Nortier about the *rooibos* tea seeds which a Hottentot woman had found in the underground larders of the ants, a remarkable discovery.* Dr. Nortier told me the whole story. From *rooibos* tea the conversation moved on to other drinks and dishes, strange and familiar. Leipoldt dominated this part of the discussion, as I hoped he would, for this was his favourite subject; even closer to his personal taste, perhaps, than medicine or botany. It gave me the chance of asking Leipoldt where he had learnt the art of cooking.

"First of all I learnt in my mother's kitchen in Clanwilliam, for here the old Cape cookery flourished," Lei-

*I gave the story of this discovery in my book *In the Land of Afternoon*, published by Timmins.

poldt replied. "I studied the oriental touch in the kitchens of the White House and the old Royal in Plein Street, Cape Town, where the superb Malay cooks followed recipes that had never been written down. Finally I graduated in the international cuisine while I was a medical student in London, washing dishes at the Savoy and other great hotels to pay my fees at Guy's Hospital. Yes, I was a pupil of Auguste Escoffier, that master chef and inventor of new dishes, the most celebrated artist of all time in his chosen profession."

Leipoldt spoke of the little-known sea foods he enjoyed as a boy when the family trekked down to Lambert Bay to escape the Clanwilliam heat. Mussel soup with milk and cream was one dish; mussel fritters was another, the shellfish blended with parsley, curry powder and wine. They ate the albatross in those days, known as *malmok*, that large and splendid ocean bird. It was hung for days, marinaded in wine vinegar, and braised with onions. Leipoldt said a *malmok* cost a tickey and was not at all fishy. Also very palatable was the white-breasted duiker. You plunged it into boiling water, pulled off the skin, feathers and all, and roasted it in an iron pot. Curried limpets appeared on the table at Lambert Bay and fish cakes with almonds and chutney. Leipoldt's favourite sea fish were the rarer sorts; the butter-fish that the fishermen take home with them and which should be fried in butter; the *baardmannetjie* with its thick snout and delicious flesh; the *bamboesvis* or sea bream which feeds on seaweed and is caught in river estuaries; the young and dainty *elf*; the dark-veined *galjoen* grilled on the beach; the beautiful roman, and the windtoy that appears before gales and is caught only in winter. Leipoldt spoke longingly of the *tambryn* or John Brown, and *kliptongvis*, a rarity with the best flavour of all. I wish that I had questioned him about the *kliptongvis*, as it must be a local name, unknown to Barnard and other authorities.

When the famous Araucaria pine was cut down outside St. George's Cathedral in Cape Town the timber provided Leipoldt with a round section which he used for cooking delicate fish such as the *baardmannetjie* and butter-fish. The plank was grooved, with a well to catch the gravy. He brushed the plank with butter, placed the fish on it, and baked it in a hot oven. Silverfish, hottentot and stumpnose were best served as *mootjies*, slices grilled brown with melted butter and parsley. Leipoldt did not object to the common fish such as *snoek*, but only the rarities appealed to his imagination, for example the scorpion fish known as the sancord, a winter delicacy. He had a contempt for electricity and gas, and declared firmly that fish should be cooked on an open wood fire. When he covered a fish in clay and baked it in the coals he thought of the treat for days afterwards.

Dr. Nortier put in a word for the freshwater yellow fish and barbel from the Olifants river, and Leipoldt agreed, though he pointed out that the muddy flavour was a disadvantage. He had caught them during his boyhood, using fruit or sweet potatoes as bait; and he said that nightlines with dead rats on the hooks were most effective in luring these huge fish. Such fish, he said, had to be marinaded in vinegar to soften the bones. They were grilled or baked whole in the pan. As a contrast Leipoldt used to catch the minnows of the Cedarberg streams in a pillowcase. These slender little fish, no larger than tadpoles, were fried in deep fat and tasted rather like the whitebait of Europe. But carp were the best of the river fish, grilled carp flavoured with herbs. Eels were unknown in the Clanwilliam area, but at the White House he had tasted marvellous eel sambals and eel pancakes.

Leipoldt recalled a peculiar sport of the Clanwilliam coloured people in his youth. Just before the swallows migrated in March they were fat and luscious. The men armed themselves with long bamboo whipsticks baited with feathers. Swallows were easily killed during a *swawel-slaan* outing, and one man might take home a couple of hundred birds. Grilled, stewed with onion and potato or roasted, the tender swallows made an excellent dish, reminiscent of the ortolans of Europe. Leipoldt said you could pickle these small birds in wine or vinegar and eat them raw as

Leipoldt had a contempt for electricity and gas and declared firmly that fish should be cooked on an open wood fire.

hor's-d'oeuvres. "All birds are edible," Leipoldt remarked. "Starlings are good provided you eat them fresh. Cranes and herons were often on sale at the old Darling Street market, where the Cape Town city hall now stands. I found them palatable, though you had to be careful not to break the heron's bones or the whole dish became fishy. Before the flamingo was declared royal game we used to feast on this splendid bird. Nothing in the world of birds can compare with breast of flamingo—except perhaps the grey lourie. Flamingo does not need much bacon. We used to fry the dark flesh of the breast and sometimes we made a rich flamingo soup, tasting rather like wild-duck soup." Leipoldt also spoke with enthusiasm of *dikkop*, for the flesh was not so dry as that of many game-birds. It was the smallest and most delicious of all the bustards. Robben Island is a haunt of the *dikkop*, and there he had eaten the birds stuffed with orange, a dish that lingered in his memory. He liked the green pigeon best, especially when it had been feeding on wild figs; it was more tender than the Cape rock pigeon. All pigeons, he said, should be baked in clay with their feathers or roasted in hot ashes. Guinea fowl was another bird that varied greatly in flavour according to its diet. Namaqua partridges, too, were usually palatable, but at times they were uneatable. Wild duck was tough. Cape quail soon decomposed and should be roasted at once with fat bacon, green vine leaves and green chillis inside.

Leipoldt said that hippo meat was on sale occasionally at the Darling Street market at twopence a pound. He had also eaten it when he was a medical inspector of schools in the Transvaal early this century, and thought the flavour was like a blend of pork and beef. Hippo fat, of course, was the finest of natural cooking fats. He knew the giraffe, too, and liked the tongue. Wildebees apart from the tongue, was not worth eating. Zebra was the best of the horse tribe. Eland was his favourite antelope, fat and beefy. Kudu had memorable marrow-bones but the meat of the springbok was much better. Leipoldt had few prejudices at the table; he loved frogs and snails, gypsy dishes such as squirrels and hedgehogs, and he described the taste of snake flesh as "peculiar, smooth and oily, reminding one of terrapin flesh". Lizard flesh he found delicate. But when I mentioned dassies Leipoldt seemed to be more interested in the historical aspect of this odd little relative of the elephant. Leipoldt was, of course, an authority on Van Riebeeck; and he recalled the meal at which the governor had said that the dassies sent to him from Dassen Island were more delicious than any other meat he had ever tasted, better than the lamb on the table that day. Dassie, declared the governor, was "more delicate than a prime young cock from the Mother Country". I gathered that Leipoldt would have chosen the lamb.

Sorrel was a plant close to Leipoldt's heart, though many South Africans have never tasted it. Sorrel was the first Cape plant to arouse the interest of learned men in Europe, for it saved the lives of sailors who called at Table Bay suffering from scurvy. Dutch and English crews, weak and ill, staggered on shore and filled baskets with sorrel on the Table Mountain slopes. Van Riebeeck and his men planted the indigenous Cape sorrels in the Company's garden. Leipoldt gathered sorrel along the Olifants river and bought sorrel leaves in the Cape Town market at a penny a bunch. Sorrel soup had the flavour of chestnuts. Sorrel softened and improved all vegetable stews. Leipoldt mentioned the shrub called *bobbejaanuintjies* that the shepherds brought into Clanwilliam at one hundred little bulbs for twopence! After twenty minutes in boiling water they tasted like new potatoes. He spoke, too, of *jakkalskos*, the fruit of a parasite growing on euphorbia roots. It had an unpleasant smell but jackals and baboons loved to dig it out. Leipoldt used to put it through a sieve to get rid of the bitter pips and make a soufflé with sherry and cream. Treated in this way, it became a luxurious dish. Leipoldt, who thrived on argument, often annoyed some people by stating emphatically that there were practically no typical South African dishes. He proved conclusively that the troubadors in the south of France eight centuries ago enjoyed a mould of mince flavoured with almonds and baked with an egg custard coloured with saffron—in other words, bobotie. Early manuscript recipes in Europe mentioned bobotie by that very name. All the *bredies*, according to Leipoldt, were almost identical with the *ollas* of Spain and Portugal. However, he was prepared to admit that a *jakkalskos* dish was unique and truly South African.

Paw-paws were grown in many Clanwilliam gardens, for the heat suited sub-tropical fruits. People called the paw-paw "bobotie fruit" because this finely-cut curried meat was often served with paw-paw leaves as a flavouring. Horses were given the leaves to make their coats shine. Leipoldt thought the paw-paw tasted at its best when mashed in a pudding with sugar and spices, ginger and eggs, and steamed in a cloth. The sauce he preferred with this pudding was made of *skilpadbessies*, the astringent berries that grow wild on the dunes. They also made a paw-paw soup in Clanwilliam, using the green fruit, and they never failed to add the right amount of sherry. Avocado pear also went into a satisfactory soup. Pomegranates were grown in Clanwilliam and made a grand stuffing for meat. Prickly pears were dried in the sun and packed flat in fruit jars; they made a useful preserve. Poor people mixed the dried and roasted prickly pear peels with their coffee beans.

The *boerewors* of Clanwilliam, I gathered from Leipoldt, possessed qualities such as city butchers have never been able to achieve. Beef gave it bulk, though pork and mutton were added; and it was flavoured with such things as powdered ginger and mace, cloves and nutmeg, fennel and coriander, thyme and rosemary, sage, mint and garlic. Wine, vinegar and brandy were worked into this heroic formula and then the whole mixture was forced into the long skins. Leipoldt declared that *boerewors* should be grilled in the open on a fire of *renosterbos*; but in Clanwilliam the sausage was sometimes sun-dried like biltong and eaten on buttered farm bread.

I also took a note of Leipoldt's own recipe for tomato *bredie*. No doubt this classic method will appeal to those who wish to follow one of the greatest authorities on Cape cookery. Peel two pounds of ripe tomatoes, cut in quarters and add a few green tomatoes. Take two pounds of thick rib of mutton, as fat as possible, cut in pieces and dust with flour. Place the meat in a shallow saucepan with one pound of sliced onions, three sliced leeks, half an ounce of green ginger, a few cardamoms, coriander seeds, peppercorns, fennel seeds and some crushed thyme, marjoram and garlic. If you like it hot, add a crushed chilli and black pepper. Braise all this with sheep fat and when the meat is nicely browned, add the tomatoes. Cover closely and simmer for several hours, shaking often. Then add salt to taste, a teaspoonful of chutney sauce, a tablespoonful of moist sugar and let it simmer for another two hours with the lid off, until it has thickened. Add a glass of wine and serve. It should then have become a well-spiced tomato puree with tender pieces of meat impregnated with flavour. A proper tomato *bredie* is never watery or greasy.

I think Leipoldt acquired a taste for curry in the East, and he was certainly an authority on all these dishes, from the *rystafel* of Java to the *kerries* of the Cape Malays. He said that curry and rice was originally the meal served after funerals at the Cape, hence the *begrafnisrys* still found in recipes; rice dotted with raisins and coloured with turmeric. As a doctor he recommended curry because the condiments stimulated the digestion. "A fine curry is the highest form of a blend," declared this epicure. He enjoyed the interesting side-dishes that accompanied curry; the indispensable rice, plain or with borrie; the lightly-fried eggs, bananas and sambals of apple, quince or cucumber. Leipoldt collected rice recipes wherever he went, for he had the true South African longing for rice at almost every meal. He found yellow rice in Turkey, where the cooks use saffron instead of borrie. I will not give you Leipoldt's recipe for rice with penguin eggs, because only the most influential people can now be sure of their penguin eggs.

Some gourmets pick at their food but Leipoldt had a huge appetite. I sat next to him long ago at a lunch in the Groot Constantia cellars, a lavish affair in honour of visiting Members of Parliament from Britain. Everything was of the best, and Leipoldt's capacity for wine and food astonished me. It was a treat in another way, for he commented so wisely, with such wealth of detail, on each course and each wine, that I left the cellar with the back of my menu covered with priceless notes. No one, not even Hildagonda Duckitt, knew half as much about the Cape dishes as Dr. C. Louis Leipoldt. Years ago a Cape Town newspaper approached Leipoldt at Christmas and asked him to suggest the ideal menu. Here is his effort:

*Green pea soup*
*Roast muscovy duck and cucumber salad*
*Rice, stewed peaches, steamed*
*marrow, potato puree, broiled*
*yellow butter beans*
*Cold Christmas pudding and sweet sauce*
*Melktert* *Fruit salad*
*Green fig preserve*
*Mealie bread*
*Coffee*

It was hardly orthodox, of course, but Leipoldt was never orthodox. I have no doubt that he would have gone through that menu course by course, missing nothing, and keeping his wine glass filled.

Clanwilliam farmers made some good dry wines last century, until the phylloxera destroyed the vineyards. Some of the old wine remained on the farms in Leipoldt's time and he spoke wistfully of these lost growths. However, there has been a revival in wine-making which would have gladdened Leipoldt. Those old farms Zeekoe Vlei and Die Berg are pressing grapes; and the stein wine from Die Berg is a well-known table wine. The copper kettles which once produced *witblits* in the Clanwilliam district are now museum-pieces. I believe that the only farm with a permit is Zeekoe Vlei, where the brandy Leipoldt loved is "stoked" in the old-fashioned way.

*Chapter Fourteen*

# BUSHMEN OF THE CEDARBERG

HAPPIEST of all the Bushmen in Southern Africa, I think, were those who lived in and around the Cedarberg before the white explorers came. This was the golden age of primitive man. They had all that Bushmen needed; abundant water in mountain streams, the Olifants river with its hippo, herds of eland and other antelope. Plants and wild fruits provided them with medicines and food. Wildbees gave them the honey that made strong drink. They had the right timber for their bows and arrows, spears and digging-sticks, wooden pestles and mortars. The great rocks, mountain slopes and the earth itself yielded those mineral ores which they needed for their paintings. In the Cedarberg there were caves which they used as art galleries, recording their fantasies and their memories of this remote paradise.

Probably the Cedarberg had been a Bushman stronghold for thousands of years before the Dutch came up from the Cape in search of treasure. It is hard to say whether the Bushmen were invaders or original inhabitants; possibly a Stone Age people were living in South Africa when the Bushmen arrived. If that was so, those people have vanished; and the Bushmen have almost disappeared from the vast hunting grounds they once knew. However, they have left many enchanting relics of their peaceful centuries in the Cedarberg, and Bushman blood still flows in the veins of descendants who stayed behind. The last clans of wild Bushmen left these mountains almost within living memory, and I gathered their story long ago from men who had watched the end of the long epic chapter.

In the unrecorded beginning the Bushmen may have been alone in the Cedarberg, or they may have fought or mingled with some unknown Stone Age race. Long afterwards came the Hottentots, and it is obvious from similarities in language and appearance that a certain amount of mixing occurred. Yet by some mysterious process the two races separated and retained their own cultures, traits, skills and ways of life. In the western Cape the Hottentots chose that coast while the Bushman clung to the mountain ranges. Both races had all the space they needed, the Hottentots for their stock, the Bushmen for their hunting. Now and again the Bushmen raided the sheep belonging to the Hottentots; but they seem to have been moved not by hunger but by sheer devilment and the craving for a change of meat. As a rule Hottentot and Bushman worked out amicable settlements. Often the Bushmen regarded the more advanced Hottentots as overlords and they never robbed the kraals of the Hottentots they served. Often the Hottentots feared the brave and elusive Bushmen and avoided conflict with them. Here in the west there was no Bantu invasion, no endless warfare. In the fastnesses of the high Cedarberg ranges the Bushmen were secure.

They were, of course, the pure Cape Bushmen, the tiny yellow fellows, most of them under five feet in height, veritable gnomes of the mountains. If they were the most primitive people on earth they had the toughness of early man and their child brains held essential knowledge and secrets which the white scientists have not yet mastered. Weak babies died, but the survivors often passed the century mark. Their teeth seldom decayed and they could still use them even when they had worn down to the gums. They had the finest eyesight on earth, deep-set mongoloid eyes that twinkled with good humour. Whorls of peppercorn hair with bald patches marked them as a race apart from the Hottentots, whose hair covered their scalps like wigs. Their limbs were slight yet powerful and they had tiny hands and feet. The body posture was peculiar, for the spine curved inwards at the waist so that the buttocks were thrust out. This ludicrous silhouette often reached the size of a deformity in the women, yet there is evidence that large buttocks were greatly admired by the male Bushmen. You might not imagine that such people would make a pleasant impression on the stranger. Their faces have been described as fox-like, with lobeless ears and broad noses. Yet I have seen the last of the Cape Bushmen and I found nothing repulsive about them. They suited the landscape with a natural beauty which the expedition I accompanied certainly did not possess. In the deserts the Bushman lives in very small clans, a few families sharing the available water and food resources. Up in the Cedarberg, a land of plenty, the Bushman clans were much larger.

Hottentots covered their huts with mats, but the Bushmen could not be bothered with weaving and they made simple skerms of poles and branches. Hottentots lived at their water-holes. Bushman hunters always put up their little villages at a safe distance so that the game could drink undisturbed—until the hunters came on the scene. Hottentots wore sheepskins; the Bushmen made their karosses from the skins of wild animals.

Narrow kloofs of the Cedarberg were ideal for the pitfalls devised by the hunters. They would build a fence of stakes right across the kloof, leaving one opening which led straight into the deep trap. Bushes were thrown over the stakes. Then, when a herd of antelope were sighted, the Bushmen would turn and drive them down the kloof into the grass-covered pitfalls. Eland was the Bushman's favourite meat in these parts, the lean and tender eland that tasted like beef. One eland often weighed a thousand pounds. The milk was rich in cream. A swift Bushman runner could drive the docile eland in any direction and it formed an easy target even for a bow-and-arrow man. Eland skins made wonderful karosses. The long ravine in the Cedarberg named Elandskloof by the early settlers must have been a great hunting ground two centuries ago. No wonder the eland was given a place of honour in so many of the Cedarberg cave paintings.

Of course the springbok migrations provided the greatest feasts. Countless thousands of springbok trotted or pounded at speed over the karoo plains just to the north of the Cedarberg range. They came unexpectedly and in such numbers that the enormous herds made a sound like the ocean breaking on the rocks. Bushman hunters came easily within bow-and-arrow range when the buck were browsing or gambolling with the dazzling white hair on their backs raised. Those migrations were tremendous events and I imagine that the Bushmen enjoyed both the spectacle of the leaping springbok and the abundance of meat.

After the feast came the music and the dancing. They had a musical bow called the *gora*, sounded by a quill held in the mouth, and this enabled them to imitate an angry ostrich or the roaring of a lion. Another type of bow with four strings and a calabash resonator was the *ramkie*; and when the strings were struck with the forefinger or tapped with a stick the musician could produce sounds like the pattering feet of a hare or antelope running. Each clan had a *rommelpot*, a taut hide fastened over the shell of a large tortoise or clay pot. Male dancers wore "Bushman bells", rattles of springbok ears sewn into bags and holding berries or pebbles. The women, clapping and singing, formed the orchestra at a dance. They danced happily under the new moon, for they welcomed the light after the darkness. They mimicked the whole animal world, from the lion to the gemsbok, grimacing like baboons, squatting like frogs, or becoming a realistic swarm of bees.

Lions must have worried the little hunters of the Cedarberg at times. When an old man-eater became a menace they would creep up on it while it was asleep and discharge a little poisoned arrow that stung no more painfully than a bee. The unsuspecting lion would fall asleep again; and on the third day after the attack it would die. At night, when lions prowled round their camps, they threw a secret medicine on the fire, a pounded root which gave out an odour the lions disliked. I am told that botanists have been unable to identify this root.

Bushmen are fond of their children but do not pamper them. Babies are rolled in the sand at birth, but bathing in water is not a Bushman custom. Feeding stops soon after the child is able to crawl. Tiny mites of two and three follow tortoises on hands and knees, tracking them by almost invisible scratches in the sand. Older children stalk mice, lizards and birds. They catch small birds such as turtle-doves by the wings with the sticky pips of the Cape mistletoe that grows on black ebony wood. They learn to eat young bees and ants, and rob the ants not only of their *larvae* but also of their stores of grass seed. This is indeed a luxury, grass-seed pounded on a flat rock, winnowed and boiled like porridge in a clay pot. During the nesting season the children robbed every bird's nest they could find. The discovery of ostrich-eggs was an event for each egg weighs over two pounds. Yet a Bushman could eat an ostrich egg at a meal.

Bushman mothers taught their children botany in a practical way that has aroused the admiration of professors. There were times when the discovery of edible plants and desert melons containing water meant life instead of death. They found roots swollen with water and the *tsamma* with a nutritious pulp that slakes the thirst; the spiny gemsbok cucumber with its flesh like jelly and pips for roasting; the bulrush with brown spikes that makes a brown porridge; the sweet bulbs of the sedge plant, food not only of the Bushmen but of the birds; the ferns that taste like lettuce; and the truffles as large as potatoes, with a delicious salty flavour, but traced only by tiny cracks in the baked earth.

Meat is grilled or buried in the embers and roasted, for wild Bushmen like cooked food. Exceptions to the rule are the flesh of the *muishond*, wildcat, jackal and hyena, which are eaten raw. Bushmen also drink the blood of these animals. They preferred meat to fish, but they trapped and speared fish in the Olifants river and other streams. Basket traps were used, stretched across a shallow part of the river, and the fish were driven into the baskets.

Bushmen never hoarded to any extent. Apparently they never discovered the preservative value of salt. Some families might dry and store wild raisins like apricots or the gum from certain thorn trees. Jan Danckaert the explorer reported meeting Bushmen who lived on dried fish and honey. But most Bushmen were incapable of thinking twenty-four hours ahead, and so their possessions were few and simple. A family could pack everything into a few skin bags and net of leather thongs and move off. They took the ostrich egg-shells that served as water-bottles; their sharp stone knives and scrapers; their digging tools and the hardwood fire-sticks they twirled in a notch of soft inflammable timber until the wood dust smouldered. Tortoise-shells served as plates and they made rough clay pots. Breast-bones and leg-bones of ostriches were their dishes.

No doubt they carried a bag of medicines wherever they went, for the Bushman's pharmacopoeia was gathered over a wide area. Pain was usually treated by applying a bag of hot sand to the affected part, a sensible remedy in some cases. They knew that the stomach was affected by wind, and thought that pains in other organs were due to the same cause. Incisions were made in the skin of the forehead for headaches. They tied a sinew round an afflicted limb to prevent the pain spreading. Buchu was a well-known remedy, plentiful in the Cedarberg; shrubs and bushes were used as poultices or decoctions. But the cure for all sorts of diseases, the "miracle medicine" of the Bushmen, was provided by the kidneys of the *bakoorjakkals*. It is clear that the Bushmen were more skilful in extracting various poisons that they were in devising curative preparations. However, their primitive surgery included several forms of trepanning. Stone flakes or shells were their instruments. New bone growth on skulls thus treated prove that some of the patients recovered. Apparently the motive was to "cast out a devil" when the person was suffering from mental illness or a tumour. Bushman skeletons have revealed other evidence of cave surgery, amputations and the treatment of fractures and dislocations. Fortunately the patients were blessed with a physique rare in civilisation. Deformities were almost unknown. Old people never suffered from high blood pressure. They all picked their teeth and cleaned them with grass, so that toothache did not occur.

In many ways the Bushmen made a fascinating study for explorers, and the Dutch soon realised that they had encountered a strange and interesting race. Several years passed before Van Riebeeck's men set eyes on the Bushmen, and at first they called them Sonquas. Long before the seventeenth century ended, however, the diary and various minutes and journals refer to "Bosjesmans" and "Boslopers". In fact, the Bushmen of those days lived in the mountains of the hinterland rather than the bush.

Van Riebeeck's explorers were the first to mention the Bushmen living in the Olifants river and Cedarberg areas. Simon van der Stel also noted the bands of Bushmen along his route to the north. He gave details of their food but his observations were naturally incomplete "They eat nothing but bulbs of flowers, which they call 'ajuntjes' (*uintjies*), also tortoises and certain large kinds of caterpillars and locusts which are found in great abundance," Van der Stel wrote. Later he mentioned honey and wild game. Cruythoff spoke of the waterfigs of the Olifants river brought to him by Bushman women. Van der Stel gave the Bushmen a sheep and noted: "They immediately cut the sheep's throat, skinned it and then cut off both the forelegs. They allowed nothing of it to go to waste except four small glands which are in the legs, which they cut out and threw away."

Jan Danckaert said that he met Bushmen who did not know how to smoke. I think there must have been some misunderstanding, for the Bushmen in the Cedarberg and elsewhere had bone or soap-stone pipes and smoked local herbs and *wildedagga* for centuries before the first white men landed. Bushmen soon recognised the superior aroma of the tobacco which they bartered from the Dutch settlers; but excavations in Bushman caves have brought to light hollow bones and carved stone pipes, gourd hookahs and other smoking devices of great age.

Van der Stel made an early mention of a Bushman dance. They placed the mutton he gave them under the ashes for half an hour and ate it with rice, bread and brandy. Then they celebrated with "dancing, singing and shouting in a very strange manner, which cannot be described otherwise than as a party of calves, just let out of their stalls".

Naturally the Bushman language called for comment.

Several Dutch writers spoke of "the cluckings of turkey cocks". It was left to later travellers to discover the dental click sounding like annoyance, the palatal click like the drawing of a cork, the lateral click such as horsemen use, the labial "kiss" click, and the snores and warbles. Before very long the Bushmen were calling the white men "thunsi", a word based on the sound of a gun being fired.

For a time the Bushmen remained on friendly terms with the Dutch strangers. Some of the little people were so frightened when they met the newcomers that they could not speak; but some bolder Bushmen visited the Castle in November 1660, bringing gifts of zebra heads. The diary reads as follows: "The Sonquas (a people who dwell in the mountains, have no cattle and are mostly robbers) promised that they would supply us with young horses from those parts and have brought us two or three stuffed heads of such horses, which are most beautifully striped but have such long ears that they look like asses. When a live specimen is brought to us we shall be able to judge better what they are like, for our men have now and then seen some of them, but only from a distance, running wild. These Sonquas often eat the meat of these animals which they declare more palatable than beef".

Dutch explorers used the Bushmen as guides and rewarded them with tobacco, bread and brandy. The guides had to be changed at frequent intervals, however, as a Bushman was unwilling to enter the hunting grounds of a different tribe. Bushman offered honey in exchange for tobacco and beads. It was not until the eighteenth century, when white settlers entered their domains, that the Bushmen became hostile. Through the centuries white observers have pointed out that the Bushmen were usually harmless people. They became vindictive when the settlers massacred the game and then they raided the white man's cattle and were dangerous enemies. Only the Bushmen could have driven the stolen cattle up the steep places of the Cedarberg to their most secret haunts. The trick some Bushmen genius invented was designed to fool the cattle into the belief that others of their kind had passed that way before them. Bushman raiders sprinkled the difficult routes with cattle droppings, and the oxen strained and panted and struggled to the heights.

So the war opened and the Bushmen were doomed. They clung to the Cedarberg strongholds for decades, and made counter-attacks. Marauding bands of Olifants river Bushmen were attacking white farmers as far south as the Berg river in the seventeen-thirties, until a commando drove them back. Slowly they were forced out of the Cedarberg into the deserts to the north, into the waste and barren plain that became known as Great Bushmanland. Late in the eighteenth century the Dutch intensified the campaign. Thunberg the botanist saw a thousand Bushman prisoners in Cape Town at this period; men, women and children. Some of the Bushmen warriors were taken to the Castle and hanged or broken on the wheel. Others had their ankle sinews cut and were imprisoned for life. Never was a more ruthless war carried on in Africa.

Heavy fighting against the Bushmen ended early last century but guerrilla warfare continued. Pockets of resistance formed in the Cedarberg and other mountains to the north. Bushmen in the mountains between Pofadder and Raman's Drift drove the white sheep farmers to Springbok for protection a century ago. Schroeder, the missionary at Pella, had to leave his station. His son was killed by a poisoned arrow. A government expedition was organised, but two years later the Bushmen were still holding out in the mountains. During a fight in the kloof near Pella three policemen and fifteen Bushmen were killed. The leader of the Bushmen then approached the police and said that his men were about to surrender. In fact he was playing for time, and the main body of Bushmen escaped. They were finally rounded up on Gaams mountain. All the men fought to the death. The prisoners were women and children.

The geologist E. J. Dunn travelled through Bushmanland in 1872 with an escort of fifteen troopers of the Northern Border Police. "So great were the depredations in this quarter, and so great was the trouble they were causing, that the police had instructions to capture or shoot any wild Bushmen they might come across," Dunn reported. In spite of his escort, Dunn said he had a narrow escape from death near Pella. On this journey Dunn saw the recent grave of a police trooper who had been killed by Bushmen while in charge of some Bushman prisoners.He also passed the spot called Renosterkop where Bushmen had murdered a Bushman girl because she would not allow them to take the goats she was guarding. Dunn visited Pella after the Bushman raid. It was burnt out, the church destroyed, the gardens ruined and water furrows choked. He found relics of the missionary's home strewn over the mountain. Bishop Simon, who took over the Pella mission, said that the Bushmen had almost vanished from that troubled area in the eighties of last century. "They became savages only because of the cruelty shown to them," stated the bishop. "The Bushmen wanted to live peacefully."

Away to the east in the Kenhardt district Bushmen were declared outlaws and shot at sight. Deprived of their game, they raided the sheep farms and were hunted by the white farmers. Throughout the remote North West Cape of those days a peculiar type of stone house was built by the farmers to protect their families. They were called *byekorf* houses because they were shaped like bee-hives, and they were really small forts which the Bushmen could not set on fire. Even the roofs were made of stone. The late Dr. W. P. Steenkamp, senator, author, hunter and medical man, told me that he was born in a *byekorf* house at a time when the Bushmen were still a menace. Keelafsny in the Kenhardt district was named after a farmer named Van der Colff had been murdered by Bushmen during the eighteen-nineties; and there was a skirmish at Kruissuid not far away, with casualties on both sides.

All the dangerous Bushmen had not been rounded up when the present century opened. The wild clans had left the Cedarberg, only tame remnants clinging to their old hunting grounds as farm servants. But in 1903 the Cape Mounted Police under a well-known frontier officer named Woon set out for the Pella area, again the scene of Bushman raids. A wounded Bushman woman was tracked for forty miles; then the blood spoor disappeared and the woman escaped. Later twenty-three Bushmen were caught and taken to Kenhardt gaol, and there all but two died. Wild Bushmen seldom survive in captivity. It would have been far better if they had remained in the Cedarberg, living on roots and honey and the food given to them by white masters.

Dunn had been in Australia before he came to the Cape, and he had studied the aborigines. He saw the pure Cape Bushmen of the same race as the Cedarberg clans, and he also observed many people of mixed descent. "The Bushman was a distinct race, having special characteristics that differentiate him from all the other South African races" Dunn wrote. "He was a yellow-skinned negroid pygmy, less than five feet in stature. He was a very primitive hunter, using stone, bone and wooden tools and weapons, the bow and poisoned arrows, and living on the animals he shot and the vegetable and other food his women gathered. The feature that distinguished him from all other primitive races was his unique skill in painting and engraving. He was a marvellous artist."

Many attempts have been made to estimate the mental age of the Bushmen, and the little people have failed lamentably in intelligence tests devised for the children of civilisation. Even the Australian aboriginal has come out years ahead of the South African Bushmen. Yet in his own surroundings the Bushman soon proved that he is not a "child of five" as the psychologists have suggested, but far superior in hunting skill and knowledge of practical botany to the scientists who have tested him. Dr. S. D. Porteus, an American scientist who compared the Bushman and the Australian aborigines, found the Bushmen were more courageous and their artistic skill greater. It was far more difficult to "educate" the Bushman, though he was highly imaginative.

"He was a marvellous artist," said Dunn. In the Cedarberg the Bushmen left many great paintings. Some of the most interesting caves are those on the farms Kromrivier and Pienaar's Vlak, reached by way of the steep passes, Nieuwoudt's and Uitkyk, over a spur of the main range and along the green vlaktes on the far side. No finer elephant herd has been discovered, say the experts. than the frieze on one of these rock shelters scooped out by the weather. Those are sites marked on maps and easily accessible, but there are hundreds of others which are known only to the few who can be trusted to keep the secret. For the story of the Cedarberg paintings is a sad one. Cave art of enormous interest has been covered with the soot of fairly recent camp fires. Thoughtless wayfarers have scrawled their names over the lovely animals. One most tragic example was reported by a retired chief justice who revisited a cave he had last seen in his youth; a cave with a rare ship painting. Bushmen watched the coming of the Portuguese and the Dutch, and if there were earlier navigators they saw them, too. That ship painting which the judge remembered vaguely had been blotted out completely by campers. It may have been a Phoenician ship. No one will ever know. So the caves discovered in recent years have not been pinpointed for vandals. Many paintings of real beauty have been copied by such artist-searchers as Townley Johnson, and other have been photographed.

Cedarberg paintings include a number of rarities. Near the Pakhuis Pass there is a cave with swallows in flight. Bushmen often painted ostriches, but for some undiscovered reason they usually ignored the birds of the air. Battle scenes, buffalo, zebra, baboons and elephant appear in other Pakhuis caves. Only the swallows and the baboons still inhabit the peaceful Pakhuis world of today. Line drawings of ships were found not long ago, sixty miles from another cave which holds a four-masted sailing ship in brick red, possibly a vessel of the Van Riebeeck period. Some of the oldest paintings are shadows now, the white and yellow pigments lost, fine detail gone, only the dark red showing up. The last Bushman artists depicted crude Voortrekkers, white men with guns and wagons. Townley Johnson followed clues for three years before he discovered a painting of a leopard entering a farmer's trap. Close by was a Bushman grave, possibly the grave of the artist.

Human figures were always among the Bushman's favourite subjects. He depicted his own race in a wishful style; slender, graceful, tall people hunting, fishing and dancing. His animals were lifelike, and there are more lions and leopards, elephant and giraffe, rhino, buffalo, eland and other antelopes in the caves than any other living things. Snakes and frogs appear now and then, but trees, landscapes and fish are as uncommon as birds. Prehistoric or extinct animals do not appear in Bushman paintings. Elephant herds and other great beasts have departed from the Cedarberg but they live on elsewhere. Note that the caves of Europe hold such wonders as the bison which I saw at Altamira, a vanished species painted twenty-five thousand years ago; thus it may be argued that there have been no dramatic changes in the fauna of South Africa for thousands of years. If the Bushman had seen pterodactyls he would have painted them. When the Hottentots and later the Bantu arrived with their domestic cattle the Bushmen painted oxen and sheep for the first time; and so certain paintings may be roughly dated. Their earliest artistic efforts were outlines of animals hacked out of the rock; or possibly they used diamonds. Sometimes they cut human feet or the spoor of game. Then came the painters, using natural earth colours at first, red and yellow ochre, and concentrating on profiles of the eland. As the centuries passed the little artists reached out for materials which would satisfy the hunger for more vivid expression. Nothing was too weird for the Bushman's palette. Hyrax urine, ostrich egg albumen, beeswax, honey, animal fat from the fat-tailed sheep of the Hottentots, the contents of gall bladders, euphorbia juice, bone marrow, ochre powdered by grinding stones and heated; all these he gathered and treasured. Instead of brushes he used feathers or the tail hair of a *wildebees*, sticks or his own fingers. Just as the great masters of fine art in Europe possessed technical secrets which died with them, so the Bushmen left mysteries which science cannot solve. They struggled for thousands of years to blend a pigment which would defy sun and rain, and they defeated the sun. Rock shelters have been lashed by sand and wind, baked by thousands of summers, snowed up and frozen. Only when the rain blew over the ancient pictures was the work of the Bushman washed into oblivion.

Years ago there was a scientist who was given a sample of a combustible mineral which, an old woman told him, was the secret ingredient used by Bushman painters. She said this basis of the pigment had been a closely-guarded secret for years; and the scientist was so impressed by circumstantial evidence that he sent the mineral to Cape Town for analysis. It never arrived. The secret, if secret it was, had been lost in the post.

Why did the Bushman paint? This is one of the deep mysteries, though I think it is obvious that he revelled in his work. Magic there may have been, some primitive belief that by painting his huge quarries he made it easier to kill them with his bow and arrow. But the more obvious magic lies in the liveliness of his work, the sense of movement. The Abbé Breuil, that lifelong student of cave art, summed it up as "a sort of moving-picture film expressing throughout *joie de vivre*, the delight of being agile, fleet-footed, supple in sport and dance, deft in shooting arrows". Walter Battiss, the South African painter and authority on Bushman art, pointed out that those who used several colours excelled all other rock painters. They had an uncanny genius for natural animal poses revealing in the simplest way the whole nature of the animal. In the beginning the Bushman artist could not portray movement. Perspective and action came in time, though centuries may have passed. Bushmen depicted hunting scenes, dances and battles in miniature, and real genius was found in delicate groups that could be measured in inches. Finally the Bushman saw the whole picture on the screen of his mind; he aimed at a large effect and achieved compostion.

Often he resorted to caricature. People he disliked, such as the Bantu, were given protruding lips and large feet. Other pictures revealed grotesque figures and the weird monsters of Bushman mythology. Battiss, like other artists, was baffled by the paint technique and said that the secret of the mixture had been lost. He admired the rare vermilion of comparatively recent cave paintings, a colour with a formula which no one could penetrate. Pure yellow, green, blue and purple were never used. Thousands of Bushman paintings were monochromes in red. Battiss longed for a "Rosetta stone", some alphabet or key to the riddles of the rocks.

Frobenius called the Bushman art the "painted rock archives" of African history. The Abbé Breuil, too, found the story of the Bushman race in the caves, migrations and battles, cattle raids, successful hunting expeditions and feasts. Other pictures were devoted to hunting magic and rain-making, sometimes with human sacrifice. He also discovered such day-to-day events as courtships, quarrels, reconciliations and initiations.

Many of the Cedarberg cave paintings are very old, yet it is clear from the later subjects that the art flourished in fairly recent years. When the Bushmen were driven from their caves they still felt the creative urge; they engraved walking-sticks with animal designs, burning the round surface or using a sharp point. Ostrich shells were also decorated instead of rock walls.

Ask almost any Bushman to draw the spoor of an animal he knows and he will demonstrate a form of primitive art which has survived. He will draw in the sand a convincing reproduction of hooves, footmarks, the path of a snake, anything from a frog to a gemsbok; and only another Bushman would be able to distinguish the copy from the real thing. But the art of the cave painter belongs to the past. Those little people needed time to develop their technique, to strive for perfection. Through the long centuries in the Cedarberg they found the sanctuary of every true artist's dreams. There in the high and hidden galleries the painters rose and flourished and created their masterpieces at last. And there, with the coming of the men with guns, their cave art died.

Naturally the Bushmen of the Cedarberg had their own names for the peaks and forests, streams and *poorts* of their mountainous home. Few of these place-names have survived; their language was too difficult for local usage by the white people. Hottentot names in their original forms, or corrupted or translated by white people, are far more common.

Like everyone else the Bushmen were fond of bestowing names as a result of encounters with animals. *Thounce* the hyena, *Koes* the jackal and *Gabee* the giraffe inspired many names. But the language of the Bushmen was too complicated for the mapmakers. "Harsh, broken, full of monosyllables which are uttered with strong aspirations from the chest and a gutteral articulation as disagreeable as it is difficult"; such was one missionary's impression. So you find Hottentot names on the Cedarberg maps, Krakadouw and others, but only the expert will detect names of Bushman origin in the mountains they once dominated.

It is said that the Bushmen had no religion. Certainly they had no organised forms of worship; but such an imaginative people possessed ideas of God and a life after death. As Dornan the anthropologist remarked: "To the Bushman everything is alive with some spirit—lightning, eddies of wind and dust, storms, thermal springs, natural phenomena." The Bushman shares with the Australian aboriginal the belief that the stars are the camp-fires of the departed. He sings to the moon to bring him luck in hunting, and moon worship is probably his nearest appraoch to religion. Miss Dorothea Bleek wrote down one of the Bushman's prayers:

*Ho, moon lying there,*
*Let me kill a springbok*
*Tomorrow,*
*Let me eat a springbok,*
*Let me eat filling my body*
*In the night which is here,*
*Let me fill my body.*

Here in the Cedarberg lived sorcerers and men who knew more of snake venoms than the scientists of our time. Here were prophets and medicine men. They told the Bushman clans that the animals were once human, that anyone who disobeyed them could be transformed into a jackal! Here they made their smoke signals; here they left sticks in the ground, pointing, telling a clear story to those who could read the message. You can still see grooves in the rocks where they sharpened their weapons, grinding and polishing the bone and flint points of their arrows. They made strong ropes of plaited grass to reach the hives of the wild bees. The ropes have gone but some of the hard wooden pegs they hammered into the cliff faces have not yet splintered.

In the Cedarberg the Bushman clans watched the lightning, kept the fire going which the lightning had started, and used their brains as no apes could have done to achieve at last the miracle of man-made fire. Here and in other mountain ranges mankind came out of far distant blackness into the daylight of recorded history. In these caves are clues to great mysteries; here one day the whole vast picture of the past may be brought into focus. They were brave little people, the Bushmen of the Cedarberg, they fought hard for the caves of their ancestors, and when they were defeated at last they went out fighting.

*Chapter Fifteen*

# LORD OF THE SKIES

*He clasps the crag with crooked hands;*
*Close to the sun in lonely lands,*
*Ring'd with the azure world, he stands.*
*The wrinkled sea beneath him crawls;*
*He watches from his mountain walls,*
*And like a thunderbolt he falls.*

ALFRED LORD TENNYSON.

OVER a valley in the Cedarberg the birds of prey were gathering. They feasted on the entrails of a small buck I had shot near the homestead, and I stood there in the evening glow with the farmer, watching the hungry ones.

"In my father's time, here in the Cedarberg, there was a greater bird than any of those eagles," declared the farmer. "I have watched a large black eagle with a klipspringer in its talons. It was so close that I could see the klipspringer twisting and hear it bleating with pain and fear—until the eagle dropped it on a flat rock and killed it. But the bird my father saw was the huge lammergeyer, the bearded vulture that has vanished from these mountains. That was the largest and strongest bird in African skies. Bushmen told my father that lammergeyers had carried off their babies and my father said he believed the story."

I had often heard of the lammergeyer and the legend of the babies, but at that time I had never seen the great bird. Long ago it nested on Table Mountain, and it still lays its eggs on ledges of remote precipices in the Drakensberg and Basutoland. It is a rare bird in Africa and Europe, but the lammergeyer floats over the summit of Everest and is often seen elsewhere in the Himalayas. I watched it first just outside Cairo, sailing over the Mokattam Hills without a flutter of the magnificent wings, soaring with poise and beauty.

By that time I had fallen under the spell of the lammergeyer, and I wanted to pierce the mysterious background and trace the legend of the stolen babies to the source. The quest has led me not only into museums and libraries, but also into the mountains. Now I, too, accept as truth the story told by the old Bushmen of the Cedarberg. Let me bring the lammergeyer and the evidence before you.

Ornithologists are irritated by the lammergeyer because it refuses to fit any pigeon-hole. No scientist can say with certainty whether it is eagle or vulture. In appearance, apart from the hooked vulturine beak, it is an eagle. Its habits are those of a vulture, but a magnificent vulture. The feathered, bearded face, the long mane of feathers behind the head, the legs with pantaloons have fascinated naturalists for centuries. Between the lammergeyer of Europe and Africa there are few differences; they are brothers rather than cousins, though the African lammergeyers have bare legs. No doubt it is a link between the true eagles and vultures, flying with all the majesty of the eagle but hunting and feeding in its own way. The lammergeyer, proud and solitary, is very different, from the vultures of Longfellow's poem:

*First a speck and then a vulture,*
*Till the air is black with pinions.*

You will never find a crowd of lammergeyers fighting over a rotting carcass as the vultures do. The lammergeyer and his mate will stand aside until the vultures have finished; then they will seize the bones and drop them on the rocks to secure the marrow. Unlike other vultures the lammergeyer will not touch putrid flesh. Possibly it is a rare bird for that reason. Great flocks of lammergeyers would not find enough food to sustain the species. Their exact diet is still controversial, but there is no doubt that some lammergeyers will attack living mammals and tortoises. Below the nest of sticks you will find a Golgotha of cracked bones of many victims. Dassie skulls are sure to be there, the fat little coneys that provide African birds of prey with meat when nobler flesh is not to be found; tiny springbok, young steenbok and the skulls of dogs and calves. A whole hare was once found in the stomach of a lammergeyer. It can swallow and digest almost anything; the stomach is so acid that a cow's vertebra presents no difficulties. A stone axe-head, however, proved too much for one ambitious bird.

Long and black, narrow and pointed are the wings of the lammergeyer. Wingspans of eight to ten feet are not uncommon, and in North Africa a wingspan of fourteen feet has been recorded. The wings, torpedo body and wedge-shaped tail make the lammergeyer easy to identify in flight. It has most remarkable eyes, red and staring, fierce and sinister. The outer part of the eye, usually described as the white, has the scarlet hue with a yellow pupil. As a rule the lammergeyer is described as a silent bird, though a long-drawn, ringing whistle has been heard. Male and female are very much alike. Round the eyes runs a black mask. Many observers have mentioned the vivid orange throat and breast, the chocolate back, the creamy neck. I studied seven lammergeyers in the Paris museum of natural history not long ago; one of them collected in Algeria by Francois le Vaillant after his South African expedition. These specimens from various parts of Europe, Tibet and Africa revealed marked differences in colouration. However, the noble lammergeyer always displays the bright underparts which take on a typical brick-red hue at sundown. The unique beard consists of a strange tassel of black bristles, a veritable *bokbaardjie* on a bird! Hence the name bearded vulture. But the lammergeyer has been confused with other birds of prey, especially in South Africa. In the old Cape Colony it was the *arend*, and in recent years the rare lammergeyer has been shot at sight by people who thought it was the more common lammervanger or martial eagle. Both the lammergeyer and *lammervanger* have been called "golden eagle", a bird which does not exist in Africa. Shepherds in the mountains of Spain call the lammergeyer *Quebrantahuesos*, the "bone-breaker", owing to its fondness for marrow. Swiss and

German farmers named the lammergeyer, the "lamb vulture" that carried off their stock. It is seen no more in the Alps, but the great red and gold bird is a wanderer, and it may breed there again one day. Bengt Berg, the Swedish naturalist, called the lammergeyer the "flying dragon", and told many stories of its ferocity. The scientific name *Gypaetus barbatus* is less dramatic, but it does away with all confusion.

All the museum lammergeyers I have seen were examples of old-fashioned taxidermy, birds with folded wings. One day I hope to see this great bird mounted with realism, settling on its nest with outspread wings, a baby antelope in its talons. Wolfe the painter showed a lammergeyer swooping down on a chamois, a most dramatic picture. The speed of a lammergeyer in a dive was estimated by a Royal Air Force pilot (who dived his aircraft not far from the bird) at more than one hundred miles an hour.

No one has ever been able to fix the life-span of the lammergeyer. The centenarian parrot has been outlived by vultures, however, so there must be a number of venerable lammergeyers in the world. Colonel Richard Meinertzhagen, one of the greatest bird observers of this century, has put forward the theory that the phoenix of the ancients was really a lammergeyer. It came to him while he was watching a lammergeyer only a few feet away against the golden infinity of a memorable sunset. The bird sat on a rocky pinnacle facing the setting sun, wings slightly drooping and half-stretched head turned up towards heaven. Brilliant golden plumage round the neck, the throat adorned with a crest, the head with a tuft of feathers; all these recalled to Meinertzhagen the bird Pliny described. "It was the finest, most beautiful and yet most terrible, the most romantic view of any bird I have seen at any time anywhere," summed up Meinertzhagen. Other naturalists have suggested that a lammergeyer was responsible for the death of Aesculus, the Greek philosopher. Aesculus was told in his youth that he would die when something fell from heaven. In his old age Aesculus was resting on the shore when a lammergeyer saw the bald head gleaming in the sun, thought it was a rock and dropped a tortoise to crack the shell. Thus the prophecy came true. Mogul emperors venerated the lammergeyer and believed that if the great shadow of the bird fell on a man he would become emperor one day.

How dangerous is the lammergeyer? Whenever this bird nests far above settled lands, there you will hear the folklore and the legends of its evil deeds. Of course the lammergeyer has its defenders. They have claimed that the lammergeyer's talons are weak and blunt; that the bird is cowardly in spite of its size; that the lammergeyer is more interested in bones than live animals or babies. Yet reliable observers have given convincing evidence of the lammergeyer's strength and daring. Layard of the South African Museum described the raids of lammergeyers in the Bain's Kloof area a century ago, and said they killed lambs and sheep. Jackson, a farmer at Nelspoort, sent specimens of the lammergeyer to the museum. Another farmer named Atmore of Blanco wrote to Layard: "We are going to lay for an *arend* tomorrow evening. He always sits on one particular yellowwood tree in the forest, but he examines the premises very carefully before he perches. What a beautiful flight they have, sailing about without even flapping a wing; and when they swoop they come out of the sky like a lightning flash. There are several here and we know of a nest." Bryden of Naroekas Poort stated that the lammergeyer bred there and was a menace to lambs and kids. Two brothers named Woodward studied the lammergeyer of Natal towards the end of last century and asserted: "It will kill and devour wild animals, which it prefers to carrion. It is hard to shoot, but is taken sometimes in steel traps baited with meat." Graham Hutchinson, a bird collector of the period, watched the lammergeyers fly into deep caverns, where they nested. Bold climbers who reached the ledges and caves favoured by lammergeyers found clear evidence that these birds of prey could lift heavy weights. In and below the nests were ossuaries which proved that the birds had carried lambs, buck, goats, dogs, tortoises and dassies to their nests.

If their feet are weak their beaks are strong. Sometimes they will sweep a lamb or buck over a precipice with a sudden blow of the wing. General Sir Ian Hamilton was attacked by a lammergeyer. "There was a tremendous swish in the air and my hat was sent spinning off my head down a precipice while I received a blow from the talons which all but made me follow it," he declared. "My shikari drove off the bird by firing a rifle." There are stories of lammergeyers throwing climbers to their deaths. Verner, the great field naturalist, gave this opinion: "After watching these powerful birds carrying the weighty limb of an animal in mid-air the idea has more than once struck me that the old tales of golden eagles carrying off children may without any great stretch of imagination find their origin in the misdeeds of the bearded vulture. The bearded vulture is very richly coloured; in brilliant sunlight the bright tawny throat and underparts assume a golden hue, far more so than the pale tawny feathers on the nape of the golden eagle." The Rev. J. G. Bruce, a missionary who camped on a mountain in North Africa, gave an account of the lammergeyer which showed the bird as anything but cowardly. A pot of steaming meat was standing in the middle of the camp, and the lammergeyer alighted on the food and scalded its feet. Bruce's servants ran for their spears. The angry lammergeyer scattered its attackers and flew off with a leg and shoulder of goat. It settled again not far away, and Bruce shot it. The lammergeyer weighed twenty-two pounds, and the wingspan was eight feet four inches.

I have traced many accounts of vultures attacking men and animals in South Africa, but it is often impossible to fix the species of the birds. A farmer carried a huge lammergeyer or *lammervanger* into the "Grahamstown Journal" office early this century and told the editor it had fought his Hottentot shepherd and a dog even after being wounded with buckshot. Some years later a huge vulture was found on a Bechuanaland farm engaged in a fierce battle with several ostriches. A Queenstown farmer named Bell heard that his sheep were being attacked by vultures. He went to the rescue on horseback and had to ride for his life when two hundred vultures flew at him. His dogs killed several vultures, but they were driven off, and eight sheep were devoured by the birds. These vultures, could not have been lammergeyers. Vultures have attacked native women and cows. Possibly the greatest flocks of vultures of all species seen in South Africa last century were those which hovered over the tracks to the diamond fields and gorged themselves on the oxen which had died in the snow.

Most famous of all the lammergeyer stories is the Swiss legend of Anna Zurbuchen of Habchern in the Bernese Oberland. This goes back to 1763, but the ornithologist Dresser investigated the details and accepted the whole story as fact. Anna was taken up the mountain by her parents when she was three years old and left asleep on the grass. Her father placed his straw hat over her face. Both parents then went up the slopes collecting herbs, and when they returned Anna had vanished. Other peasants joined the panic-strickened father and mother, but they searched in vain. Meanwhile one Heinrich Michel was following a narrow path in the neighbourhood when he heard the cry of a child. He ran towards the sound and a lammergeyer rose and soared away. Michel found Anna at the very edge of a precipice. Apparently the bird had seen the bare limbs of the little girl and had mistaken her for some animal. Anna was uninjured apart from deep scratches on the left arm and hand. The precipice where Anna was found was fourteen hundred paces from the spot where she had been lifted into the air while asleep. This episode occurred on July 12, 1763. Anna was known for the rest of her life as Lammergeyer Anna. Dresser declared that he had found other authentic records of small children being attacked by lammergeyers. The story of Anna was also accepted by Naumann, author of "Naturgeschichte der Vögel Deutschlands".

Large eagles and vulture have given so many proofs of their strength that their ability to carry off lambs and babies cannot be denied. They still tell the story in Calvinia of a black eagle caught in a jackal trap to which four other traps had been attached. The total weight of the traps was thirty pounds. In its efforts to escape the eagle lifted all five traps fifteen feet into the air. A zoo curator noted an attack on one of his keepers by a golden eagle. The bird weighing ten to twelve pounds was able to knock down a one hundred and forty pound man by hurling itself from a distance of a few feet. "It is easy to believe that by a swoop from a great height at terrific speed the bird might well knock down and stun a small animal such as a lamb—or a human baby," declared the curator. "It is possible that under exceptional circumstances it might carry the victim away. But the circumstances would certainly have to be exceptional."

In the Himalayas there are stories of lammergeyers flying off not only with sheep and goats but with ibex and young bears. Dr. T. C. Jerdon, who studied the lammergeyer in India last century, asserted that it was fearless of man when bent on securing flesh. He quoted a Bishop Heber who had reported that a tiny child had been seized by a lammergeyer in a street in Almora and carried off. This bird was shot later; it had a wingspan of thirteen feet. I have also read a number of news stories in American newspapers giving full details of small children being lifted by eagles. Tests carried out by scientists in the United States with a captive eagle and a dummy ended with this finding: "If a baby weighing six pounds was left on an exposed mountainside it might conceivably be carried off by an eagle." If an eagle can do it, the powerful lammergeyer could accomplish the same feat with ease.

The habits of such a rare mountain bird as the lammergeyer must remain controversial. There are enormous gaps in its distribution, and no one can say why it clings to the great widely-separated African peaks and ranges where it is still found.

No doubt the lammergeyer was driven out of Switzerland because of its sinister reputation. Africa shelters both the European lammergeyer (in the Atlas mountains) and the southern species in Egypt, Abyssinia, Kenya, Tanganyika, South West Africa and South Africa. Some authorities believe that the lammergeyer found its way to Africa during one of the Pleistocene ice ages, and that the route to the ancient colonies has been preserved. It has often been said that the species is on the verge of extinction, apart from those nesting in Asia. Dr. Gustav Rudebeck, the Swedish expert, who was among my companions on a zoological expedition, thinks that the lammergeyer should survive in the Drakensberg if it is protected. He counted twenty-one lammergeyers in twelve days along the Basutoland border. Mount Morosi is their home. Rudebeck watched the lammergeyers searching for food, skimming close to the ground with hardly a movement of the wings, following every curve of the hillsides. He thought they needed little food, as they spent most of the time, like other birds of prey, soaring and gliding, finding pleasure in the air currents. One lammergeyer settled among a herd of goats and the goats went on grazing unafraid.

Some say there are probably no more than twenty pairs of lammergeyers in the whole of Southern Africa today. However, the great bird has a way of remaining hidden in a secret kingdom of high places above settled areas. Now and again a lone lammergeyer surprises ornithologists by revisiting haunts from which the species departed many decades before. If it returns to the Cedarberg with a race memory of fat Bushmen babies it will be disappointed.

Naturally the eggs of a rare bird nesting in almost inaccessible places must be extremely rare. So it is with the lammergeyer's eggs. If they do not rank with the dodo, there are probably more eggs of the extinct great auk in the world's collections than there are of the living lammergeyer. I have set eyes on these large dull white eggs only three times in my life. Dresser stated that the enormous prices obtained for lammergeyer eggs, and the killing of the birds for their feathers, were responsible for the species abandoning many old haunts in Europe.

Museum curators wrote to Layard from many parts of the world a century ago begging for specimens of the southern lammergeyer. At that period the lammergeyer was fairly common in the Cedarberg, at Bain's Kloof, Caledon, Swellendam, Graaff Reinet and other places. Layard collected a number of specimens and exchanged one for an Alpine lammergeyer. Probably the first lammergeyer's egg known to have been secured in South Africa was a specimen which Henry Jackson of Nelspoort sent to Layard for the South African Museum about a century ago. Graham Hutchinson, the pioneer Natal egg collector, found a lammergeyer's egg in 1883 at Bushman's Nek near Matatiele, and this is to be seen in the Transvaal Museum. Few eggs of this species have been collected in South Africa since then. Dr. Austin Roberts described a creamy white egg with purplish grey and brownish yellow markings, collected in Basutoland.

Only in 1941 was a lammergeyer egg taken in Kenya. The nesting site in the Nanyuki district was discovered by a Kikuyu named Ali. This fearless native was lowered over a precipice to the eyrie at great risk. As he reached the nest a lammergeyer flew off. This specimen was presented to the Coryndon museum in Nairobi. Two years later an ornithologist named Pollard climbed Mount Kenya. He had reached the glaciers at sixteen thousand feet when a lammergeyer suddenly appeared, shot past him, rolled and twisted down the face of a thousand foot vertical cliff. He saw another lammergeyer, gleaming with gold and black, preening itself on a cliff face; and then he realised that he had come upon a nesting site. Pollard returned in 1944 and secured a single egg. James Ferguson-Lees, a British authority, says that only three lammergeyer eggs are known to have been collected in India.

Photographs of the lammergeyer on its nest are even rarer than the eggs. Verner was defeated again and again in Spain, year after year. After thirty years of effort he found a nest littered with the feet of sheep and goats, all the bones picked clean. His photographs were failures, but he found two eggs, one broken, richly marked with shades of yellow and brown. Verner risked his life and injured his left arm for these eggs, which are now in the British

Museum. Verner intended to shoot a lammergeyer, but he had to wait ten years before he encountered one at close quarters. He was on a mountain, surveying a plain dotted with brood mares, cattle and droves of pigs. Through his glasses he picked up a large bird flying with marvellous ease, more gracefully than a golden eagle. It winged towards him and he saw that it was a lammergeyer. On came the great bird, unaware of his presence. Verner raised his gun. When the bird was fifty yards away he became aware of its full beauty; the fierce, handsome head, silvered crown and black moustaches, the rich throat and breast, the sweeping black pinions. It was making for a crag just above his head and he could have shot it easily. Verner found that he was unwilling to squeeze the trigger. Suddenly the lammergeyer checked its flight, swung round with a rush of wings and whirled away. Verner also witnessed a mid-air duel between a lammergeyer and an old female griffon vulture. The griffon was obviously in deadly fear as the bearded vulture attacked and struck out vigorously. Locked together, the birds fell, then separated. The griffon made off at full speed and escaped. "Of all the great birds of prey the lammergeyer appeals most to the popular imagination," said Verner. "It is credited with almost supernatural powers and a sinister interest in infants."

Most successful of all lammergeyer photographs were those taken in July 1961 by Mr. P. R. Barnes, game ranger of the Giant's Castle reserve, and three other bold mountaineers. They had studied the pages of a previous ranger's log-book, and an entry made early this century gave them a clue to the nesting site. It was in a hole on the face of a six hundred foot Drakensberg precipice, two hundred feet from the summit. The men had to endure sleet and snow and precarious holds, but they took a number of magnificent colour and black and white pictures at a distance of ninety feet before returning shaken after the dangerous effort. They had observed a single egg in the nest. Five weeks later two members of the expedition climbed again and photographed the young bird. This was described as the "only picture in the world of a lammergeyer chick". Evidently the pictures taken by Eric Hosking in Spain a few years before had been overlooked. Hosking photographed one of the parents and a chick about ten weeks old on the nest. An old rope sandal was found in the nest, but Hosking reported: "Fortunately there was no trace of the owner." Photographs of lammergeyers on their nests had also been taken in India by Lowther and Bengt Berg.

Seldom does the lammergeyer lay more than one egg. When there are two (or even three) only one young bird is reared. An incubation period of three weeks is followed by three months or more in the nest. The nesting materials often include hooves, bones and sticks lined with sheeps' wool or goats' hair, and are designed to protect the young one from falling. Lammergeyers roost in the same nests for years even when they are not breeding. They choose small caves or a ledge below an overhang when available. Sometimes the nests are fourteen thousand feet above sea level, and the lammergeyer has been observed flying at twenty-five thousand feet. Young birds are covered with greyish-white down, changing to brown; they gain adult plumage after five years. While they are in the nest the young eat voraciously, the parents bringing them several pounds of meat a day. At one period the young bird is too fat to move. Little is known of the lammergeyer's first flight, though obviously this must be carefully timed to avoid disaster.

Gaze upon a lammergeyer egg, largest and most impressive of all eggs laid by the birds of prey, and you cannot fail to visualise the lord of the skies. Those legends you hear from the Alps to the Cedarberg were once real enough, the tragedies of bygone peoples. Look down the long corridors of time and strange tales come true.

*Chapter Sixteen*

# VERLOREN VLEI, THE "LOST WORLD"

I AM still in the Leipoldt country, south of Leipoldtville, the village named after the poet's father.* In this unspoilt stretch of the Sandveld between the mountains and the flamingo coast there are a number of pans and vleis, lagoons and little rivers which attract vast numbers of waterfowl and other birds. Verloren Vlei is the great spectacle in this little-known water wonderland.

They called it the "lost vlei", perhaps, because it loses itself among the dunes when it reaches the coast. Some old maps show it as Verloren Vallei, the "lost valley", off the beaten track, a remote place unexplored by travellers following the main route to the north. This is more romantic. Before the days of motor-cars, before farm gates were almost abolished, Verloren Vlei was more than a lost vlei or lost valley; it was a remote, inaccessible "lost world". The vlei, of course, is in reality a little river, the Kruis river. It rises to the north of Piketberg and flows lazily on its north-west course for fifty miles to Eland's Bay. Quaecoma, the Hottentots called the river. Olof Bergh named it "Sand or Zeekoeien" river in 1682; and three years later Simon van der Stel called it the "Cleyne Oliphants River off Zeekoe Vallei." First to describe the river was Starrenburg the landdrost and cattle trader early in the eighteenth century. "On the eastern side of the Piketberg are many cattle posts," he wrote. "The soil would produce good wheat if manured, as it is a light clay. The mountains have many kloofs, from each of which runs a small

*Brandwacht farm at Leipoldtville was occupied by Jacobus Louw in 1746 and is still owned by the Louw family. In the old days the farmers in the remote Sandveld went to Cape Town by ox-wagon once a year; later they went to Tulbagh or Malmesbury for *nagmaal*. Old people spoke of the long period of isolation as the days "when farming was farming".

brook wending towards the plain where they unite to form the source of the river. It flows round the north end of the mountain receiving on the way water from some springs and forms the large Quaecoma river, whose estuary we saw on the sea beach." Starrenburg, a keen plant collector, had with him Jan Hartog, sailor and master gardener. They were visited by a rhino while gathering seeds and plants beside the vlei, but the rhino retired quietly when fires were lit. Starrenburg and Hartog then shot flamingoes, wild geese and duck for the pot. Ensign Rhenius passed that way in 1724 and he was responsible for naming the Verloren Vallei. The name Kruis came later, but it was certainly in use two centuries ago. Het Kruis was the spot where the Kruis river joined the small Berg Vallei river, not to be confused with the Great Berg river to the south. Het Kruis is now the name of a railway station on the line to Namaqualand, the only place-name in the official list with the prefix "het". (How "de" and "het" baffied me at school!) Some miles farther north you find Verlorevlei station (official spelling).

Follow the river down the "lost valley" and you will soon come to the thatched homestead of the Schrik van Rondom farm. Some names on this old northern route were bestowed so long ago that the meanings have become legends or guesswork. Schrik van Rondom ("fear on all sides") appears to have been taken from a biblical text. The original grant is dated 1839, so that the farmer of those days may have been menaced by Bushmen; but I would like to learn the true origin. Schrik van Rondom was once a goldmine, one of many in the Cape and just as disappointing as the others. Doyle, a hopeful prospector from England, sunk two vertical shafts; another optimist drove a tunnel into a hillside during the last years of last century. They can show you the heavy iron pestle and mortar used to crush the quartz. Yes, there was gold in the earth of Schrik van Rondom, but never enough to pay for the shafts and the two hundred and fifty feet of tunnel.

Dr. A. W. Rogers summed up Schrik van Rondom in

two shrewd sentences: "The quartz obtained from near the surface would have given all the information required to determine whether further expense should be incurred. In this case, however, as in several other unsuccessful ventures, the ruling idea was that rock which is perhaps worthless at the surface may contain untold riches at a depth only reachable by the expenditure of much money."

Thank heaven this "lost world" landscape of the Cape west coast has never been wrecked by mine dumps. Their onions, so the Sandveld farmers claim, are among the finest in the world, and some weigh more than two pounds. Along the Verloren Vlei they cling to thatch and gables and whitewash and mules and the hammer-guns their grandfathers used. One family, the Louws, have been in the "lost valley" for eight generations. They founded the village of Redelinghuis, the "capital" of this secluded valley, eighteen miles from the sea; Redelinghuis with its church spire and shady Voortrekker Straat. When I first drove through the "lost valley" nearly thirty years ago I had to open a gate to enter Redelinghuis, and there were so many gates across the valley road that a trip to the seaside was an ordeal. Now the gates have gone, the summer typhoid has been conquered and there are other signs of the right sort of progress. But the outboard motor-boats which have appeared in the quiet world of birds are as unhappy a contrast as the mine shafts of Schrik van Rondom.

Verloren Vlei still has the sort of homesteads and cottages you would expect to find in a "lost world" of the Cape. Schrik van Rondom is a good example for the original small and picturesque home must have been built in the first half of last century and rooms were added at intervals. Koopmanskraal, not far away, may well have an eighteenth century origin. It has end gables and an unusual arrangement of wings at the back. Showplace of the Sandveld is the large farm St. Helenafontein, on the coastal route to Verloren Vlei. The old farmers in this district could seldom afford ornamented gables and those other outward signs of wealth found in Constantia and Stellenbosch. Thatch and plain limewashed plaster gave dignity without grandeur. St. Helenafontein, however, is a handsome late Georgian homestead with beautiful doors and small panes in the sash windows. One of the Cruywagens was granted the farm more than two centuries ago and an early Martin Melck followed; but the present house was probably built by Pierre Rocher about 1835, and the Rochers are still there. A second storey has been added without spoiling the charm of the place. Near by is Rocherspan, a bird sanctuary which may be regarded as a satellite of Verloren Vlei.

Rocherspan, also known as "Die Panne" or Bokram, is a vlei fed by a river that once emptied itself directly into the sea. After a rainy season Rocherspan becomes a series of broads close to the dunes that stretch along the beach. Here are green banks of grass, fine patches of open water, wooded side pools, and sandy flats with masses of wild flowers. At times Rocherspan has been filled over a north and south distance of seven miles, while the widest part has measured seven hundred yards. Low islands of sedge and bush rise above the surface. The banks are sheltered by fringes of reeds and clumps of rushes, nesting places of the smaller birds. In parts there is wild dense bush. The pride of Rocherspan is the flamingo colony, often two thousand strong. Shepherds employed by the Rocher family have acted for many years as gamekeepers, so that thousands of wild duck and geese still fly in, line after line. Here, too, are the Damara terns that are always found near salt water; the bold sandplovers, including the handsome dark-ringed sandplover; tall black-headed stilts; coot nesting on floating islands; moorhen and wagtails among the reeds.

Here you are sure to find the Cape shoveller, essentially a bird of Southern Africa, and after the *geelbek* the most abundant wild duck in these parts. Until recently this duck was regarded by ornithologists as "the rarest and least-known of the shovellers". However, the full-scale report by Mr. W. R. Siegfried of the Cape department of nature conservation has solved most of the mysteries. One observer found thirty-one Cape shoveller nests on an island two hundred square yards in area at Rocherspan. They are brown duck, fast on the wing, fine table birds when in good condition. Apart from the water-birds the Rocherspan neighbourhood attracts many other species. Bustards, the huge *gompou*, trek in from the north in times of drought and may be seen running for shelter or standing in the shade of a bush until you approach. Then they rise in a sideways and almost noiseless flight; a remarkable feat for such large birds. Francolins cackle in the thick bush and quail call in the wheat. Storks have been seen at Rocherspan, but these are rare and shy. Eggs of wild birds used for research in hatching and breeding are secured at Rocherspan. The area deserves full protection, and it is highly probably that it will be purchased by the Provincial Council and declared a sanctuary.

Verloren Vlei has a long narrow course, but as you approach the sea you observe a fine sheet of water. For some miles it is five hundred yards wide, dammed back by the dunes, fringed by sedge and reed. During heavy winter rains, of course, the water floods down the valley and breaks through the blind mouth to join the South Atlantic. Then the carp emerge from their muddy pools. Birds and men catch all the freshwater fish they need when the vlei is full.

Eland's Bay, nearly sixty miles from Piketberg, is a fast run nowadays for those who do not care to gaze on the old homes, the gardens with palms and bananas and the turkeys which thrive in the sheltered valley. Cape Deseada, the Portuguese called this bold brown headland; but the country people have another name, Baboon Point. When I trudged over heavy sand to the point before World War II the fishermen were risking their lives to land their catches. Now there is a factory but they still have to hoist their boats on to jetties. Wheat growing close to the dunes; snoek and crawfish in the cold ocean; these are the golden harvests that have outlasted the pitiful gleams of gold at Schrik van Rondom.

Verloren Vlei is now recognised as the great wildfowl

haunt of the west coast. Ornithologists camp in the low scrub, rise before dawn and listen to the whirring of the sand grouse, "like the winding of an enormous clock," as one bird-lover said. Here, too, you will surely hear the alarm call of Le Vaillant's warbler. That controversial Frenchman was the scientific discoverer of this valley when it was a true bird sanctuary; and this is the right place to study the man and his work. For in spite of all his faults, Francois Le Vaillant was the pioneer of bird study in South Africa. He has also been described as "the most widely-read traveller of the eighteenth century." Le Vaillant crossed and re-crossed the serpentine Kruis river in 1783, during the journey which took him to Heerenlogement and on to the Orange River. The sand was deep and loose, his wagons sank in to the axle-trees, and he had to secure four more oxen for each team of twelve to continue the trek. At this difficult stage he formed an unfavourable impression. "There are men who inhabit this district, sandy and miserable though it is, and cultivate a few spots of less barren land," Le Vaillant wrote. He met Hans van Aardt and Hermanus Louw at Lange Vallei. He camped on a dry plain where he could find no water for his cattle. When he shot thirty partridges the smell of the meat attracted jackals and hyenas, and his dogs drove them off. But the roasting of the birds on spits brought more carnivorous animals to the camp, and he was kept awake by the barking of the dogs. Roused by the loud cry of a *bergeend* next day, he followed the shelduck on horseback and found a badly-needed pool of rainwater. On his return from the north he decided to travel down the Verloren Vlei, which he described as "an extensive lake separated from the sea by a narrow border of sandy downs." He was impatient to return to the Cape, but soon he was gripped by the rich bird life of the vlei, and he summed up as follows: "Verloren Vlei is the only place for an ornithologist to fix his residence who would wish in a short time to procure a complete collection of the web-footed and shore birds of Africa."

On the beach at Elands Bay the French naturalist saw

the jackass penguins he had observed previously at Saldanha; "fat, a lucrative article of trade, so tame they suffer being knocked on the head without stirring." He collected a species of penguin he had never seen before, "with a crest of long, narrow feathers covering its eyes and the sides of its head, a creast it can erect and lower at will." Le Vaillant obviously did not realise that this was a great rarity. Nearly two centuries have passed since his visit to Elands Bay, and I doubt very much whether another such penguin has tumbled out of the surf there since then. For this turned out to be a rockhopper penguin, recorded five times along the South African coast during one hundred and fifty years. It breeds on Tristan da Cunha and other lonely isles. (I brought a rockhopper mat away from Tristan with me; made of rockhopper feathers including the pale yellow eye plumes Le Vaillant mentioned.) As a rule the rockhopper swims in the seas of the Antarctic; and when Dr. Leonard Gill of the South African Museum saw one of these rare visitors on a Cape Peninsula beach he thought some ship must have brought it. Indeed it is a long voyage for a lone, flightless bird. However, a stray rockhopper comes up from Tristan, Prince Edward or Marion about once in every thirty years. Le Vaillant was lucky. A South American jackass penguin with two cross-bands across the ventral white part of the body was seen in June 1963 on the guano island at Lambert Bay to the north of Elands Bay. There was no doubt about this report, for the bird was photographed. The nearest breeding-ground is in the Falkland Islands,. This was the first of the species recorded in South Africa.

I have called this long shore the flamingo coast, but it is also the coast of penguins. Diego Cam, first of the Portuguese explorers to set foot on the coast, saw penguins at Cape Cross. Diaz and Da Gama killed and salted penguins when they were short of food. Kolben, more vivid than most travellers of his day, remarked: "The Europeans at the Cape call them pinguinen, a name which, I fancy, was given them on account of their being generally extremely fat. The feathers are ash-coloured and have very much of the appearance of hair . . . All the day this bird is near or upon the water watching her opportunity to catch fish, which is all her food. Her wings are so short that she cannot fly. The utmost she can do, in order to escape her pursuers, is to hop and flutter along. But on the water she is very nimble and very quick at the catching of fish. The eggs are as large as ducks'-eggs and are delicious food. The Cape Europeans get and present several thousand of them every year to the Governor, and they are looked upon as a fine present. But the flesh of these birds tastes so fishy that it is no manner of value at the Cape."

For eleven days Le Vaillant wandered along the sedge-beds and rushes of this entrancing vlei. He was especially impressed by the purple gallinule he saw there, that large and beautiful rail which lives on snails and water-plants and nests among the reeds. It is known to the farmers as the *koning riethaan*, and they know what the epicure Le Vaillant found, that the flesh makes an excellent dish. The tinkling grass-warbler named after Le Vaillant is the most common at Verloren Vlei of the great family of these little birds. Lively and colourful in its bright chestnut feathers, it has a chirpy warble sounding like "chi chi cherruee". Le Vaillant was delighted with the vlei, and recorded that he saw there all the birds he had noted previously at Groen river in Namaqualand, and also the coot of Europe, and different species of grebes, a small crested falcon that fed on crabs and fish, and many web-footed and shore birds. While he was at the vlei he added one hundred and thirty-two birds to his collection.

Le Vaillant's six quarto scarlet morocco volumes entitled *Histoire Naturelle des Oiseaux d'Afrique*, with three hundred colour plates, contained accurate descriptions of many South Africa birds collected at Verloren Vlei and elsewhere. This was the most important work of its kind the world has seen up to that time, and it is unfortunate that Le Vaillant included a number of birds which were unknown in Africa. Apparently he was shown these specimens when he returned to Paris and incorporated them in the belief that they were African birds. Le Vaillant has also been denounced for various inaccuracies and exaggerations in his travel books. He was a vain philanderer and revealed his weakness when he listed the merchandise carried in his wagons: "All these articles which the wives and daughters of the planters incessantly ask from travellers are necessary to gain their affection and perhaps something more when the opportunity offers." He did not care to mention the thrashing with a *sjambok* given to him by a Widow van der Westhuizen in the Kamiesberg for making improper advances to her daughter. Nevertheless, his work has great historical and scientific value in spite of the blemishes.

Many leading South African ornithologists have followed Le Vaillant's tracks down the "lost valley". Andrew Smith was there in midsummer 1829 shooting the red-billed kaffir rail in the reeds. The "South African Commercial Advertiser" reported his discoveries when he returned to Cape Town in April. Edgar Layard, consul, traveller and prince of ornithologists, went to Verloren Vlei when he was writing his classic "Birds of South Africa", the first complete account and the foundation of all modern works. Dr. Emil Holub, that tireless and enterprising Czech collector, trekked up into the Sandveld and added to his thousands of specimens. W. L. Sclater was there, watching the African darter, the heron they call "snake bird"; watching and finding the dense masses of sticks used as nests; and finally remarking that "all the herons are first rate, very delicate eating." Your modern ornithologist seldom comments on the edible qualities of his specimens. Sclater enjoyed the flesh, and declared that the green eggs were prized by the farmers. Dr. C. J. Uys, a fairly recent visitor, listed more than one hundred bird species and twenty-four nests in three days at Verloren Vlei. Like previous bird-watchers he was troubled by the mosquitoes at night and listened to the wild cries of the fish eagles by day.

Ornithologists like to record such rarities as the white-faced whistling duck that make history when they come down from the north at intervals of decades to mingle with common shelduck, *geelbek* and Cape teal. Whistling duck really do whistle in three syllables. Cape widgeon are seen on the vlei, though they are not common.

I doubt whether the herons cast a mystic spell over those patient watchers who sit behind the tall plumed rushes with fieldglasses. Herons are rowdy and their haunts are malodorous. They strike down into the vlei with sharp beaks to impale their fish. Swallowing its prey at a gulp, it regurgitates the food to feed the young in the nests. Herons are best admired at a distance. Dr. Uys has pointed out that herons depend on the presence of others of the same species to maintain the breeding drive. Thus you have well-populated heronries, secluded and surrounded by open water, where the large flat nests are built. One observer, however, noted a solitary nest of the purple heron five miles from Redelinghuis, a floating platform of reeds anchored to the vegetation of the vlei. This nest was occupied by a well-feathered young bird in October that year.

Verloren Vlei knows the grey heron as a *blou-reier*, but they are cosmopolitan rather than South African. This very bird was caught by falcons over London for centuries and served at royal banquets. Leipoldt, who knew the vlei well, never thought much of the dark, oily flesh of the heron. Farmers dislike the grey heron as it has been known to devour chickens; but the more common black heron or *swartkop-reier* is welcome, for it prefers mice and large insects. Malachite sunbirds nest there, the green and glossy birds known to the farm people as Jan Groentjie. In the spring they seek nectar from the flowers with long curved beaks. Lizards and insects are welcome items of food at all times. Malachite kingfishers burrow in the river banks; they are true river birds, climbing high like brilliant blue and red jet flyers, flashing down to secure their small fish.

Boldest of the birds nesting at the vlei, perhaps, is the jackal buzzard. It howls like a jackal, soaring over the water, swooping on rodents and snakes, frogs and lizards, game birds and hares. A jackal buzzard will tackle a black eagle when its domain is invaded. These buzzards occupy the same nests year after year, on ledges along the ridges that shelter Verloren Vlei. They are demons for poultry. The black-shouldered kite also nests at the vlei but farmers do not regard it as an enemy. It hovers and pounces on insects and mice, never on tiny turkeys. Cape longclaws are there, too, mewing and whistling. They are called *kalkoentjie* because they have red throats like turkeys. Mountain chats sing beside the vlei at sunrise. They fascinate the watchers, for their changes of plumage are inexpliciable. Fairy flycatchers nest there, too, small and lovely birds with a pleasant song. Do they migrate? The mystery of this little member of a large family remains unsolved. Avocets are seen in flocks hundreds strong, waders in search of water animals. Dabchicks, too, favour this large expanse of water. These grebes are clumsy on shore, and they prefer the water to the air. They nest in the reeds where their musical laugh may be heard.

Years ago the flavours of all the edible birds of Verloren Vlei, not only the game birds but many others, were known to the people of the "lost world". Great shoots were held, the farm labourers cracking long wagon whips in the rushes, the guns in ambuscades along the banks. On these occasions the birds would come up in thousands, flying backwards and forwards, and extraordinary tales are told of the numbers shot. Egyptian geese were there in vast flocks, the large, shy *berggans*, cackling and honking. Buckshot was needed to bring them down, for the thick plumage and tough flesh are hard to penetrate. Only the young ones are worth eating. Another tough bird with a far better flavour is the spurwing goose or *wilde-makou*, a large green bird with a wingspan of almost six feet. Farmers love to shoot them for they graze on their crops. Pochards, chocolate coloured and fast, often escape by diving when wounded. Opinions of epicures differ on this bird. Major Boyd Horsburgh, who shot nearly everything in South Africa early this century, declared that the Cape pochard was "a poor fowl to eat, tasting strongly of mud."

About the yellowbill duck or *geelbek* there is no argument. This high-flying two-pounder is a well-known favourite among hunters. They are usually roasted, lemon and port wine being used in the process. Leipoldt had a poor opinion of all the water-birds, however, and declared they were only fit to eat after they had been soaked in vinegar to remove the muddy taste. He was in favour of disguising them in *ragouts* and *bredies*. Needless to say the waters of the "lost valley" have long known the white pelican and the flamingo. Let us hope there is no more hunting of the flamingo tribe.

I often saw this delectable stretch of Cape countryside from the air at one period of my life. Piketberg mountain rose from the ocean of wheat like an island. On the summit of the high island were two or three dozen farms which, I learnt later, were growing millions of apples, fine pears and peaches, apricots and plums. I was often puzzled by pock-marks in the wheatfields, circular patches of a different and darker colour from the surrounding soil. Farmers told me that the wheat sown on these patches grew better there than elsewhere, but they were unable to explain the phenomenon. Some thought there were once kraals on those spots, and a legacy of fertiliser had caused the richer growth. Long afterwards a scientist found the explanation. He sat thinking for hours beside a patch, where a road had been cut throught the circle. It all seemed lifeless, but at last he saw little particles of earth moving. Then the head of a "soldier ant" appeared, with a smaller ant shovelling earth. The dark soil consisted of tiny black grains of ants' excreta and other rubbish from a huge colony of ants far below the surface. Here was the fertiliser that made the wheat grow so well. The riddle of the rings had been solved.

You look down on a wide and wonderful countryside when you fly over Verloren Vlei and the Sandveld. Because of the sand the city motorist has still to discover such far corners as Aurora and Papkuilsfontein, Klein Tafelberg and Caesar's Kraal, on the track to Verloren Vlei. If you are seeking adventure it can still be found within a few hours of Adderley Street; the sort of adventure that takes you back suddenly to last century. You lose the harsh odours of the city and breathe in the aromas of vlei and dune, the water lilies and the bush, the strong tang of the sea mingling with thatch and bluegums. As you stand beside some old homestead asking the way to Verloren Vlei you may find yourself thinking how different life at the Cape was when that house was built. And how much better.

*Chapter Seventeen*

# BEHOLD THE GREAT BERG RIVER

BEHOLD another and greater body of water, the Berg river, sometimes called the Great Berg River. This is a South African rarity, a navigable river. Not for all of its two hundred miles, of course, but for about thirty miles from the mouth which opens into St. Helena Bay. Portuguese explorers gave the bay that name because they first saw it on the Saint's day; and the river they called Santiago after Sant' Iago (St. James the Great) patron saint of Spain. But the explorers sent out by Van Riebeeck named the river Berg, and Santiago vanished.

I have navigated the Berg myself, and I am more interested in the seaward end than the source. Nevertheless, the story of a river must have a beginning, a middle and an ending. The source of the Berg is in the steep Drakenstein and French Hoek mountain ranges about thirty-five miles east of Cape Town. Climbers struggle up through the tree-ferns and forests to places with tremendous views, Bushman's Castle and Bushman's Tooth, and then look down on the streams and pools and waterfalls and winter snows of the Berg near its source. The river enriches the old Huguenot farms of the French Hoek valley and flows northwards to Paarl and Wellington. It must have been a magnificent spectacle before the hand of man changed the natural beauty of the valley and destroyed the trees. William Burchell and botanist crossed the Berg early last century and described the water-jungle: "The ford which had rather the appearance of a lane led us through the tall thick palmites (i.e. *palmiet*, a mass of rushes) with which the river was in part so choked up that its waters seemed as if struggling to find a passage between the stems. It would be very unsafe, without great care, for a traveller to ford a river of this kind, for should he by the force of the stream be carried into the palmites he might find the greatest difficulty in extricating himself and his horse."

West of Tulbagh the Klein Berg river flows through the lovely pass to join the Great Berg. Pieter Potter, the surveyor of the Van Riebeeck period, discovered and mapped this area. He saw "wild horses of a dapple grey colour, fat and beautiful, but very wild and not easily to be caught." Next day Potter and his men passed the spot where Hermon now stands and found the Klein Berg "which comes forth from the mountain range which is cut in two and with sides like a huge wall." Here I must mention Vogelvlei, the lake in the Tulbagh mountains that helps the flow of the Berg in summer. Thomas Baines, the explorer and artist, suggested a conservation scheme at Vogelvlei more than a century ago. Now the natural lake has been transformed into a reservoir more than four miles long and holding eleven million gallons of water. Carl Thunberg gave an early description of the lake as he saw it two centuries ago: "a kind of swamp which lay at the foot of the mountains and was frequented by sea-fowls and snipes." Two decades later John Barrow saw "ducks, geese and teal and also the great white pelican, the *onocrotalus* and the rose-coloured flamingo." (*Onocrotalus* is the so-called European pelican, a restless bird which probably remains within the African continent). Today the birds are still there, many of those you saw at Verloren Vlei and others. Vogelvlei was also once the scene of annual massacres of birds. Now it is an official sanctuary, though poachers still pick off some of the wild duck. Fishing is allowed; bass and blue-gills are abundant. Sailing men and botanists also find great pleasure on and around this fine, hidden sheet of water.

Now the stronger Berg turns north-west across the golden ocean of wheat. You come to Misverstand, the drift Simon van der Stel used on his Namaqualand journey. Five miles lower down the river there is the century-old iron bridge, the *Ou Brug* I crossed so often on the way to Piketberg before the concrete bridge was built a few miles to the west. Soon the river takes you back into the

Sandveld, going westwards to the sea. Thirty miles across country, but twice that distance to the sea if you paddle along like the young men do in the tough canoe race every year. Near the farm Caledonia, which is twenty miles from St. Helena Bay in a direct line, the Berg begins to flow slowly at sea level across a flood plain. This zone is one of the most interesting stretches of the river in winter, when salt pans and vleis are filled and the broads attract thousands of waterfowl. June to August is the flood period. If you strike the river seven miles to the north of Hopefield you are in the region where the river floods the marshes and reed-beds beside its course, thus creating secluded backwaters where almost every species of water bird finds peaceful breeding conditions. Here, as at Verloren Vlei, are the herons and duck. Red-knobbed coot work on their floating nests in the rushes while plovers and sanderling trot briskly on the sandy river beaches. Bee-eaters in brilliant green plumage nest in the banks and fly low in hundreds over the poppies in the wheat fields. The huge *gompou* and that smaller bustard the *korhaan* trek in from the north, lured by the expanse of fresh water.

Buzzards and small hawks are numerous in the Sandveld to the north of the Berg but birds of prey are rare south of the river. Mrs. M. K. Rowan, M.Sc., research officer at the Percy Fitzpatrick Institute of African Ornithology, noticed that the small rats known to scientists as gerbilles were destroying crops in the south. Grainfields were riddled with their burrows, wheat was eaten before it could be reaped, and strychnine had failed to keep the pest in check. Gerbilles occur to the north, but they are not a menace and Mrs. Rowan is convinced that they are under the natural control of the birds of prey. In the early nineteen-fifties she recorded a dense population of birds of prey in the southern area; black harriers, eagle owls, jackal buzzards and others. They were shot off, many owls were run down by motorists, and other birds died after feeding on poisoned rodents. It seems clear that birds of prey are very important in helping man to keep the gerbilles within bounds.

You have already met Carl Thunberg, the learned Swede who became known as the "father of Cape botany". He came to the Berg river in springtime nearly two centuries ago with Auge the gardener and a well-equipped expedition. In his covered ox-cart he had "necessary clothes, as well as with boxes and bags for collecting roots and seeds, with boxes and pins for insects, a keg of arrack for preserving serpents and amphibious animals, cotton and boxes for stuffing and keeping birds in, cartridge paper for the drying of plants, tea and biscuits for my own use, and tobacco to distribute among the Hottentots together with firearms, and a large quantity of powder, ball and shot of various kinds". Thunberg, a keen observer, noticed huge flocks of goldfinches in the wheat. They lived along the Berg, weaving nests with long entrances to keep birds of prey from their young. Ostriches were common, and Thunberg found their nests, trampled in the sand, each with twenty to thirty eggs. Large packs of jackals hunted the antelope on the plains. The jackals had a "regular cry" when they surrounded the game at a distance; then they narrowed the circle and went in to create havoc. South-east winds had scattered seeds and the plains were adorned with wildflowers. Thunberg noted that the root of the aromatic *anys wortel*, with its flavour of aniseed, was eaten by the people of the river, and had a pleasant taste when roasted in the embers, boiled in milk, or stewed with meat. The farmers made their slaves dig up large quantities for sale in Cape Town. The root of the *gatagay* was also roasted, but this Thunberg disliked. Farmers also gathered *raapuintjies* (*Cyanella capensis*) a kind of onion. Thunberg said the Hottentots in this district wore leather round their legs as they were afraid of serpents. He crossed the Berg by ferry at Piet Joubert's farm. Farmers on the north bank paid Joubert eight guilders a year to keep the ferry in order.

Captain Paravicini di Capelli, aide-de-camp to General J. W. Janssens, governor of the Cape in 1803 and 1804, kept a journal of his visit to the Berg and St. Helena Bay. He visited the patriarch Jacob Laubscher at the famous old farm Langrietvlei on the south bank. Granted in 1715 to the wealthy landowner Hendrik Oostwald Eksteen, it had become a huge and flourishing estate with more than one hundred labourers. Laubscher grew wheat and kept eighty horses, about seven hundred head of cattle, thousands of sheep and goats. The house built by Eksteen stood too close to the river, and the great floods of 1788 swept it away. A fine homestead built the following year remains almost unaltered to this day. Jan Jurgen Kotze, a horse-breeder, bought Langrietvlei and five other farms in 1833, and his descendants still own the farm. Capelli met a slave at Langrietvlei, a Javanese who had been at the Cape for a century and whose age was estimated at more than one hundred and twenty years. The slave declared that when he first saw Cape Town there were only a few houses apart from the Castle. He had set up the Dutch East India Company's beacon at St. Helena Bay in 1733. Though his eyes were weak, his memory was clear. He had a wife of fifty and a son of thirty. Laubscher informed Capelli that the hippo in the Berg river estuary had recently attacked a boat and left some of its teeth embedded in the timber. Members of Laubscher's family were in the boat at the time. Soon afterwards Capelli visited the farm Kersefontein and heard the hippos roaring at night.

Kersefontein (over the bridge from Berg river railway station nowadays) is another old river farm. It was included in Eksteen's grant in 1715, but the first Martin Melck bought the farm in 1770 and an unbroken line of seven Martin Melcks have possessed the lovely farm for two centuries. I have a picture on my wall of one of the Kersefontein outbuildings with steps to the loft, a boy above and a shapely young girl leaning against the shadowed wall. It is an Arthur Elliott coloured photograph with the beauty of an oil painting. Kersefontein has a grand coach-house, a slave bell and other relics of its long, calm watch beside the river. You can smell the sea breeze there, for the river has only twelve miles of country to cross; but when I cruised up the Berg in a yacht the river curved and wriggled so much that the distance was more than doubled. It was so pleasant on the river that the voyage did not seem long. Tidal movements can be observed at Kersefontein in the dry season. The farm runs along the north bank of the Berg for fifteen miles. In the primitive parts, among the rushes and in the thick bush, are wild long-horned aboriginal cattle, a legacy from the Hottentots who once had their kraals along the coast. They are red cattle, with long legs and savage natures. Shooting has reduced the herd, for they are useless, but for sentimental or other reasons a number remain. Wild pigs are found there, too, and they are not likely to become extinct. Partridge, guinea-fowl and francolin potter and crow round the homestead like tame birds. A most unusual place is Kersefontein, "the fountain of the wild cherry bush". The homestead has some fine old Cape furniture, a seventeenth century armoire, a Huguenot *rusbank*, an antique copper chandelier, an old chest of Coromandel wood, Cape silver and Persian carpets.

Turn back to the early years of last century and you find Dr. Martin Lichtenstein, the German physician and traveller, calling on Jacob Laubscher at Langrietvlei. He described the farm as "a State in minature." Laubscher, he said, only needed the outside world when he was short of cloth, linen, hats, arms, tea, coffee, sugar, spices, iron, pitch and rosin. The house was surrounded by all sorts of workshops. Cattle were sent to this district when disease broke our elsewhere. *Lamsiekte* was unknown. Ten or twelve hippos remained in the river, protected since Governor Tulbagh's day by a fine of one thousand guilders. They came on shore at night, ate the young corn and trampled down the crops. Occasionally a hunt was allowed and the skin, skeleton and entrails were sent to Cape Town. Lichtenstein secured a license but could not find a hippo. He was then invited by Frederick Kirsten to see his estate Viswater at the mouth of the river. Here the Berg was one hundred and sixty feet wide, but it was choked with sandbanks and at low tide there were two feet of water on the bar. M. de Grandpré, a French visitor, had suggested cutting a passage through the sand bar for ships, but

Lichtenstein sneered at the very idea. "It must be obvious at the first glance that this was the idea of a man wholly ignorant of the subject of which he pretended to treat," declared Lichtenstein. Indeed there are great hazards involved when man challenges sand and the forces of the sea. More than a century and a half passed before the funds were voted (hundreds of thousands of pounds) and engineers blasted a new channel linking the Berg with St. Helena Bay.

After inspecting Kirsten's cattle Lichtenstein and his retainers crossed the Berg. The men used boats, the horses swam. Wagons were unloaded and floated across with the aid of empty casks. Along the north bank Lichtenstein noted the sandy veld with its patches of bright pelargonium. Moles were a nuisance, for the horses were in constant danger of stumbling owing to the holes. Somewhere to the north of the river Lichtenstein encountered the first Bushman woman he had seen. She was skinning a lean hare. The doctor wrote: "The greasy swarthiness of her skin, her clothing of animal hides, as well as the savage wildness of her looks and the uncouth manner in which she handled the hare presented altogether a most disgusting spectacle. Now and then she cast a shy leer towards us."

John Barrow (later Sir John), explorer and ruthless critic, was among those who surveyed the Berg river mouth early last century. "Though an immense mass of water, it is so sanded up that boats can only enter at high water," wrote Barrow. "Game of every kind is plentiful towards the mouth of the river. The two large antelopes, the hartebees and the gemsbok, are occasional visitors to this part of the country."

One master mariner who gave a favourable account of the Berg was Captain Benjamin Morrell of the American schooner *Antarctic*. This old sealer came up from the southern ocean islands in 1824 and anchored in St. Helena Bay. "Ships in want of fresh water I would recommend to anchor near the bar," Morrell advised. "There are three feet of water at low tide. Send the casks into the river on the flood tide, ascend the stream for five miles, remain until nearly the last of the ebb and knock out the bungs. The water is excellent and will keep as sweet as any ever taken to sea. The next ebb will take the casks down to the ship. I have filled fifty casks at this river. I purchased fine fat bullocks at four dollars each, sheep at one dollar, fine lemons and oranges at half a dollar a hundred."

Naturally the fresh water of the Berg has inspired many ambitious brains. Theunis Smit, a wealthy farmer of Klipfontein (near the present Langebaanweg air station) drew up a scheme in the middle of last century. He proposed to build a wall across the river about five miles from the mouth to prevent the salt water flowing upstream. He engaged J. C. Poortermans the lithographer to design a lock or *sluis*, covered with a pivot bridge, similar to the Nieuw Diep lock at Amsterdam. Smit pointed out that Dr. Daly, the only physician in the area, lived on the north bank, and the bridge would enable him to reach his patients more easily. "With this plan the land along the river will increase in value," Smit argued. "Irrigation will become possible, the farmers will have gardens instead of sending to town for potatoes and cabbages." Nothing came of the scheme, but Poortermans painted several amusing and atmospheric water-colours depicting life in the district.

Miss Hildagonda Duckitt, author of the most famous of all Cape cookery books, came on the Berg River scene about a century ago. She set out one December with other members of the family in a wagon drawn by eight horses. They left the Duckitt farm Groote Post in the Darling district and reached the Berg on the evening of the fourth day. Of course there had been a number of halts for refreshments, and Hildagonda described (with an enthusiasm which I share) the unpacking of the food hamper. "Bread, butter, hard-boiled eggs, corned breast or ribs of mutton; fricadels, that is minced mutton with bread crumbs and spices made into little balls and fried—they are excellent for travelling." The journey ended at Kersefontein. "The lovely Berg river winds in and out, running level with its banks, which are wooded with willow, blue-gum and blackwood, forming a lovely oasis,"

Hildagonda wrote. "The soil is very rich, being much mixed with limestone, and grows fine crops of wheat, oats, rye and barley. Vineyards do not thrive there but apricots, peaches and lemons flourish. It is a lovely homestead, known far and wide for its hospitality. Shooting is a favourable pastime, game abounding. On this farm ostriches roam in large droves. They find their own food here, the saline bush with succulent leaf grows all along the banks of the river."

Lovers of sailing craft manned by fine seamen must have known happy, crowded days along the Berg river throughout the second half of the last century. In spite of the sand bar, many types of ships entered the river. Among the small craft on the Berg river run in the middle of last century was a sailing cutter named *Alabama*. I have failed to trace her owner or skipper, but the memory of the *Alabama* was clear in the minds of old people who knew the west coast fleet. Now she is a legend, and also the origin of a legend. The little *Alabama* carried many cargoes. Often and often she came into Table Bay loaded with *dek-riet*, the thatching reed that grows in the Sandveld. She also brought *matjiesgoed* for tying the bundles of reed; it is stronger than any twine, as the good thatchers knew very well. These cargoes were not only used by thatchers and basket-makers. The Alabama brought also the raw materials of romance. One type of Berg river reed formed part of the beds made specially for Malay brides. Wedding guests would feast on chicken curry and *buriyani;* then they would be shown the "Alabama bed" covered with white and silver spreads of exquisite workmanship. Malay choirs often sang a folksong in honour of the cutter that Malay brides had such good reason to gaze upon with happy eyes:

*Daar kom Alabama, Alabama kom oor die see*
*Nooi, nooi die rietkooi nooi, die rietkooi is gemaak,*
*Die rietkooi is vir my gemaak,*
*Om daarop te slaap.*

That is the true origin of the *Alabama* legend. Prescott, the American historian, once remarked: "History is often more accurately told in folksongs than in libraries." What a perfect example! I have gone through most of my life believing the well-known story that the Malay song arose spontaneously among some of those who watched the Southern commerce-raider *Alabama* entering Table Bay in 1863 with the Northern barque *Sea Bride* as her prize. Over the years the ships and the brides became confused. Only recently was it discovered that the *Alabama* of the Malay song sailed into Table Bay years before the raider of the same name. This is the death of a legend, but for once the truth is more glamorous.

No doubt the flat-bottomed *Alabama* sailed in and out of the Berg easily enough. Carl Stephan, shipowner and uncrowned king of the Cape west coast, sent his fleet of schooners, cutters and fishing boats over the bar regularly in spite of hazards. Stephan's headquarters were at Laaiplek, the "loading place" just inside the mouth. Perhaps there was more water on the bar in those days. Stephan's skippers certainly possessed a degree of skill which has vanished, for nearly all of them had to rely on sail alone. Carl Stephan had one small steamer on the Berg, however, a cargo-carrier named *Spes Bona*. I am told that during one flood season she reached Hopefield and loaded wheat there for Table Bay. It is hard to imagine anything larger than a rowing-boat at Hopefield, but Carl Stephan was a most enterprising man. From the year 1873 onwards the *Spes Bona* was a familiar sight on the lower Berg, carrying all sorts of farm produce from oats to eggs down to Laaiplek for transhipment into the larger vessels of the Stephan fleet. In those days of ox-wagons, long before the railway had even reached Malmesbury, sea transport paid handsomely.

One of Carl Stephan's most successful business deals, combined with a feat of seamanship, was the purchase in 1878 of the French three-masted barque *Neree* of three hundred tons. She had run ashore in Table Bay and had been condemned. Stephan bought her at a bargain price and sailed her up to Laaiplek himself. I would like to have seen him doing it. He must have chosen the right period during an exceptionally high tide, and his crew must have been wonderful sailormen. There is a sharp bend in the river at the mouth. Under sail, the manoeuvre would call for masterly timing. It would be a nightmare if anything went amiss.

Yes, there were dramas at the river-mouth, and the Berg watched many wild and dangerous episodes when Laaiplek was a busy, roaring harbour. Seaman went out from there across the oceans to Rio in the west, to Mauritius in the east. Carl Stephan made a great deal of money out of salt fish and sugar and coffee. Runaway seamen, many of them Italians, came to Laaiplek in search of a life easier than the deepwater windjammers gave them; and they found a sort of sanctuary in Carl Stephan's domain at the Berg river mouth. Once there was more Italian spoken there than Afrikaans; now there are only the Italian names. Some of the old settlers were boat-builders, and descendants have inherited their craftmanship. They have a language of their own, peculiar Afrikaans phrases which would not be understood elsewhere to describe the river they know so well, the boats, the fish and the vicissitudes of the ocean beyond the river mouth. They remember the old ships and the old people. Carl Stephan's house now forms part of an hotel at Laaiplek, and the bones of the *Neree* lie on the river bed.

Outside the river runs the curve of the great bay of St. Helena, stained with the waters of the Berg in flood seasons. Only recently there has come to light an English translation of the sailing directions compiled by Joao de Lisboa, the pilot who accompanied Vasco da Gama. He told those who followed him that St. Helena Bay could be identified by a hill in the south like a large castle with towers. "At the point," he warned, "there are some shoals a bombard shot to sea." In the bay towards the north John of Lisbon noted a great hill like a ship's prow. He laid down clear instructions regarding the anchorage: "Know that the anchorage in this bay is on the south-eastern side of you and if you anchor you shall do so near the islets that lie south-east of you. On the eastern side of this bay there is a river that has two-and-a-half fathoms at the entrance at high water during the neap tides." So they knew the Berg, those old Portuguese, and with eighteen feet of water on the bar some of their ships might have sailed in to a more secure anchorage than the bay offered. However, there were dangers everywhere along the uncharted coast, and so they left the unknown river to the sailors of the Dutch period.

Professor Andrew Young the geologist believed that the Berg was once one of the world's greatest rivers, possibly the greatest. He found huge, water-rounded boulders in the Berg which could only have been shaped by a tremendous flow of water. From this and other evidence he estimated that the Berg must once have been forty feet deep, running at fifty miles an hour. The water came from ice that melted when the Karoo ice age came to an end. At that period the whole Karoo was a dam, the largest in the world.

A last glimpse. On the map, along the south bank near the mouth, there is the farm Carl Stephan once owned, Flaminkvlei. Wherever you go on this coast there are the flamingoes, rising on crimson wings.

*Chapter Eighteen*

# THE QUACK

MY favourite little settlement along the whole Berg river is Olifantskraal, the place where I met the resourceful vagabond who called himself Professor Nicholas Culpepper. Olifantskraal is possibly outside your experience. It is just a group of white buildings under tall bluegum trees on the south bank about eight miles from the mouth.

I had cruised up from Table Bay in the small yacht I mentioned earlier. After the pounding and buffeting of the ocean the river was tranquil and we followed the many bends slowly, exploring the backwaters, watching the birds, diving over the side at intervals to take out a kedge-anchor and free the yacht from sand-banks. Olifantskraal had a wooden jetty, an hotel of a sort and a cheerful bar where the Sandveld characters gathered at week-ends. In a little cemetery close by there was a headstone bearing the date 1825; and the barman at the hotel said he was specially interested in that grave. It was one of his predecessors, born in Somerset, England, according to the inscription, and killed by a hippo while swimming in the river. Olifantskraal became our base. We left the yacht there for some weeks, driving up at week-ends, sauntering along the river and receiving visitors who had never seen a yacht there before. One Saturday morning we set eyes on the strangest visitor of all. He was a hunchback, not an embittered hunchback but one with a ruddy, benevolent face, aquiline nose and merry black eyes. It was midsummer, and he wore an unsuitable top-hat and frock coat. "I'm Professor Nicholas Culpepper," he announced briskly with an American accent. "That's my chariot up there, and as you can see, I'm a herbalist." Sure enough there was an old, high-roofed motor-caravan standing near the hotel, the sides decorated with symbols of Culpepper's profession. A painting of an apricot tree stood out with brilliant green leaves and attractive fruit against the black background. "Apricots will save your life," declared the slogan. I was reading this message with some visible doubt, for I had often suffered from *appelkoos-siekte*. The professor gave me a reassuring wink. "They will do you no harm as long as you don't eat them raw," he said firmly. "Of course I have ways of treating the simple apricot and transforming it into a valuable medicine. But at the moment I would like to invite your co-operation in a herbal expedition. You are voyaging along the river? Excellent! I would be most grateful if you would allow me to accompany you so that I may add to my *materia medica*, my stock of health-giving plants and herbs of the veld."

It was a memorable cruise. We towed a dinghy, and when Professor Culpepper sighted wild growths and shrubs with marvellous properties we put him on shore to fill his boxes and bags. His eyes gleamed with pleasure as he worked. Neither his frock-coat nor his deformity hampered his activities, and he shouted happily at each fresh discovery. Soon our little saloon was filled with pungent aromas. As we moved gently downstream on the return to Olifantskraal the professor looked over his specimens and gave us a lecture on the art of the herbalist.

"Here in these bags I have the very foundation of medical science," Culpepper began portentously. "Here are the living herbs, not the unnatural products of the laboratories. I need hardly tell you how the doctors secured their modern remedies. You know that colchicum for gout is simply the autumn crocus discovered by tribal medicine men thousands of years ago. Apricot mould, used by old wives in every countryside for centuries, has become the modern panacea for many infections and diseases, the strain Fleming called *Penicillum notatum*. Buchu, which you find in the pharmacopoeia as the great diuretic, was the medicine of the Hottentots long before they saw a white man. Quinine was another gift of nature used by happy savages in South America before the *conquistadores* descended upon them. Tannic acid occurs in bark, and was extracted by primitive races to treat burns. All this is nature's chemistry, essential for the health of mankind."

I listened spellbound. Professor Culpepper was a quack, but not an ignorant quack. "How do you reach your patients?" I asked. "Will you be holding a meeting at Olifantskraal?" The professor nodded. "To-night when they come to the bar they will also attend my lecture," he replied. "I shall remain on the scene for a week or two so that those who have benefited from my remedies may send their friends for treatment."

"You bear the name of a famous English herbalist of the seventeenth century," I pointed out. "Any relation? You are an American, I take it?"

"Nicholas Culpepper may have been an ancestor—I have never inquired," Culpepper answered airily. "Yes, I was born in the United States but I am a child of nature and citizen of the world. The Culpepper you have mentioned was an astrologer. I will have no truck with that nonsense. I am a lecturer, phrenologist, bone-setter and herbalist—not a quack."

We made the yacht fast to the jetty at Olifantskraal. I walked up to the caravan with Culpepper and watched him stowing away his plants in labelled boxes and bottles. The hunchback was enormously proud of his collection. It almost filled the caravan, leaving room only for a small old-fashioned brass bedstead, copper pots and stone jars, a stove and a cupboard for clothes. When he opened the cupboard door to hang up his frock-coat a penetrating scent flooded out. "No moths in here—that's *akkwanie*, a root that keeps them away. I draw on the herbal kingdom for nearly all my needs. No ailment can harm me for long. I can deal with anything from influenza to snakebite. If I am hungry the *anys-wortel* is my turnip, the *doring-komkommer* is my cucumber, and I can make a full meal of *jakkals-kos* cooked under the embers of my campfire. When the wild blackberries ripen in January I have my jam—and a very useful medicine for a certain intestinal complaint. I quench my thirst with *ghaap*, the carrion flower that cures piles when infused with brandy. The root called *hotnotskool* is my asparagus. I love the *suurbessies* which yield vinegar, and the wild plum with its red fruit and kernel that I press for oil. There is a shrub called *boesmanstee* that tastes far better than anything from India or Ceylon; and if I feel like a change of flavour I gather the *hotnotstee* shrub on the Cape mountains. I know every mushroom on the veld from the shaggy inkcap to the blusher; and no panther or death-cup will ever end my life. Apricots have a special meaning for me, and if you care to attend my lecture tonight you will hear my views on that luscious fruit."

I asked Culpepper to show me some of his favourite medicines. He reached into a drawer and brought out a bottle marked *geneesbos*. "My patients like to have everything labelled in the language they understand," Culpepper remarked. "Actually this is the *Lobostemon fructicosum*, a bush with a pretty blue and pink flower that country people call *agt-dae-geneesbos*. Boil the leaves and you have a liquid which you can drink to treat eczema—and the same liquid may be applied to the skin to hasten the cure."

I felt that Culpepper had some belief in his own remedies though he was a natural actor. There was a note in his voice which might have been genuine enthusiasm. I sat entranced, taking an occasional shorthand note so that none of his wisdom would be forgotten, while Culpepper ranged through the lore of the herbalist from Hottentot figs (for diptheria) to *brandblaar*, the anemone that raises a blister and is said to cure rheumatism. I saw the *sandolyf*, a decoction used as a purgative in fevers; the *kruidjie-roer-my-nie* or "touch-me-not" plant like myrrh which makes a gargle for sore throats; leaves of *heuningtee*, which form a sweet infusion swallowed by victims of catarrh. Culpepper was a wild tea specialist. He had *stekeltee* from Table Mountain, a shrub with prickly leaves known as an asthma treatment and also as a gentle diuretic; the well-known *kaffertee* and *blommetjiestee* for various chest ailments. When I asked him about toothache he produced the *tand-pynwortel*, a root which is chewed; but I gathered that he could extract teeth as skilfully as any dentist in places so remote that no one was likely to report him to the police. Sore eyes? He produced the *lantana* plant known as "bird's brandy" and declared it would kill bacteria. Tonics? He showed me the carrot-shaped root called *bitter-wortel*. "Grate it and take it in wine," Culpepper said. "The milky juice is a great medicine. Or you could try *paddaklou*, though that plant suits some people and not others. I have known people who could not sleep or eat restored to health by this plant with flowers like a frog's claw. Paralysis? Wild cardamom or *knophout* is the very thing, for the aromatic fruit has cured generations of sufferers." I tested Culpepper from many angles and never found him a loss. Under the high roof of that lumbering caravan he had classified and stored everything from cedar gum for rheumatism to the different types of buchu. He had *soethout-bossie* roots, rather like licorice, for wasting diseases and the nauseous *dawwetjies wortel*, one of the old Hottentot remedies for snakebite, dropsy and bladder troubles. Other diuretics, possibly less drastic, were the ice plant, *wildeselery* and the *platdoring* or *sieketroos*, rather like sarsaparilla. I admired the zeal which had driven this hunchback to penetrate ravines and search the veld and the dunes, the edges of vleis and the banks of rivers for rare or useful herbs. He had found the handsome red flowers of the mistletoe called *voëlent* with its astringent stems and leaves; a single parasite regarded as a cure for such different conditions as epilepsy in children, loose bowels and St. Vitus's Dance! On the Cape Flats in summer he had gathered the *wildekamille* with its volatile oil, the great digestive remedy. In this old caravan the industrious Culpepper had pounded the leaves and stalks of *wilde-als*, the balmy-smelling wild wormwood to make a medicine for swollen tissues. He had extracted the strong resin from *wurmkruid* which undoubtedly had the power to expel worms. Here he had brought *wilde roosmaryn* and the volatile oil called bellis. He pored over his phials and bottles and jars of *kruisement* and saffron tasting *geel-blommetjies* like a miser over gold. Here were purgatives and emetics, nuts and fruits, some harmless as *bossies-stroop*, others poisonous as *wolveboon*, used to destroy hyenas. "You have to go to the Gifberge, the poison mountains near Vanrhynsdorp, to find that bush," remarked Culpepper. "It grows nowhere else. But I've travelled far and wide in search of herbs. I've been to Swellendam for *bospeper*, the hot berries that cure stomach troubles, and to Riversdale for aloes. Now I can supply anything my patients ask for. Of course I'm not allowed to diagnose or prescribe."

I watched the humorous face of the hunchback for a smile or a wink, but he remained impassive. Here was a quack who knew how to remain within the law. "You have put in an enormous amount of work, studying the Cape herbs," I pointed out. "How did you do it?"

"I am not a pioneer in this branch of healing," Culpepper replied. "Here is my library. I have the good Dr. Ludwig Pappe's work, published in the middle of last century and as true today as when it was written. Orthodox medicine shifts and changes, but the herbalist is on firm ground, close to nature, following principles that remain the same through the years. But the herbalist in all countries relies largely on common sense and the physical senses. Among thousands of plants you find the specific remedies by taste and smell. The valuable plant is usually pungent or bitter, acid or astringent or aromatic. I have risked my life, perhaps, carrying out experiments on my own body before passing on a medicine to my patients. Now and again I have found natives, Hottentots and others, willing to share their heritage of experience with a stranger. Deep in the country, far away from the chemists and the doctors, there are farmers who will show you their medical legacies. Of course they have ridiculous beliefs, too, such as dog's blood for fits, goat's dung for measles and vulture's fat for lumbago. I have watched them rubbing tortoise-blood into a child stung by a scorpion and I have seen a snakeskin wrapped round a rheumatic limb to ease the pain. One can only deplore a belief in animal droppings or crawfish-eyes as medicines. That is witchcraft, not science. You might as well tie a rope round your forehead for headaches. Oh yes, they do that, and if you can get hold of a hangman's rope so much the better."

In the face of these old *boere-rate* I began to see Professor Nicholas Culpepper as a true scientist, a man dedicated sincerely to the traditional art of healing. No doubt they spoke of him in many small places such as Olifantskraal as a *wonderdoener*, a man who left a trail of small miracles behind him. True, the phrenologist's chart hanging inside the caravan looked suspiciously like quackery. Culpepper followed my glance and spoke up in defence of the pseudo-science. "Yes, I know phrenology has fallen into disrepute," he began. "And yet how true it is! The small and villainous retreating forehead, the humps of self-esteem and genius, benevolence and crime—there are sermons in skulls, my friend, and no observant being can ignore the evidence before his very eyes."

This was rather more than I could stomach. I promised Culpepper that I would attend his lecture and returned to the yacht. All that afternoon, I noticed, Culpepper and a coloured man with grey peppercorn hair were standing over flaring pressure-stoves, cooking-pots and the abracadabra of herbalism. Sometimes the aroma was that of a jam-factory rather than a laboratory, and then I saw baskets of apricots being emptied into a cauldron.

I was in the bar before dinner. Culpepper was there, too, proving that a true herbalist was fully aware of the value of the grape when properly distilled. The bar was crowded and everyone seemed anxious to pay for Culpepper's drinks. Culpepper was in genial mood, looking over the company, summing them up. "Come to my lecture—I'll deal with that point," he told each anxious inquirer. I shall never forget that lecture under the tall bluegums at Olifantskraal. Culpepper had placed his caravan against the fence. The caravan had a sort of rear-end balcony where Culpepper stood under a wooden canopy as though in a pulpit. Electricity had not reached Olifantskraal, and the hunchback depended on flaring naptha lamps. The light gave a dramatic effect. Culpepper was no longer a

I shall never forget that lecture under the tall bluegums at Olifantskraal . . . Culpepper was a quack but he was no ordinary quack.

little hunchback tricked out in a frock-coat. He towered over his audience with the aid of a hidden box and the height of the caravan balcony. On a table below stood a vast array of bottles and other labelled containers. Beside the table stood Culpepper's old coloured man David, dressed for the occasion in starched white coat. A hush fell over the gathering as Culpepper struck a tuning-fork. It seemed to me that the sound created just the right wavelength for Culpepper's brand of mass hypnosis.

"The Lord hath created medicines out of the earth and a wise man will not abhor them," began Culpepper in a rich and sonorous voice that commanded instant attention. "My friends, I come before you not to make money. I am not trying to sell medicines. Please do not call me doctor. It so happens that I am a doctor, graduate of a famous American university, and my diploma hangs there in the caravan for all to see. But owing to professional jealousy among medical people—and you all know how bitter that can be—my doctorate is not recognised everywhere. So I come before you merely as Professor Culpepper, a lecturer, and I shall now give you my greatest lecture free of charge."

When the expected applause had ended Culpepper went on. "I come before you as one who bears the Balm of Gilead. My whole life is wrapped up in these blessed herbal decoctions and my one motive is to improve the health of humanity. Death only comes through the defiance of nature's laws. Are there any doctors in the audience? I am sure they will bear me out."

Culpepper paused, though he knew full well that the few scattered practitioners in that large district were far from Olifantskraal that night. "The doctor is your friend," went on Culpepper magnanimously. "You have fine doctors in this district. I have not come here to compete with them or to sell a cure-all. Each ailment, each disease, calls for a special remedy. Every bottle, every tin of ointment, every box of powder on that table is worth a sovereign and more. I'm not going to charge you a sovereign. Nothing costs more than half-a-crown, and I return your money as freely as you give it if my cures fail. Now you, sir, did you ever feel under the weather?" (Culpepper had selected one of the bar's regular customers.) "I know what's wrong with you sir! Pains all over when you wake up in the morning, dizziness, spots in front of the eyes. Am I right? Of course I'm right. David, hand the gentleman a bottle of my number one tonic. A bottle for you, sir? And another? And another? My friends, you're not healthy—and all because you're not taking the herbs that nature provided for you, the marvellous remedies I've brought to Olifantskraal. A bottle for you sir? Now I see some of you are wavering. All I ask is that you stop and listen. Germs cause disease. Kill the germs and you cure the disease. I'm asking a beggars' fee—for this! First dose will make a new man of you and I'll not be here again for a long time, my friends. Buy now and you'll never regret it. A bottle for the gentleman at the back, David. Sold, sold, sold!"

"Sold out professor," called David as he took half-a-crown from the gentleman at the back. "No more number one tonic, professor." Culpepper and David had timed it skilfully. They could not have sold another bottle anyway. Every tonic buyer in the crowd had paid his half-a-crown.

"So now I come to another rich gift to mankind," Culpepper's sonorous voice boomed on. "You all know the apricot. Some of you grow apricots. You know the aperient properties of apricots, whether, fresh, dried, boiled or stewed. Most of you realise that you can give up taking aperients if you eat apricots regularly. The apricot stimulates the liver—but it does more than that. Yes, my friends, the apricot holds the secret of long life. I have extracted from the apricot the active principle that makes one bottle of my apricot elixir equal to a thousand fresh apricots. After all, you cannot eat apricots all day and every day. You would defeat the purpose of the fruit by becoming satiated. But one dose of my elixir taken once a day acts like a wagon-load of fresh apricots. It regenerates the blood more effectively than a diet of fresh liver. It keeps your weight down. It is the essence of the juicy, aromatic apricot—the secret of long life. This is powerful stuff, my friends, and I am almost giving it away in the belief that after a few doses you will come back for more. Yes, I shall be here for a few days to provide you with special remedies for various complaints. Just a few days, and I know you'll keep me busy all the time. Now you can have a trial bottle of my apricot elixir for two shillings. Never mind the expense—I'll recover my outlay on the turnover, because there will be a huge demand for this elixir once you have tested it for yourselves. Two shillings, my friends, for the secret of long life."

With these beautiful words ringing in my ears I left the scene of Culpepper's triumph and went on board the yacht. We cruised down the river under the moon. Culpepper had turned Olifantskraal into a noisy metropolis, and we sought a quiet backwater for the night. I never saw Culpepper again, but I often thought of him. Years afterwards I read a news message from India stating that scientists had been studing longivity in a tribe of Pakistanis known as Hunzas. Their exceptional health was investigated years ago by Sir Robert McCarrison, a distinguished medical officer, and the records of longivity in the tribe have been maintained since then. Recent scientific research has shown that the Hunzas eat large quantities of apricots. Samples were analysed, and the main elements were found to be iron and silver.

Professor Nicholas Culpepper was a quack, but he was no ordinary quack.

*Chapter Nineteen*

# EGGS OF GREAT PRICE

ANOTHER very different personality was at work along the Berg river during one of my visits years ago. He was James Drury, the South African Museum taxidermist for almost half a century. Drury was a true artist in the world of natural history. He knew the deserts of Southern Africa and the flamingo coast; the wild Bushmen and the great beasts. I met him at Laaiplek in search of very much smaller specimens, namely birds' eggs.

When men are gripped by the collecting mania their passion surpasses the love of women. So it is with the oologists, the collectors of bird's eggs. Drury regarded the business calmly, but he assured me that eggs were Nature's masterpieces, surpassing in beauty of form and colouring the purest gemstones, the loveliest seashells, the most gorgeous butterflies. He said that eggs were rivalled only by the flowers. "Eggs? I've handled the largest and the smallest," Drury told me with pride. "That priceless *Aepornis titan* egg from Madagascar, six times the size of an ostrich egg, was my discovery. I found it unlabelled and forgotten in a storeroom at the museum, an egg twelve inches long, laid by a gigantic bird that became extinct five hundred years ago, an egg worth hundreds of pounds. What about the smallest? Well, you need a magnifying glass when you're working on the eggs of humming-birds or a penduline tit—they're only half an inch long. And they're all exquisite."

Drury also loved the flavours of certain eggs unknown to the ordinary man. The green eggs of the African darter or snake bird were among the delicacies he had enjoyed. On the bird islands he had eaten the nourishing eggs of all the seabirds; penguins and cormorants, black-backed gulls and petrels, finding no "fishiness". He said the large eggs were most satisfactory. The small eggs of the oyster-catcher and other little shore birds were often bitter. Drury pointed out that the early Dutch settlers at the Cape had been saved from starvation by the seabirds' eggs they gathered on the islands. "They got sick of them, but I have seldom had enough to satisfy my appetite," said Drury.

South Africa has nearly a thousand species and sub-species of birds. When you see their eggs arranged in cabinets you are gazing at Nature's greatest achievements. Science can account for the shapes of the eggs but the colours, the miraculous colours, remain a mystery. Birds that nest on high ledges of rock lay eggs with the axis placed so that the egg will spin in the wind but will not roll over the edge. Eagles lay one or two eggs because their eyries are safe, but their food supply is insufficient for a large brood. The vulnerable partridge lays up to twenty eggs, and it can always feed the surviving chicks. Birds that use dark places and holes lay white eggs, which would be conspicuous if they were not hidden. It is clear that there is a relationship between surroundings and the colours of an egg, but the details of avian camouflage cannot be explained. Why is the egg of a red-legged partridge speckled? Why does the golden oriole lay a lilac and brown spotted egg? There is infinite variety in birds' eggs; the smooth eggs and the glossy, the chalky and the dull, the granulated and the pitted. Markings of the same species often vary according to locality. And the colours are beyond the ingenuity of a painter; the pale green eggs of the cormorant; the blue green eggs of the grey heron; the beautiful yellow eggs, smeared with red-brown, laid by the lanner falcon in old nests on high cliffs. Yes, the egg-collector loves those pigments, but he cannot tell you how they are formed. Patterns vary from egg to egg, and all those colours have a meaning. It may be that white enables the birds to see their eggs in the dark; that heavy screens of colour protect the unborn chicks from strong sunlight. Those pigments may come from the blood stream of the parent bird. Colour is not the whole secret of the charm which egg-collecting holds for some people. But those colours are fascinating, whether they are subdued or brilliant. Some eggs have the burnish of glazed porcelain. The kingfisher's egg has a translucent outer layer. Here is a theme which still baffles the world of science.

Rarity means far more to the collector than beauty. Africa has only one egg which may be compared with the Great Auk's egg (worth more than a thousand pounds), and that is the dodo egg from Mauritius. Fossilized eggshells found near the Etosha Pan in South West Africa may have been laid by a giant species of bird known as *hepyorinthirformes*, previously identified only in Madagascar; and these must rank high among the rarities. I asked several leading ornithologists to name South Africa's rarest eggs, and they found this a difficult question to answer except in general terms. "The more precarious a bird's existence, the more demand there is for the eggs," said one authority. Others pointed out that the eggs of some species are entirely unknown. The eggs of certain eagles and vultures are rare because the nests are so difficult to reach. Mr. C. J. Skead, field research officer of the Percy Fitzpatrick Institute of African Ornithology, suggested the egg of Neergaard's Sunbird as one which should be placed near the head of the list. Captain C. D. Priest, a great authority on eggs, said that the bluish-white eggs of the Maccoa duck were extremely rare anywhere. This duck breeds in swamps and makes a floating nest of reeds. Other eggs were rare because certain birds seldom breed in South Africa; for example the blue-green eggs of the great white egret. Rhodesian collectors prize the eggs (dirty white with brown marks) of the African hawk eagle. The chat-warbler of that territory lays oval eggs of light pink, spotted and marbled all over with reddish-brown and purple blotches. Years pass without a single nest of the brown-headed parrot being found. Eggs of Smith's and Bennett's woodpeckers and the grey hornbill are other rarities.

South Africa's most ardent egg-collector of last century was Edgar Leopold Layard, first curator of the South African Museum. He was a great ornithologist, author of the first complete standard work on South African birds. Layard came on the scene in the middle of last century and inspired many helpers with his own enthusiasm; captains of ships calling at remote places, farmers and many others. He sent duplicates to museums all over the world, exchanging Cape birds' eggs for Arctic bearskins and a male wolf from Switzerland. The famous Cape schooner *Silver Cloud* brought him butterflies from Rio, while Captain Nolloth of H.M.S. *Frolic* contributed eggs of the wandering albatross, dull white with brown spots, from the Tristan da Cunha group. These islands have provided museums with interesting exhibits; and many years later Drury mounted a pair of flightless rails from Tristan, great rarities in the bird world The master of a sealing schooner gave Layard seabirds' eggs from the bleak Crozet isles. Captain Roe of the schooner *Telegraph* collected a number of pelicans, sacred ibis and their eggs on the Cape guano islands. Dyer's Island on the Bredasdorp coast yielded the creamy white chalky eggs of the mitred pelican.

Long-desired eggs of birds of prey were presented by Mr. Henry Jackson of Kamfers Kraal, Beaufort West. These birds nested on a fearful precipice on Nelspoort mountain. Aasvoëlkrans as it was called, could be seen for miles, as the birds had bred there for centuries and the face of the cliff was white with their droppings. It was a dangerous climb, and Jackson risked his life in vain during August 1868, for all the eggs he found were addled. Another expedition was planned, and an Irish ex-sailor offered to tackle the precipice. He went over the edge clinging to a rope and returned with thirty-four eggs in his wool-lined knapsack. Thus the South African Museum received its first specimens of lammergeyer and other vultures eggs, and the eggs of the Senegal eagle, black eagle and tawny eagle.

Berg river farmers were great egg-collectors in Layard's day. Members of the Melck and Kotze families sent in hundreds of specimens, including some which Layard had not seen before. These included the eggs of the rare booted eagle, which bred near the Berg river in the spring; two immaculate white eggs of the white-bellied eagle; the white eggs, streaked with brown of the Cape kite; a fine series of heron's eggs; and the eggs of the little river duiker. Some of the eggs baffled Layard, especially a series of brilliant red eggs which Kotze had labelled "Blaauw Valk". The eggs of a mysterious wader, possibly a redshank, also puzzled Layard. He visited the Berg river himself in November 1869 and collected more than eight hundred eggs. Many of his duplicates went to the British Museum at this period. A Malmesbury farmer sent in a box of eggs which included a noble specimen of the Egyptian vulture.

Francois le Vaillant mentioned a small flycatcher in his book, a bird which he called "Le Molena" (the miller) because its note resembled the grinding noise of millstones. Le Vaillant failed to discover the nest, but one of Layard's helpers located it. "The nest was an exquisite structure of fibre lined with hair," Layard wrote. "It was covered with lichens outside to resemble the swelling in a tree. The dull white eggs were tainted with green, with pale brown spots." Layard also welcomed the eggs of the crested Kaffir crane as a prize; and he was delighted when Miss Annie van der Byl of Fairfield, Bredasdorp, sent him the first eggs of the blue heron ever seen in South Africa. The same district provided an egg of the giant heron, another rarity. Layard was able to exchange a coveted egg of a Verreaux's eagle with a museum in Saxony for a golden eagle's egg. Among rare birds and eggs sent in from Colesberg was a bird described early last century by Sir Andrew Smith as a *tink-tink*. It had not been seen for more than forty years. Layard was an exponent of the ethics of zoology at a time when few people had considered this aspect of egg-collecting. He exchanged eggs with boys who were anxious to learn natural history, but he declared firmly: "We utterly deprecate the barbarous practice of robbing birds of their eggs for the simple purpose of stringing them on a thread and hanging them up on a wall."

Sclater, who followed Layard as director of the South African Museum, travelled widely in search of specimens. He took Drury with him early this century, when the railway to the Victoria Falls was opened; and together they collected weaver birds, Ruppell's vulture, the hooded vulture and a number of rare eggs along the Zambesi.

Egg-collecting is often an adventure. About sixty years ago several pairs of Verreaux's eagles were seen to be nesting between Table Mountain and Cape Point, and a one-armed man named C. E. Lane-Poole tried to secure an egg. He had observed a pair of eagles carrying green branches of *renosterbos* for their nest to a ledge on a Cape Point precipice. Lane-Poole was lowered by a rope, a shotgun fastened to his back, a sheer drop of six hundred feet below him. Instead of the expected egg he found a very young bird and the remains of a number of dassies. The parent birds flew round and seemed about to attack, but Lane-Poole did not have to use his gun. He was hauled back to the summit with the young eagle in his bag. The lighthouse-keepers had complained that the eagles were killing their poultry, and they wished to get rid of them. However, the young eagle was kept as a pet, eating raw meat ravenously until a spell of wet weather set in; then it died.

Among the most determined South African egg collectors for many years was Mr. R. E. Symons, conservator of the Giant's Castle game reserve on the Natal side of the Drakensberg mountains. He was stationed at one of the most remote spots in Natal, with his nearest neighbour twenty miles away. Early this century he had no car and had to ride everywhere on horse-back. Bored with his isolation, Symons decided to take up oology as a hobby. He studied books on the subject; bought sixty yards of Manila rope, an egg cabinet, a set of blow-pipes and other equipment; aneroid and hunting belt, field-glasses, compass, camera and egg-boxes. "These mountains, rising to eleven thousand feet above sea-level, formed a virgin field—and I soon discovered that egg-collecting on those cliffs was a perilous business," said Symons.

First he marked down the nests of black eagles and jackal buzzards. Natives lowered him over the cliffs. During one early descent his rope jammed in a crevice in the rocks above him, and he was unable to climb and free the rope because of an overhang. For a time he hung suspended. After much shouting he persuaded one of the natives to climb down and jerk the rope out of the crack. Symons and his cousin were after vultures' eggs some weeks later. His cousin went down first, and Symons followed, using the same rope. Very soon Symons came upon a vulture's nest. He then let the rope go and held on to a bush growing out of a large rock. To his horror the rock moved slightly and gave signs of coming away from the cliff face. Symons called to his cousin to return at once. Both of them reached safety before the loose rock fell into the valley with a mass of debris. That was his narrowest escape.

Symons owed his life to his habit of examining every inch of the ropes he used. He also carried iron dog-spikes for climbing the tall yellowwood trees where the martial eagles, fish eagles and crown eagles nested. These trees had no projections near their bases, so Symons hammered a spike into the trunk at intervals of three feet as he climbed. Now and again the spikes worked loose and fell out under pressure, leaving him with serious problems far above the ground. Once he was robbing a wryneck nest in a tree-trunk only ten feet above ground level when his right arm became jammed inside the hollow trunk. His body was twisted awkwardly round the trunk, and most of his weight was resting on his left arm. If he had let go, his right arm would have been broken. "It was no use shouting for help, as no one would have heard me," Symons remarked. "The evening was wet and misty and there was a strong wind blowing. I had never been nearer complete loss of nerve in my life. My only chance of escape lay in wriggling my arm and hauling occasionally to free it from the timber vice of the tree-trunk. For a time I had no luck. The pain was excruciating and I felt that the moment was coming when I would have to make a desperate effort. At last I put my whole remaining strength into a final tug and brought my arm out with most of the skin torn off."

Snug dome-shaped nests built by the *hamerkop* often hold unpleasant surprises. The outer nest is constructed of sticks, bones, twigs and stones; but the small inner sanctum is neatly plastered with mud. When the birds depart a mamba seeking refuge from the winter cold may take up residence in the nest. Symons probed this type of nest with a stick before feeling round with his hand for eggs. The collector also meets scorpions, bees and wild beasts. Symons travelled widely in search of eggs. He camped in the deserts of South West Africa and went through the surf to Dyer's Island. There he found birds from distant places, the Kerguelen tern, the roseate tern (known to seamen as the bo'sun bird), and Tristan birds such as the giant petrel mollymawk and Cape hen. Mitred pelicans breed on Dyer's Island, as I have recorded, but the eggs are destroyed by the headman because this bird devours the valuable guano-producing birds and their eggs. Here, too, are the swift terns, known locally as "small mutton birds" because of their flavour. There is also a "large mutton bird", the Caspian tern. After nearly a quarter of a century of egg-collecting Symons had gathered one of the finest private collections in Southern Africa. Then his lonely homestead was burnt out and he was able to save only a small part of his collection.

Oologists have never been so numerous as the stamp-collectors, the hoarders of match-boxes or sea-shells or antiques. Mr. C. J. Skead informed me that he regarded Mr. Hubert James of Salisbury, Rhodesia, as one of the leading oologists in Southern Africa; a man who committed his knowledge to paper. Other great names in this select field are those of Dr. Pitt Fennell of Kefani and Mr. D. C. H. Plowes of Umtali. There is a P. A. Sheppard collection of birds' eggs in the Natal Museum, Pietermaritzburg and a Bell-Marley collection in Durban. No doubt other museums have benefitted as the result of the efforts of expert amateurs.

South African oologists encounter many mysteries. Why has the cuckoo's egg came to resemble the eggs of its victims? How do you account for the wide variations found in the eggs of the mossie, ranging from white to black? Why is the black African rook the only crow in the world that lays pink eggs?

Egg-collectors have been classed with kleptomaniacs and those primitive races which gloried in securing the scalps or wives of their enemies as trophies. It is true that some oologists regard the filling of the cabinets as far more important than the preservation of a rare species of bird. Their greed is uncontrollable, and such collectors have caused great damage in the past. All the tricks devised by low cunning have been used to secure rare eggs. Sometimes a bird has been led to produce six clutches in one season, a great strain on the vitality. Yet it is probable that rats, snakes, lizards, ants, monkeys and marauding birds take more eggs than the most reckless collectors.

Eggs must be collected, identified, measured and studied if the secrets of the birds are to be solved. Eggs are a great help in the classification of the birds that lay them. Oologists have made their contributions to science, especially in their discoveries of the nesting sites of rare species. Eggs often provide clues to the relationship of the species. There is a type of collector, of course, who keeps his discoveries to himself for fear of putting rivals on the track of rarities; but the field naturalist who shares his knowledge works in the cause of science.

Colonel Willoughby Verner, whose quest of the lammergeyer I have already mentioned, was such a keen egg-collector that he pursued his hobby while on active service during the South African War. The search for rare species moved him to climb mountains, explore remote marshes and make adventurous sea voyages. For him, the fascination lay in personal experience. He was satisfied only when he had located the desired species, studied and recorded its habits, followed it to the nest and discovered its secrets. Verner looked with contempt on collectors who exchanged eggs to fill the gaps in their cabinets. He bought a Great Auk's egg because it was clearly impossible to find one by his own efforts; other eggs he took from their nests with his own hands. So the true collector may earn a high reputation as an ornithologist. He knows that wild birds are a public heritage; that the secret of a bird is in its flight and song, and not in its corpse. He collects with a definite purpose, to secure knowledge. The vivid eggs in his cabinets recall the strange places where he has swung perilously in mid-air to reach the nests; the sun and the winds of far corners; the myriads of birds wheeling round him, the glamour of their voices as he reached some lonely breeding ground.

"I think if required on pain of death to name the most perfect thing in the Universe I should risk my fate on a bird's egg," wrote T. W. Higginson a century ago. Indeed the charm of a beautiful egg is no mere childish fancy, no schoolboy's whim. There you have mystery in the most appealing shapes, in a blaze of colour that no artist could surpass.

*Chapter Twenty*

# ON WINGS OF FIRE

SUNSET, a calm September sunset over the Berg river, and the gold in the water is matched by a sky aflame with scarlet wings. Here are the flamingoes again, those unpredictable birds you have seen in desert places along a thousand miles of coastline. They are streaming down the hills, dipping over the dunes, skimming across the vleis in huge formations. You may see a leader with a thousand silent followers making for the water of his choice; silent but for the beating of all those exquisite black and scarlet pinions.

As the light fades the flamingoes settle for the night and give tongue at last. You hear chuckling noises, with a constant bugling sound mixed with loud "quark-quarks." At times their raucous voices are indistinguishable from the honking and gaggling of geese. Hide in the reeds, allow the flamingoes to surround you, and you are overwhelmed by colour and harsh croaking. Strange that such lovely birds should pour out such a cacophony. When you stand up and walk towards them the sentinel flamingoes will give their alarm call, the "kronk kronk" that raises every neck. For a moment or two they are all facing you and listening, heads turned and bent at remarkable angles. Then a great red wall of birds is on the move, echoing the "kronk kronk" of the sentinels. They lurch and tumble like a chaotic panic-stricken mob, their feet churning the mud so that you can smell the vlei. Some birds find room to stretch their long necks and beat the air as they run. Suddenly they are airborne and streamlined, a graceful contrast with the ludicrous spectacle of a few seconds ago. They are roaring and whirring away like noisy aircraft. Though they may settle a mile away you will still hear them like surf on a distant beach.

Dear old James Drury was the man who aroused my interest in flamingoes. He told me that the first birds he skinned and mounted in Africa were flamingoes, back in 1900 when he was a gunner in the Cape Garrison Artillery stationed at Walvis Bay. "Flamingoes are large and conspicuous, yet very little is known about them", Drury remarked. "They have caused bitter controversies among naturalists. Their structure and habit. are extraordinary. How did they evolve? We don't know. Their nesting and breeding habits in Africa form a mystery though Africa is their home. Not so long ago nobody knew how they hatched their eggs. The flamingo, in fact, is a well-known stranger".

Thus inspired I looked into the life of the flamingo along the flamingo coast and elsewhere. Drury had sent me on an absorbing quest. Though some of the mysteries have been solved in recent years, a number of riddles have never been answered. Those who count the birds (surely a difficult occupation) say that the world has one million greater flamingoes and five times as many of the lesser species, nearly all of them in Africa. But their migrations and feeding habits are unpredictable. Their life-span is a matter of guesswork, though one eminent ornithologist thinks the lesser flamingo may become a centenarian. Even in closely-settled Europe the flamingo has contrived to outwit those who have tried to pry into its life and habits. Bird-watchers sought the flamingoes for years in the salt marshes of the Camargue to the west of Marseilles. They found three hundred abandoned eggs in that strange and lonely region in 1924, but they had to wait another twenty three years before a breeding-colony was located. It appears, however, that the flamingoes of Europe do not keep up their numbers by breeding there. They rely on reinforcements from Africa.

Flamingo is a Portuguese word meaning "flame-like". Some call it the "red goose", but it comes in between the storks, ducks and geese. The Spanish describe them as *solitarios y tranquilos*, solitary and tranquil. Man has always been the main enemy of the flamingoes. Primitive hunters painted their brilliant shapes on cave walls five thousand years before Christ. Early in the Christian era men identified the flamingo with the phoenix, flame of the sunset sky.

I like to watch the flamingoes, the ballerinas in pink, in their solitudes. Yet in spite of their well-founded fear of mankind they are to be seen almost on the doorsteps of South African cities. Hundreds of them have visited Rietvlei in recent years, though this stretch of water close to Table Bay is no longer safe for birds. Rondevlei on the Cape Flats is a sanctuary, and there the flamingoes are nearly always to be seen. Flamingoes settle on the mine dams of the Rand, and Durban harbour has heard their chatter.

One of the great flamingo disputes old Drury mentioned to me was started at the end of the seventeenth century by none other than William Dampier, the buccaneer. Dampier combined a life of fighting and adventure with a deep study of navigation and natural history. When he was in the Cape Verde Islands, off the west coast of Africa, he found a number of abandoned flamingo nests and described them correctly. There were no eggs to be seen. As you may know, the nest is a mound of mud, a raised platform on which the egg is safe if the water rises slightly. When a breeding colony settles on a secluded island or sandbank in shallow water the birds work feverishly to build a city of mud and feathers; and within twenty-four hours their stronghold is complete. Dampier studied his flamingoes late in the season, for the incubation period of one month was over and the young birds were in their brown plumage. He wondered how the long-legged flamingo could sit on such a high nest. After much thought he started the "riding astride" myth which was regarded as fact for two centuries. "When incubating they stand with their legs in the water, resting themselves against the hillock and covering the hollow nest upon it with their rumps", wrote the imaginative buccaneer. "Their legs are very long, and building thus as they do upon the ground they could neither draw their legs conveniently into their nests nor sit down upon them otherwise than by resting their whole bodies there, to the prejudice of their nests and their young, were it not for this admirable contrivance which they have by natural instinct."

Two centuries passed and Abel Chapman the ornithologist and author crept up on a breeding colony of flamingoes in Spain and exploded the absurd story. He observed the mother flamingo sitting with her long legs doubled beneath her; folded up exactly like a domestic fowl, and not dangling a la Dampier. So firmly was the Dampier version established, however, that an editor threw doubt on Chapman's description. Chapman sued for libel and won the case.

In Africa and elsewhere the quest for nests of the flamingoes went on much longer. Audubon, the indomitable American naturalist, searched the backwaters of Florida in vain for years and died without finding a nest. East Africa revealed the secret in recent years. The shy flamingo frequent certain lakes there in numbers running into millions. One of the great sights of the Pretoria to Cairo wartime flights which I remember was the Nakuru flamingo colony. Some of the Lodestar pilots flew low, to the consternation of bird-lovers and the delight of those who gazed spellbound at this vast concourse of birds rising in rocket bursts and filling the air with flame. Elspeth Huxley has estimated that one and a half million flamingoes may be seen in the alkaline shallows of Nakuru at one time. Lake Natron on the Tanganyika—Kenya border is another great flamingo haunt, and it was there in 1953 that the bold and resourceful ornithologist and wine-lover Leslie Brown discovered the hidden breeding-places. He nearly lost his life during the search, for the soda in the lake burnt his feet and the mud was as dangerous as quicksand. In the end Brown secured a small aircraft and located the nests. Both the greater and the lesser flamingo breed there, though Lake Natron is mainly a lesser flamingo breeding-ground. Brown found many greater flamingo eggs on a rocky island in Lake Elmenteita near Nakuru. Colonel Meinertzhagen had eaten flamingo eggs for breakfast in that area some years previously, but had failed to locate the nests. The white, chalky eggs are elongated, and have a blood-red yolk. Fish eagles, eagles, vultures, hyenas, jackals and serval cats prey on the young flamingoes when the shallow soda lakes dry up. Sometimes a rise in the level of a lake destroys thousands of nests in a day. However, the flamingo does not have to nest every year to maintain its numbers. The capricious, observant birds are sensitive to water levels, and they will only nest when they decide that the water and feeding conditions are exactly right. They have always sought the lonely places, in deltas, lakes and lagoons, moving from one sanctury to another; and so they eluded those who sought their breeding-grounds.

Some eminent South African ornithologists made up their minds years ago that the flamingo was a migrant, breeding far to the north of the Limpopo, or possibly in the Kalahari. They held this view firmly in spite of some other evidence. The Swedish explorer and ornithologist C. J. Andersson saw a few young flamingoes barely able to to fly near Walvis Bay in the middle of last century and surmised that they nested along the coast on rare occasions. Lake Ngami, he said, was their breeding-ground. They winged away to the north at the approach of the breeding season in February and returned at the end of October, the old birds arriving first. Anderson studied the flamingoes at various places along the coast of South West Africa, and called them "a perfect gem among the feathered tribes". He said the lesser flamingo was comparatively rare along that coast. "The young are not bad eating, but being rather fishy require to be well-cooked and spiced after all fatty matter has been removed," declared Andersson. That was a personal view. The meat became so popular in the German colonial days that a fine of three hundred marks (fifteen pounds) was imposed for shooting a flamingo. Phoenicians sailed to Cornwall with cargoes of dried flamingo meat, for in those days the flesh was regarded as a passport to immortality. Romans relished the pickled tongues of flamingoes. At last the hunted birds became almost unknown on Mediterranean shores. They had found peace in Africa.

Edgar Layard tried to find the flamingo breeding-ground while he was curator of the South African Museum in the middle of last century. He, too, was impressed by the discovery of young birds along the west coast, but he could not find the nesting area. Many people assured Layard that the flamingoes nested at Verloren Vlei. A Miss Boonzaaier of Hoedjies Bay presented the Museum with a flamingo egg from the Saldanha district, but even this clear piece of evidence failed to convince later ornithologists. They said the egg must have come from somewhere else. I have a friend who lived for a quarter of a century beside the Langebaan lagoon. This must have been a flamingo haunt long before the first white man set eyes on the sandbanks and shallows, and the flamingoes are still there. My friend once informed some visiting ornithologists that the flamingoes bred there, on the low and inaccessible islets at the head of the lagoon. The experts laughed at this statement and declared that it was impossible. So my friend gave no further information. He told me, however, that while paddling his canoe among the islands he had seen the broken eggshells, the young birds and the typical nests.

Mr. W. L. Sclater, director of the South African Museum early this century, was inclined to agree with Layard about the flamingo breeding in the Cape, and Layard also gave Lake Chrissie in the Transvaal as a breeding site. Yet in 1942 no less an authority than Dr. Austin Roberts asserted: "Eggs have not yet been taken in South Africa." In the nineteen-fifties a survey party from the University of Cape Town reported a flamingo nesting site near the Orange River mouth. Large flocks of flamingoes gather there in the channels and on the islands and swamps. Thanks to the rich diamond areas close by, the birds are effectively protected from poachers. Officers of the Department of Nature Conservation tried to locate the breeding site but failed. This bird paradise lies on the migration route of the flamingoes, and so many young birds have been seen there, some barely fledged, that a nesting site must have existed not far away. It is also worth recording the fact that Bushmen in many desert areas have spoken of their liking for flamingo eggs, and they were not likely to have been mistaken about an item of food. Not until the spring of 1960, however, was a successful mass breeding colony discovered on the farm Reinerskraal in the Bredasdorp district. This was certainly the first authentic report of such an event on a large scale in Southern Africa. Four ornithologists from the University of Cape Town headed by Professor C. J. Uys noticed the first nesting activity on a low island in a vlei. They found fifty nests but only two eggs. About five weeks later, however, there were three hundred nests, and the first young appeared in December. A peninsula half a mile away had been selected by another breeding colony, and there four hundred and forty five nests were counted. In both the colonies there was one nest containing two eggs. All the rest had one egg, thus confirming previous records in other parts of the world. Some of the young flamingoes were able to fly within three months of hatching. Once a black-backed gull was seen pouncing on a young flamingo and flying off with it. Gulls, sacred ibises and herons preyed on the eggs. Caracals, genets and polecats were also in attendance. Young flamingoes looked rather like goslings, covered with greyish down. They took to the water in "raft" formation, guided by adults. A second attempt at mass breeding was observed in November 1961, but all the eggs were destroyed by predators. Probably the flamingoes selected Reinerskraal because the area is secluded. They also found the rich food they needed in the brown water of the vlei. This area has long been frequented by enormous flocks of water fowl. Professor Uys observed flocks of flamingoes three to four thousand strong.

All the breeding pairs at Reinerskraal were greater flamingoes (Phoenicopterus ruber). You can distinguish between greater and lesser flamingo (Phoenicopterus minor) by their sizes, as the greater is about five and a half feet in height, the lesser about one-third smaller. At a distance the greater flamingo looks white, the lesser pink. The greater has yellow eyes and beak; the lesser ruby red eyes and beak. Their beaks and feeding habits differ considerably. The greater has thin horny plates acting as a sieve, but not set close together, so that small crustaceans and insect larvae may be swallowed. The lesser has its plates set more like a filter, and it lives on diatoms and microscopic plant growths from the surface of the water. Flamingoes do not feed on fish and frogs as many people suppose. Those queer angular beaks have to be turned upside down before they can draw in their food. They have been compared with the *balaena* whales which sift their food in the same way, passing minute particles through narrow gullets to their stomachs. However, the greater flamingo has a strong beak and uses it as a rake and a spade as it searches the vlei floor, squeezes out the mud, and retains the nourishment. You see them straightening up, removing the mud from their food with a hissing sound, raising their heads and gulping their delicacies. But in spite of this process a good deal of mud reaches their stomachs. The flamingo is graceful one moment, grotesque the next. Necks and legs are twisted into fantastic, serpentine postures. They march and counter-march with absurd pomposity. One naturalist who came suddenly upon a huge gathering of flamingoes said that it was like a strange composite monster with a thousand legs. They strut and prance, giving the "wing salute" that entrances watchers, when they open and shut their wings like gorgeous fans. Always the flamingo has splendour in reserve. As evening approaches the feeding multitude becomes restless. Some distant and hidden patch of water is calling them for the night, and already the birds on the outskirts, are running and taking to the air. When the light is right the water becomes a mirror, a fairyland of colour under the rush of wings. Flight after flight, squadron after squadron, join the airborne armada until the flamingoes go hurrying away in a formation greater and finer than all mankind's air fleets. Those who have seen the flamingoes under a full moon say that this is the most powerful spectacle of all, for even the night cannot rob them of all their ravishing colour. The birds that were mincing and gossiping along the vlei, tearing up grasses, standing on one leg, wading and swimming; these slender birds of the shadows go streaming into the sky like flaming javelins.

# *INDEX*